한국의 토익 수험자 여러분께,

토익 시험은 세계적인 직무 영어능력 평가 시험으로, 지난 40여 년간 비즈니스 현장에서 필요한 영어능력 평가의 기준을 제시해 왔습니다. 토익 시험 및 토익스피킹, 토익라이팅 시험은 세계에서 가장 널리 통용되는 영어능력 검증 시험으로, 160여 개국 14,000여 기관이 토익 성적을 의사결정에 활용하고 있습니다.

YBM은 한국의 토익 시험을 주관하는 ETS 독점 계약사입니다.

ETS는 한국 수험자들의 효과적인 토익 학습을 돕고자 YBM을 통하여 'ETS 토익 공식 교재'를 독점 출간하고 있습니다. 또한 'ETS 토익 공식 교재' 시리즈에 기출문항을 제공해 한국의 다른 교재들에 수록된 기출을 복제하거나 변형한 문항으로 인하여 발생할 수 있는 수험자들의 혼동을 방지하고 있습니다.

복제 및 변형 문항들은 토익 시험의 출제의도를 벗어날 수 있기 때문에 기출문항을 수록한 'ETS 토익 공식 교재'만큼 시험에 잘 대비할 수 없습니다.

'ETS 토익 공식 교재'를 통하여 수험자 여러분의 영어 소통을 위한 노력에 큰 성취가 있기를 바랍니다.

감사합니다.

Dear TOEIC Test Takers in Korea,

The TOEIC program is the global leader in English-language assessment for the workplace. It has set the standard for assessing English-language skills needed in the workplace for more than 40 years. The TOEIC tests are the most widely used English language assessments around the world, with 14,000+ organizations across more than 160 countries trusting TOEIC scores to make decisions.

YBM is the ETS Country Master Distributor for the TOEIC program in Korea and so is the exclusive distributor for TOEIC Korea.

To support effective learning for TOEIC test-takers in Korea, ETS has authorized YBM to publish the only Official TOEIC prep books in Korea. These books contain actual TOEIC items to help prevent confusion among Korean test-takers that might be caused by other prep book publishers' use of reproduced or paraphrased items.

Reproduced or paraphrased items may fail to reflect the intent of actual TOEIC items and so will not prepare test-takers as well as the actual items contained in the ETS TOEIC Official prep books published by YBM.

We hope that these ETS TOEIC Official prep books enable you, as test-takers, to achieve great success in your efforts to communicate effectively in English.

Thank you.

입문부터 실전까지 수준별 학습을 통해 최단기 목표점수 달성!

ETS TOEIC® 공식수험서 스마트 학습 지원

www.ybmbooks.com에서도 무료 MP3를 다운로드 받을 수 있습니다.

ETS 토익 모바일 학습 플랫폼!

ETS 토익기출 수험서 어플

구글플레이

앱스토어

교재 학습 지원
- 교재 해설 강의
- LC 음원 MP3
- 교재/부록 모의고사 채점 분석
- 단어 암기장

부가 서비스
- 데일리 학습(토익 기출문제 풀이)
- 토익 최신 경향 무료 특강
- 토익 타이머

모의고사 결과 분석
- 파트별/문항별 정답률
- 파트별/유형별 취약점 리포트
- 전체 응시자 점수 분포도

ETS 토익 학습 전용 온라인 커뮤티니!

ETS TOEIC® Book 공식카페

etstoeicbook.co.kr

강사진의 학습 지원 토익 대표강사들의 학습 지원과 멘토링

교재 학습관 운영 교재별 학습게시판을 통해 무료 동영상 강의 등 학습 지원

학습 콘텐츠 제공 토익 학습 콘텐츠와 정기시험 예비특강 업데이트

토익,

실력과 점수를 한 번에!
출제기관이 만든
진짜 문제로 승부하라!

왜
출제기관에서
만든 문제여야
할까요?

2,300

2,300명의 시험개발 전문가!

교육, 심리, 통계, 인문학, 사회학 등
2,300여 명의 전문 연구원이 모인 ETS.
토익 한 세트가 완성되려면 문제 설계 및 집필,
내용 검토, 문항의 공정성 및 타당성 검증,
난이도 조정, 모의시험 등 15단계의 개발공정에서
수많은 전문가의 손을 거쳐야 합니다.

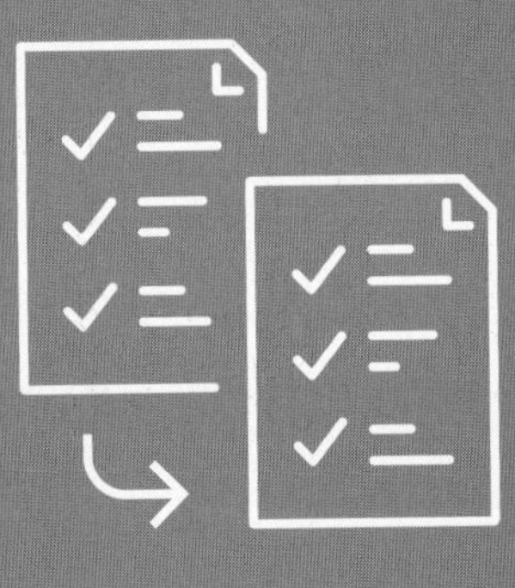

100%

싱크로율 100%

ETS TOEIC 교재의 모든 예문과 문항 및 해설은
100% ETS TOEIC 정기시험 개발부서에서
개발 및 검수되었습니다.
그러므로 사진, LC 음원, 문항 유형 및 난이도 등
모든 면에서 실제 시험과 싱크로율 100%입니다.

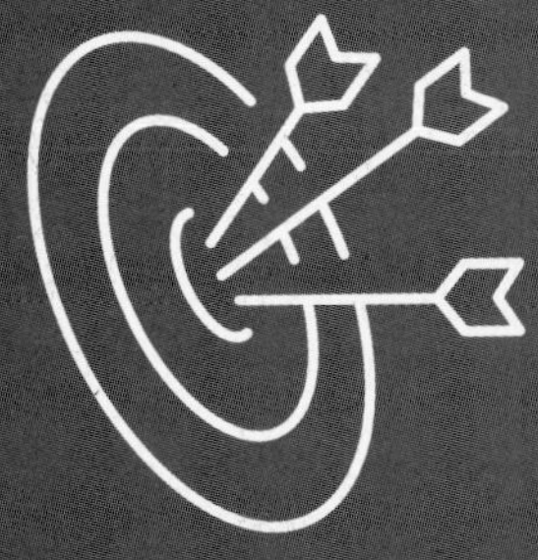

최고의 적중률!

최고의 정기시험 적중률!

기출 문항을 변형한 복제 문항이 아닌,
ETS 토익 출제팀이 만든 원본 문항 100%로,
시중의 어느 교재와도 비교할 수 없는 압도적으로
높은 적중률을 보장합니다.

발행인 허문호
발행처 YBM

편집 윤경림
디자인 DOTS
마케팅 정연철, 박천산, 고영노, 김동진, 박찬경, 김윤하

초판발행 2021년 12월 10일
7쇄발행 2024년 12월 5일

신고일자 1964년 3월 28일
신고번호 제 1964-000003호
주소 서울시 종로구 종로 104
전화 (02) 2000-0515 [구입문의] / (02) 2000-0345 [내용문의]
팩스 (02) 2285-1523
홈페이지 www.ybmbooks.com

ISBN 978-89-17-23858-7

toeic®

토익® 정기 시험 LC 기출입문서

PREFACE

Dear test taker,
Here is a test preparation book created to help you succeed in using English as a tool for communication both in Korea and around the world.
This book will provide you with practical steps that you can take right now to improve your English proficiency and your TOEIC® test score. Now more than ever, your TOEIC® score is a respected professional credential and an indicator of how well you can use English in a wide variety of situations to get the job done. As always, your TOEIC® score is recognized globally as evidence of your English language proficiency.

With the TOEIC® Starter Listening, you can make sure you have the best and most thorough preparation for the TOEIC® test. This book contains key study points that will familiarize you with the test format and content, and you will be able to practice at your own pace. This book exclusively contains a number of actual items which are carefully selected according to the beginners' level. Beginners can familiarize themselves with the characteristics of the actual TOEIC® test.

The TOEIC® Starter Listening includes the following key features.

· A number of actual items which are carefully selected according to the beginners' level
· Analyses of the TOEIC® question types and preparation strategies
· Specific explanations for learners
· The same voice actors that you will hear in an ETS test administration

Use the TOEIC® Starter Listening to help you prepare to use English in an ever-globalizing workplace. You will become familiar with the test, including the new test tasks, content, and format. These learning materials have been carefully crafted to help you advance in proficiency and gain a score report that will show the world what you know and what you can do.

출제기관이 만든
국내 유일 기출 토익 입문서!

토익 입문자들에게 최적화된 구성

토익을 처음 접하는 입문자들이 학습에 어려움을 느끼지 않도록
수준별, 단계별 학습을 제공합니다.

기출 문제 국내 유일 독점 수록

입문자도 풀 수 있는 엄선된 기출 문제를 통해
진짜 토익을 접하고 실전에 대비할 수 있습니다.

정기시험과 동일한 음원

이 책의 문제들은 토익 실제 시험과 동일한 음원이므로
실전에 완벽하게 대비할 수 있습니다.

ETS만이 제시할 수 있는 체계적인 공략법

토익 각 파트에 대한 이해를 높이고
원하는 점수 달성을 위한 체계적인 공략법을 제시합니다.

토익 최신 경향을 반영한 명쾌한 분석과 해설

최신 출제 경향을 완벽하게 분석하고 반영하여
고득점을 달성하게 해줄 해법을 낱낱이 제시합니다.

CONTENTS

청취 기초학습 18

PART 1

Part 1 개요

PART 1 시험은 이렇게 나와요 30

ETS가 제안하는 꿀팁! 31

기초학습

시제 익히기 32

수동태 익히기 35

UNIT 01 사람 중심 사진 38

UNIT 02 사물·풍경 중심 사진 46

ETS 파트별 모의고사 54

PART 2

Part 2 개요

PART 2 시험은 이렇게 나와요 60

ETS가 제안하는 꿀팁! 61

기초학습

질문 잘 듣기 62

답변 잘 고르기 63

UNIT 01 Who/What·Which 의문문 64

UNIT 02 When/Where 의문문 72

UNIT 03 How/Why 의문문 80

UNIT 04 Be동사/조동사 의문문 88

UNIT 05 부정/부가의문문 96

UNIT 06 제안·요청문/선택의문문 104

UNIT 07 간접의문문/평서문 112

ETS 파트별 모의고사 119

PART 3

Part 3 개요

PART 3 시험은 이렇게 나와요 122
ETS가 제안하는 꿀팁! 123

기초학습

Paraphrasing(바꿔 표현하기) 익히기 124

문제 유형

기본 문제 유형 알아보기 126
고난도 유형 알아보기 132

UNIT 01 직장 내 업무 138
UNIT 02 인사 144
UNIT 03 회의/행사 150
UNIT 04 기타 사무실 대화 156
UNIT 05 여가/여행 162
UNIT 06 교통/주거 168
UNIT 07 쇼핑/주문 174
UNIT 08 식당/호텔 180
UNIT 09 각종 편의시설 186

ETS 파트별 모의고사 192

PART 4

Part 4 개요

PART 4 시험은 이렇게 나와요 198
ETS가 제안하는 꿀팁! 199

기초학습

Paraphrasing(바꿔 표현하기) 익히기 200

문제 유형

기본 문제 유형 알아보기 202
고난도 유형 알아보기 208

UNIT 01 전화 메시지 212
UNIT 02 공지 218
UNIT 03 광고/방송 224
UNIT 04 회의 발췌 230
UNIT 05 연설/강연/소개 236
UNIT 06 관광·견학/설명 242

ETS 파트별 모의고사 248

ETS 실전 모의고사 254

WHAT IS THE TOEIC?

TOEIC은 어떤 시험인가요?

Test of English for International Communication (국제적 의사소통을 위한 영어 시험)의 약자로서, 영어가 모국어가 아닌 사람들이 일상생활 또는 비즈니스 현장에서 꼭 필요한 실용적 영어 구사 능력을 갖추었는가를 평가하는 시험이다.

■ 시험 구성

<table>
<tr><th>구성</th><th>Part</th><th colspan="2">내용</th><th>문항수</th><th>시간</th><th>배점</th></tr>
<tr><td rowspan="4">듣기(LC)</td><td>1</td><td colspan="2">사진 묘사</td><td>6</td><td rowspan="4">45분</td><td rowspan="4">495점</td></tr>
<tr><td>2</td><td colspan="2">질의 응답</td><td>25</td></tr>
<tr><td>3</td><td colspan="2">짧은 대화</td><td>39</td></tr>
<tr><td>4</td><td colspan="2">짧은 담화</td><td>30</td></tr>
<tr><td rowspan="5">읽기(RC)</td><td>5</td><td colspan="2">단문 빈칸 채우기
(문법/어휘)</td><td>30</td><td rowspan="5">75분</td><td rowspan="5">495점</td></tr>
<tr><td>6</td><td colspan="2">장문 빈칸 채우기</td><td>16</td></tr>
<tr><td rowspan="3">7</td><td rowspan="3">독해</td><td>단일 지문</td><td>29</td></tr>
<tr><td>이중 지문</td><td>10</td></tr>
<tr><td>삼중 지문</td><td>15</td></tr>
<tr><td>Total</td><td colspan="3">7 Parts</td><td>200문항</td><td>120분</td><td>990점</td></tr>
</table>

■ TOEIC 접수는 어떻게 하나요?

TOEIC 접수는 한국 토익 위원회 사이트(www.toeic.co.kr)에서 온라인 상으로만 접수가 가능하다. 사이트에서 매월 자세한 접수일정과 시험 일정 등의 구체적 정보 확인이 가능하니, 미리 일정을 확인하여 접수하도록 한다.

■ 시험장에 반드시 가져가야 할 준비물은요?

신분증 규정 신분증만 가능
(주민등록증, 운전면허증, 기간 만료 전의 여권, 공무원증 등)
필기구 연필, 지우개 (볼펜이나 사인펜은 사용 금지)

■ 시험은 어떻게 진행되나요?

09:20	입실 (09:50 이후는 입실 불가)
09:30 - 09:45	답안지 작성에 관한 오리엔테이션
09:45 - 09:50	휴식
09:50 - 10:05	신분증 확인
10:05 - 10:10	문제지 배부 및 파본 확인
10:10 - 10:55	듣기 평가 (Listening Test)
10:55 - 12:10	독해 평가 (Reading Test)

■ TOEIC 성적 확인은 어떻게 하죠?

시험일로부터 10~11일 후, 오후 12시부터 인터넷 홈페이지와 어플리케이션을 통해 성적을 확인할 수 있다. TOEIC 성적표는 우편이나 온라인으로 발급 받을 수 있다(시험 접수시, 양자 택일). 우편으로 발급 받을 경우는 성적 발표 후 대략 일주일이 소요되며, 온라인 발급을 선택하면 유효기간 내에 홈페이지에서 본인이 직접 1회에 한해 무료 출력할 수 있다. TOEIC 성적은 시험일로부터 2년간 유효하다.

■ TOEIC은 몇 점 만점인가요?

TOEIC 점수는 듣기 영역(LC) 점수, 읽기 영역(RC) 점수, 그리고 이 두 영역을 합계한 전체 점수 세 부분으로 구성된다. 각 부분의 점수는 5점 단위이며, 5점에서 495점에 걸쳐 주어지고, 전체 점수는 10점에서 990점까지이며, 만점은 990점이다. TOEIC 성적은 각 문제 유형의 난이도에 따른 점수 환산표에 의해 결정된다.

학습 플랜

20일 완성

· 하루 3~4시간 학습

· 매일 '문제 풀이 전략 → 연습용 문제 → 실전형 문제'의 단계를 밟아가며 학습하는 단기 집중형 스케줄

	☐ Day 1	☐ Day 2	☐ Day 3	☐ Day 4	☐ Day 5
1주	청취 기초학습 Part 1 기초학습 Unit 1	Unit 2 ETS 파트별 모의고사	Part 2 기초학습 Unit 1 Unit 2	Unit 3 Unit 4	Unit 5 Unit 6
	☐ Day 6	☐ Day 7	☐ Day 8	☐ Day 9	☐ Day 10
2주	Unit 7 ETS 파트별 모의고사	Part 3 기초학습 문제 유형	Unit 1 Unit 2	Unit 3 Unit 4	Unit 5 Unit 6
	☐ Day 11	☐ Day 12	☐ Day 13	☐ Day 14	☐ Day 15
3주	Unit 7 Unit 8	Unit 9 ETS 파트별 모의고사	Part 4 기초학습 문제 유형	Unit 1 Unit 2	Unit 3 Unit 4
	☐ Day 16	☐ Day 17	☐ Day 18	☐ Day 19	☐ Day 20
4주	Unit 5 Unit 6	ETS 파트별 모의고사	ETS 실전 모의고사	Part 1, 2 복습	Part 3, 4 복습

40 일 완성

· 하루 1~2시간 학습
· 매일 부담 없는 학습량을 꼼꼼히 학습하는 심화 학습형 스케줄

	☐ Day 1	☐ Day 2	☐ Day 3	☐ Day 4	☐ Day 5
1주	Part 1 단어 암기 및 Test (PDF 또는 어플 활용)	청취 기초 학습 Part 1 기초학습	Unit 1	Unit 2 ETS 파트별 모의고사	Part 2 단어 암기 및 Test (PDF 또는 어플 활용)
	☐ Day 6	☐ Day 7	☐ Day 8	☐ Day 9	☐ Day 10
2주	Part 2 기초학습 Unit 1	Unit 2	Unit 3	Unit 4	Unit 5
	☐ Day 11	☐ Day 12	☐ Day 13	☐ Day 14	☐ Day 15
3주	Unit 6	Unit 7	ETS 파트별 모의고사	Part 3 단어 암기 및 Test (PDF 또는 어플 활용)	Part 3 기초학습 문제 유형
	☐ Day 16	☐ Day 17	☐ Day 18	☐ Day 19	☐ Day 20
4주	Unit 1	Unit 2	Unit 3	Unit 4	Unit 5
	☐ Day 21	☐ Day 22	☐ Day 23	☐ Day 24	☐ Day 25
5주	Unit 6	Unit 7	Unit 8	Unit 9	ETS 파트별 모의고사
	☐ Day 26	☐ Day 27	☐ Day 28	☐ Day 29	☐ Day 30
6주	Part 4 단어 암기 및 Test (PDF 또는 어플 활용)	Part 4 기초학습 문제 유형	Unit 1	Unit 2	Unit 3
	☐ Day 31	☐ Day 32	☐ Day 33	☐ Day 34	☐ Day 35
7주	Unit 4	Unit 5	Unit 6	ETS 파트별 모의고사	Part 1 복습
	☐ Day 36	☐ Day 37	☐ Day 38	☐ Day 39	☐ Day 40
8주	Part 2 복습	Part 3 복습	Part 4 복습	ETS 실전 모의고사	오답 정리 및 확인

점수 환산표 및 산출법

점수 환산표

이 책에 수록된 Final Test를 풀고 난 후, 맞은 개수를 세어 점수를 환산해 보세요.

LISTENING Raw Score (맞은 개수)	LISTENING Scaled Score (환산 점수)
96 – 100	475 – 495
91 – 95	435 – 495
86 – 90	405 – 470
81 – 85	370 – 450
76 – 80	345 – 420
71 – 75	320 – 390
66 – 70	290 – 360
61 – 65	265 – 335
56 – 60	240 – 310
51 – 55	215 – 280
46 – 50	190 – 255
41 – 45	160 – 230
36 – 40	130 – 205
31 – 35	105 – 175
26 – 30	85 – 145
21 – 25	60 – 115
16 – 20	30 – 90
11 – 15	5 – 70
6 – 10	5 – 60
1 – 5	5 – 50
0	5 – 35

READING Raw Score (맞은 개수)	READING Scaled Score (환산 점수)
96 – 100	460 – 495
91 – 95	425 – 490
86 – 90	400 – 465
81 – 85	375 – 440
76 – 80	340 – 415
71 – 75	310 – 390
66 – 70	285 – 370
61 – 65	255 – 340
56 – 60	230 – 310
51 – 55	200 – 275
46 – 50	170 – 245
41 – 45	140 – 215
36 – 40	115 – 180
31 – 35	95 – 150
26 – 30	75 – 120
21 – 25	60 – 95
16 – 20	45 – 75
11 – 15	30 – 55
6 – 10	10 – 40
1 – 5	5 – 30
0	5 – 15

점수 산출 방법

아래의 방식으로 점수를 산출할 수 있다.

자신의 답안을 수록된 정답과 대조하여 채점한다. 각 Section의 맞은 개수가 본인의 Section별 '실제 점수 (통계 처리하기 전의 점수, raw score)'이다. Listening Test와 Reading Test의 정답 수를 세어, 자신의 실제 점수를 아래의 해당란에

	맞은 개수	환산 점수대
LISTENING		
READING		
총점		

기록한다. Section별 실제 점수가 그대로 Section별 TOEIC 점수가 되는 것은 아니다. TOEIC은 시행할 때마다 별도로 특정한 통계 처리 방법을 사용하며 이러한 실제 점수를 환산 점수(converted[scaled] score)로 전환하게 된다. 이렇게 전환함으로써, 매번 시행될 때마다 문제는 달라지지만 그 점수가 갖는 의미는 같아지게 된다. 예를 들어 어느 한 시험에서 총점 550점의 성적으로 받는 실력이라면 다른 시험에서도 거의 550점대의 성적을 받게 되는 것이다.

▼

실제 점수를 위 표에 기록한 후 왼쪽 페이지의 점수 환산표를 보도록 한다. TOEIC이 시행될 때마다 대개 이와 비슷한 형태의 표가 작성되는데, 여기 제시된 환산표는 본 교재에 수록된 Test용으로 개발된 것이다. 이 표를 사용하여 자신의 실제 점수를 환산 점수로 전환하도록 한다. 즉, 예를 들어 Listening Test의 실제 정답 수가 61~65개이면 환산 점수는 265점에서 335점 사이가 된다. 여기서 실제 정답 수가 61개이면 환산 점수가 265점이고, 65개이면 환산 점수가 335점 임을 의미하는 것은 아니다. 본 책의 Test를 위해 작성된 이 점수 환산표가 자신의 영어 실력이 어느 정도인지 대략적으로 파악하는 데 도움이 되긴 하지만, 이 표가 실제 TOEIC 성적 산출에 그대로 사용된 적은 없다는 사실을 밝혀 둔다.

LC

청취 기초학습

LISTENING PRESTUDY

- 미국식 발음 VS. 영국식 발음 비교 체험
- 유사 발음 비교 체험
- 긴 문장 청취를 방해하는 연음 듣기
- 문장 이해의 필수, 내용어 듣기

미국식 발음 VS. 영국식 발음 비교 체험

토익 시험의 Listening은 미국, 캐나다, 영국, 호주 네 나라의 성우가 녹음하게 되는데, 캐나다는 미국식 발음과, 호주는 영국식 발음과 크게 차이가 없습니다. 따라서 수험자들은 미국식과 영국식의 두 가지 발음만 신경 써서 학습하면 됩니다. 지금부터 가장 두드러지게 차이가 나는 미국식 발음과 영국식 발음들을 알아보도록 하겠습니다.

1 자음 r

P0_01

- **미국식** : r을 항상 발음한다.
- **영국식** : r 또는 re 다음에 자음이 오는 경우에는 발음하지 않는다.

	enter	there	bird	carefully
미국식	[엔터r]	[데어r]	[버-r드]	[케어r플리]
영국식	[엔터]	[데어]	[버-드]	[케어플리]

A **bird** is flying to the sky. 새가 하늘로 날아가고 있다.
Stand in line over **there**. 저기 줄에 서 있으세요.

2 자음 d/t

P0_02

- **미국식:** 미국식 영어에서는 '모음+d/t+모음'인 경우에 d/t를 r로 발음한다.
- **영국식:** 영국식 영어에서는 '모음+d/t+모음'이라도 d/t를 d/t로만 발음한다.

강모음 + d / dd, t / tt, rt / rd + 약모음

	riding	ladder	waiting	letter
미국식	[롸이-링]	[래러r]	[웨이링]	[레러r]
영국식	[롸이-딩]	[래더]	[웨이팅]	[레터]

I've been **waiting** for a bus for almost thirty minutes. 저는 거의 30분 동안 버스를 기다리고 있는 중이에요.
I've decided to start **riding** the bus. 저는 버스를 타기 시작하기로 결정했어요.

3 모음 a

P0_03

- **미국식:** a는 여러 발음이 있으나 짧은 [애 æ]로 발음하는 경우가 가장 많다.
- **영국식:** a 다음에 다음 5개의 자음 [f, n, mp, s, th]이 오면 길게 [아 a]로 발음한다.

	afternoon	plant	sample	class
미국식	[애(f)프터눈-]	[플랜ㅌ]	[쌤쁠]	[클래ㅆ]
영국식	[아-(f)프터눈-]	[플란-ㅌ]	[쌈-쁠]	[클라-ㅆ]

I have some time this **afternoon** to review the report. 오늘 오후에 보고서를 검토할 시간이 좀 있어요.
Has this **sample** been tested? 이 샘플은 검사가 되었나요?

4 모음 o

P0_04

- **미국식:** [아]로 발음한다.
- **영국식:** [오]로 발음한다.

	job	stop	box	copy
미국식	[잡-]	[스땁-]	[바-악스]	[카-피]
영국식	[좝]	[스똡]	[복스]	[코피]

Do we need to **stop** for fuel? 주유를 하기 위해 멈춰야 하나요?
I'll print a **copy** for the meeting. 제가 회의를 위해 복사를 하겠습니다.

5 특이한 발음

P0_05

	schedule	garage	laboratory	advertisement	vase
미국식	스께쥴	거롸지	래브러토리	애드버타이즈먼트	베이스
영국식	쉐쥴	게롸지/게리지	러보러츄리	어드버-티스먼트	바-즈

I need to **schedule** a meeting with the managers. 관리자들과의 회의 일정을 잡아야 해요.
I'm not using Terry's **garage** anymore. 저는 더 이상 테리의 정비소를 이용하지 않아요.

미국식 발음 VS. 영국식 발음 비교 체험

P0_06

문장을 듣고 빈칸을 채우세요. 음성은 두 번 들려드립니다.

1. ________ is a path near the ________.

2. Mr. Roth is leaving this ________ for a two-week vacation.

3. I'd like you to type up this memo and make ________ that every department head gets a ________.

4. I'll finish the ________ quickly.

5. A ________ has been set up next to a lamppost.

6. A ________ leads to the ocean.

7. These fabric ________ are ready to go.

8. I'll get my ________ out of the ________.

9. Did you see the new soap ______________?

10. I was wondering if you've received my ________.

정답 및 해설 p. 2

유사 발음 비교 체험

영어에는 우리말에 없거나 구분이 명확하지 않은 유사한 발음들이 많은데, 토익 Part 1과 Part 2에서는 이러한 발음들을 이용한 오답들이 자주 출제됩니다.

1 [p] vs. [f]

P0_07

[p]는 입술을 붙였다가 공기를 터트려서 발음하며, 우리말의 'ㅍ' 소리에 해당된다. [f]는 우리말에 없는 소리로 입술을 약간 벌린 채, 윗니를 아랫입술에 살짝 대고 그 사이로 공기를 내보내면서 발음한다.

[p]	**copy**[kápi] 사본; 복사하다	**pull**[pul] 당기다	**pile**[pail] 더미, 쌓다
[f]	**coffee**[kɔ́:fi] 커피	**full**[ful] 가득한	**file**[fail] 파일; 철하다, 정리하다

She's making **copies**. 여자가 복사를 하고 있다.

She's having some **coffee**. 여자가 커피를 마시고 있다.

→ 가산명사인 copy는 a copy나 copies로 사용하고, 마시는 커피는 coffee나 some coffee로 사용한다.

2 [b] vs. [v]

P0_08

[b]는 [p]와 같은 방식으로 입술을 붙였다가 터트리면서 발음하며, 우리말의 'ㅂ' 소리에 해당된다. [v]는 [f]와 같은 방식으로 윗니를 아랫입술에 살짝 대고 그 사이로 공기를 내보내면서 발음하되, 목이 떨리는 소리가 되어야 한다.

[b]	**curb**[kə:rb] 연석	**base**[beis] 맨 아래 부분	**globe**[gloub] 지구본
[v]	**curve**[kə:rv] 곡선, 휘다	**vase**[veis] 꽃병	**glove**[glʌv] 장갑

There is a line of cars at the **curb**. 연석을 따라서 한 줄의 차들이 있다.

The road **curves** into the distance. 도로가 멀리 굽이치고 있다.

3 [s] vs. [θ]

P0_09

[s]는 혀가 윗니 뒤쪽에 닿지 않게 하면서 발음하되, 강하게 숨이 새나오도록 한다. [θ]는우리말에 없는 둔탁한 소리로, 입술을 약간 벌린 상태로 윗니와 아랫니 사이로 혀를 살짝 내밀어 발음하되, 가볍게 숨이 새나오도록 한다.

[s]	**sink**[siŋk] (부엌의) 싱크대	**pass**[pæs] 통과하다, 건네다	**sought**[sɔ:t] 찾았다
[θ]	**think**[θiŋk] 생각하다	**path**[pæθ] 길	**thought**[θɔ:t] 생각했다

What do you **think** of the new warehouse? 새 창고에 대해서 어떻게 생각해요?

The **sink** is full of dishes. 오답 싱크대는 접시로 가득해요.

It's bigger than the old one. 정답 예전 것보다 더 커요.

→ think와 발음이 유사한 sink를 이용해 혼동을 유발하고 있다.

4 [l] vs. [r]

P0_10

[l]은 혀를 뻗어서 윗니 뒤쪽에 대면서 발음한다. [r]은 혀를 안쪽으로 살짝 말되 입 천장에 닿지 않게 해서 발음한다.

[l]	**l**ate[leit] 늦은	**l**amp[læmp] 전등	**l**earn[lə:rn] 배우다
[r]	**r**ate[reit] 비율, 요금	**r**amp[ræmp] 경사로	**r**un[rʌn] 달리다

There's so much to **learn** about this job. 이 일자리는 배울 것이 매우 많네요.
Yes, I like to **run**, too. 오답 네, 저도 달리고 싶어요.
Do you like it so far? 정답 현재까지 괜찮아요?
➜ learn과 발음이 유사한 run을 이용해 혼동을 유발하고 있다.

5 [ou] vs. [ɔ:]

P0_11

o, oa를 [ou]로 발음하는 경우, '오'로 시작한 뒤 뒤에 '우'를 가볍게 붙여서 발음한다. 이러한 이중 모음은 하나의 모음처럼 발음하되 앞의 모음을 강하게 발음하는 것이 특징이다. a, au, o, ou를 [ɔ:]로 발음하는 경우, '오'를 길게 끌어서 '오-'로 발음한다.

[ou] o, oa	c**o**ld[kould] 추운	cl**o**thes[klouðz] 옷, 의복	c**oa**t[kout] 코트
[ɔ:] a, au, o, ou	c**a**lled[kɔ:ld] 전화했다	cl**o**th[klɔ:θ] 천, 옷감	c**au**ght[kɔ:t] 잡았다

It's **cold** today, isn't it? 오늘 춥네요, 그렇지 않나요?
Yes, I **called** him this morning. 오답 네, 제가 오늘 오전에 그에게 전화했어요.
Yes, you'd better wear a sweater. 정답 네, 스웨터를 입는 것이 좋겠네요.
➜ cold와 발음이 유사한 called를 이용해 혼동을 유발하고 있다.

6 [i] vs. [i:]

P0_12

i를 [i]로 발음하는 경우, 입술과 혀를 긴장시키지 말고 가볍게 입을 벌리고 '이'라고 짧고 강하게 발음한다.
ea, ee를 [i:]로 발음하는 경우, 입술을 좌우로 당기고 혀를 긴장시켜 '이-'라고 길게 끌어서 발음한다.

[i] i	s**i**t[sit] 앉다	l**i**ve[liv] 살다	f**i**ll[fil] 채우다
[i:] ea, ee	s**ea**t[si:t] 앉히다	l**ea**ve[li:v] 떠나다	f**ee**l[fi:l] 느끼다

Do you prefer the window or aisle **seat**? 창가 좌석을 원하세요, 아니면 통로 좌석을 원하세요?
Of course, you can **sit** here. 오답 물론, 이곳에 앉으셔도 됩니다.
Either is fine with me. 정답 둘 다 괜찮습니다.
➜ seat와 발음이 유사한 sit를 이용해 혼동을 유발하고 있다.

Q 유사 발음 비교 체험

P0_13

문장을 듣고 빈칸을 채우세요. 음성은 두 번 들려드립니다.

1. She is shopping for ________.

2. She's searching through some ________.

3. She's ________ on protective ________.

4. A ________ has been turned on next to a bed.

5. What will the new corporation be ________?

6. Why did you ________ so ________ last night?

7. Do you need to ________ immediately?

8. Aren't they going to build a bicycle ________ along the main road?

9. A ________ leads into the back of the truck.

10. A car is being ________ up at a fuel station.

정답 및 해설 p. 4

긴 문장 청취를 방해하는 연음 듣기

영어 문장을 빨리 읽다보면 단어들을 붙여서 읽게 됩니다. 이때 이어지는 여러 단어의 발음이 연결되어 마치 한 단어처럼 소리나는 것을 연음이라고 하는데, 토익 Listening은 단어가 아닌, 문장 듣기 시험이기 때문에 반드시 이 연음을 잘 들어야 문장의 내용을 제대로 파악할 수 있습니다.

1 끝자음과 첫모음이 만났을 때

P0_14

앞 단어가 자음으로 끝나고 뒤에 오는 단어가 모음으로 시작되면 연결하여 발음한다.

	각 단어의 소리	연음
is adjusting	[이즈 / 어저스팅]	[이저저스팅]
look around the store	[룩 / 어라운드 / 더 / 스토어]	[루커롸운 / 더 / 스토어]
half an hour	[해(f)프 / 언 / 아워]	[해(f)퍼나워]
in a new	[인 / 어 / 뉴]	[이너 / 뉴]
ask about	[애스크 / 어바우(ㅌ)]	[애스커바우(ㅌ)]

The speaker **is adjusting** the microphone. 연사가 마이크를 조정하고 있다.
They are **looking around** the furniture showroom. 그들은 가구 전시장을 둘러보고 있다.
The meeting is in **half an hour**. 회의는 30분 후에 있습니다.

2 동일하거나 유사한 발음의 자음이 만났을 때

P0_15

같거나 유사한 자음이 연달아오면 발음을 편하고 자연스럽게 하기 위해서 앞의 자음을 발음하지 않고 뒤의 것 하나만 발음한다.

	각 단어의 소리	연음
need to	[니ㄷ / 투]	[니투]
glad to	[글래(ㄷ) / 투]	[글래투]
told that	[토울드 / 댓]	[토울댓]
next time	[넥스트 / 타임]	[넥스타임]
convenience store	[컨비니언스 / 스또어]	[컨비니언쓰또어]

You **need to** call the bank immediately. 즉시 은행에 전화하셔야 해요.
Next time I'll check the traffic report before I leave. 다음 번에는 출발 전에 교통 방송을 확인할게요.
I'm **glad to** hear that. 그 소식을 들으니 기뻐요.

3 끝자음 d와 t가 y를 만났을 때

P0_16

앞 단어와 뒷 단어의 소리가 서로에게 영향을 주어서 같거나 비슷한 소리로 변하는 경우도 있다.

		각 단어의 소리	연음
	Did you	[디드 / 유]	[디쥬]
d+[j] → [dʒ]	**need you**	[니드 / 유]	[니쥬]
	told you	[토울드 / 유]	[토울쥬]
	meet you	[미ㅌ / 유]	[미츄]
t+[j] → [tʃ]	**put you**	[풋 / 유]	[푸츄]
	let you	[렛 / 유]	[레츄]
	this year	[디스 / 이어]	[디쉬어]
s+[j] → [ʃ]	**miss you**	[미스 / 유]	[미슈]
	promise you	[프라미스 / 유]	[프라미슈]

Did you hear when the project will start? 프로젝트가 언제 시작하는지 들었나요?
I'll **let you** know tomorrow. 내일 알려드릴게요.
Are you planning to attend the seminar **this year**? 올해 그 세미나에 참석할 계획인가요?

4 n과 t가 만났을 때

P0_17

- n과 t가 연속해서 -nt- 형태로 만나면, t를 발음하기도 하고 생략하기도 한다.

	center	[쎈터] / [쎄너]
-nt-	**twenty**	[트웬티] / [트웨니]
	in front of	[인 / (f)프런트 / 어브] → [인 / (f)프러너브]

We only have enough chairs for **twenty** people. 20명이 앉을 의자밖에 없어요.
She's seated **in front of** the computer monitor. 그녀는 컴퓨터 모니터 앞에 앉아 있다.

- n과 t가 서로 위치를 바꾸어 -t-n 형태로 만나면, 소리를 잠깐 멈춘 상태에서 콧속에서 터지듯이 소리를 내면서 발음한다.

-t-n	**mountain**	[마운튼] → [마운(ㅌ)은]
	fountain	[(f)파운튼] → [(f)파운(ㅌ)은]
	certain	[서어튼] → [서어ㄹ-(ㅌ)은]

I'm **certain** I mailed it to you on Monday. 확실히 월요일에 그것을 당신에게 우편으로 발송했어요.
Some people are relaxing by a **fountain**. 몇몇 사람들이 분수대 옆에서 쉬고 있다.

문장 이해의 필수, 내용어 듣기

문장에는 비교적 잘 들리는 단어와 그렇지 않은 단어가 있습니다. 잘 들리는 내용어는 핵심 내용을 담고 있는 말로서 길고 크게 들리며, 잘 들리지 않는 단어는 기능어로서 내용어들을 문법적으로 연결해주는 장치이며 상대적으로 덜 중요해서 소리를 작게 내면서 빠르게 말하거나 때로는 생략하기도 합니다. 초보자들은 우선적으로 내용어를 잘 듣는 데 중점을 두어야 합니다.

1 내용어와 기능어

내용어	역할	핵심 내용을 담고 있음
	강세	문장 강세를 받아서 길고 크게 소리 들림
	품사	명사, 동사, 형용사, 부사, 의문사, 숫자, 부정어 등
기능어	역할	핵심어를 연결하는 기능
	강세	문장 강세를 받지 않아서 빠르게 지나가며 소리가 작고 생략되기도 함
	품사	대명사, 관사, 소유격, 조동사, 전치사, 접속사 등

2 내용어와 기능어 구분하기

P0_18

The **concert starts** at **7 o'clock**. 콘서트는 7시에 시작한다.
내용어 및 핵심 내용: concert(콘서트), starts(시작), 7 o'clock(7시) → 길고 크게 잘 들린다.
내용어에 따른 결론: 콘서트 7시 시작
기능어: The, at → 빠르게 지나가며 소리가 내용어에 비해 작아서 잘 안 들린다.

All seats are being **used** at the **moment**. 모든 좌석들이 현재 사용 중이다.
내용어 및 핵심 내용: All(모든), seats(좌석들), used(사용), moment(지금)
내용어에 따른 결론: 모든 좌석들 지금 사용
기능어: are being, at, the

When will **Peter** be **returning** from his **vacation**? 피터는 언제 휴가에서 돌아오나요?
내용어 및 핵심 내용: When(언제), Peter, returning(돌아오나), vacation(휴가)
내용어에 따른 결론: 언제 피터 휴가 돌아오나
기능어: will, be, from, his

Isn't there a **coffee machine** on this **floor**? 이 층에 커피 자판기가 있지 않나요?
내용어 및 핵심 내용: Isn't there(있지 않나), coffee machine(커피 자판기), floor(층)
내용어에 따른 결론: 커피 자판기 (이) 층 있지 않나
기능어: a, on, this

Q 연음 듣기 / 내용어 듣기

PO_19

문장을 듣고 빈칸을 채우세요. 음성은 두 번 들려드립니다.

1. A technician ________ ________ some laboratory equipment.

2. I want to ________ ________ unloading our equipment.

3. I ________ ________ get this package to Hong Kong as quickly as possible.

4. I ________ ________ to start contacting candidates today.

5. I'll ________ ________ downstairs at five.

6. You can use our training ________.

7. Are you ________ that we need to advertise more?

8. I won't forget to write it ________ ________.

9. Do you have any brochures about trips to the ________?

10. ________ ________ know that a new vice president has been chosen?

정답 및 해설 p. 6

LC

PART 01

사진 묘사

기초학습
UNIT 01 사람 중심 사진
UNIT 02 사물·풍경 중심 사진
ETS 파트별 모의고사

PART 1 | 사진 묘사

6문항

Part 1 시험은 이렇게 나와요

사진을 보고 들려주는 4개의 보기 중 사진을 가장 잘 묘사한 것을 고르는 문제입니다.

문제지

음원

Number 1. Look at the picture marked number 1 in your test book.

(A) She's sweeping the floor.

(B) She's stacking some chairs.

(C) She's picking up a menu.

(D) She's serving some customers.

ETS가 제안하는 꿀팁!

1 사진을 먼저 파악하고 정답 표현을 예상해보세요

사람 중심 사진에서는 사람의 동작이나 상태, 사물·풍경 중심 사진에서는 사물의 위치와 상태에 유의하세요.

They're looking at a display. (O)
사람들이 진열품을 보고 있다.

Products have been displayed. (O)
상품이 진열되어 있다.

2 객관적인 묘사가 정답이에요!

사진에 보이지 않는 것을 추측하는 주관적인 묘사나 추상적인 묘사는 오답이니 주의하세요.

The people are preparing some ~~food~~. (X)
사람들이 음식을 준비하고 있다.
→ 사진에 음식이 보이지 않음

The people are ~~leaving~~ the lobby. (X)
사람들이 로비를 떠나고 있다.
→ 떠나려는 건지 확실히 알 수 없음

The people are standing at the counter. (O)
사람들이 카운터에 서 있다.

3 혼동 어휘를 사용한 오답에 주의하세요.

발음이 비슷한 단어나 다의어를 사용하여 얼핏 정답으로 혼동하기 쉬운 오답도 종종 등장하니 유의하세요.

They're writing ~~letters~~. (X)
사람들이 편지를 쓰고 있다.
→ 사다리(ladder)와 비슷한 발음의 letter로 혼동을 주는 오답

They're ~~walking up~~ stairs. (X)
사람들이 계단을 걸어 올라가고 있다.
→ 작업하고 있다(working on)는 말과 비슷한 발음의 walking up으로 혼동을 주는 오답

They're working on a house. (O)
사람들이 집을 공사하고 있다.

기초학습

시제 익히기

영어에는 시간을 문법적으로 규정한 여러 가지 시제가 있습니다. 그러나 Part 1에서는 현재진행, 현재, 현재완료 3가지 기본 시제가 주로 출제됩니다.

① 현재진행

현재진행 시제는 Part 1에서 가장 많이 출제됩니다. '남자가 손을 올리고 있다'와 같이 현재 진행 중인 동작이나 '기술자가 실험복을 입고 있다'와 같은 현재의 상태를 나타내는 데 쓰입니다.

주어+is[are]+동사-ing	주어가 ~하고 있다

They **are working** outdoors.
사람들이 야외에서 일하고 있다. (일하는 동작)

Many passengers **are standing** in line outside. 많은 승객들이 밖에 줄 서 있다. (서 있는 상태)

- A woman **is cutting** a customer's hair. 여자가 손님의 머리를 자르고 있다. (동작)
- A man **is writing** on a notepad. 남자가 메모장에 글을 쓰고 있다. (동작)
- He's **holding** a cane. 남자가 지팡이를 잡고 있다. (상태)
- Some boats **are floating** in the water. 배 몇 척이 물에 떠 있다. (상태)

is wearing vs. is putting on

is wearing은 이미 착용한 상태를 나타내는 반면, **is putting on**은 착용하고 있는 동작을 나타낸다는 점에 주의하세요.

- The cashier **is wearing** a watch. 출납원이 시계를 착용하고 있다. (착용한 상태)
- He **is wearing** a long-sleeved shirt. 남자가 긴소매의 셔츠를 입고 있다. (입은 상태)
- She **is putting on** a hat. 여자가 모자를 쓰는 중이다. (쓰고 있는 동작)

② 현재

현재 시제는 Part 1에서 두 번째로 많이 출제됩니다. '남자가 가방 하나를 가지고 있다'거나 '의자가 비어 있다'와 같이 주어의 현재 상태를 나타내는 데 쓰입니다.

주어+is[are] ~	주어가 ~에 있다 / 주어가 ~한 상태이다
주어+일반동사 현재형	주어가 ~한다 / 주어가 ~하고 있는 상태이다
There is[are]+주어 ~	~에 주어가 있다

Each of the apartments **has** a balcony.
각각의 아파트는 발코니를 가지고 있다.

- Some merchandise **is** on display. 물건들이 전시되어 있다.
- **There is** a plant on the table. 테이블 위에 화분이 하나 있다.
- **There are** some shelves beside the bed. 침대 옆에 몇 개의 선반들이 있다.

③ 현재완료

현재완료 시제는 정답보다는 오히려 오답으로 많이 출제됩니다. '남자가 지붕에 올라갔다'거나 '일꾼들이 일을 멈췄다'와 같이 과거에 이루어진 동작이나 상태가 현재까지 이어지는 것을 나타내는 데 쓰입니다.

주어+have[has]+p.p.	주어가 ~했다

The clouds **have settled** onto the hilltop.
구름들이 언덕 꼭대기에 자리잡았다.

- A man **has picked up** a phone. 한 남자가 전화기를 집어 들었다.
- A train **has arrived** at a platform. 열차 한 대가 승강장에 도착했다.
- Some people **have gathered** under a tent for a meal. 몇몇 사람들이 식사를 위해 텐트 아래에 모였다.

시제 익히기 PRACTICE P1_01

각 사진을 묘사하는 문장을 듣고 빈칸을 채우세요. 음성은 두 번 들려드립니다.

1

They're _________ a _________ at the office.

사람들이 사무실에서 **대화를 하고 있다.**

2

There _________ some chairs and a table alongside the van.

승합차 옆에 의자들과 테이블 하나가 **있다.**

3

Some customers _________ _________ up to the counter.

몇몇 손님들이 계산대까지 **다가섰다.**

4

She's _________ _________ some glasses.

여자가 안경을 **써 보고 있다.**

정답 및 해설 p. 8

수동태 익히기

영어에서는 '누가 무엇을 ~하다'라는 문장 형태를 '무엇이 (누구에 의해) ~되다'라는 문장 형태로 바꿔 표현하기도 하는데, 이 두 가지 문장 형태를 각각 '능동태'와 '수동태'라고 합니다.

능동태	수동태
주어 + 동사 + 목적어 누가 무엇을 ~하다	주어 + is[are] +p.p.+(by 행위자) 무엇이 (행위자에 의해) ~되다
He sets the table. 그는 상을 차린다.	The table is set (by him). 상이 (그에 의해) 차려진다.

앞에서 배운 현재, 현재진행, 현재완료 시제는 능동태뿐만 아니라 수동태로도 출제됩니다.

① 현재 수동태

현재 수동태는 사물 중심의 사진에서 자주 출제됩니다. '책상들이 연달아 놓여 있다'거나 '라운지가 칸막이로 나뉘어 있다'와 같이 주어의 위치나 상태를 나타내는 데 쓰입니다.

주어+is[are]+p.p.	주어가 ~되어 있다

The house **is reflected** in the water.
집이 물에 반사되고 있다.

- Some chairs **are arranged** on the lawn. 몇 개의 의자들이 잔디에 정렬되어 있다.
- Cars **are parked** along the street. 차들이 도로를 따라서 주차되어 있다.
- Bottles **are lined** up on shelves. 병들이 선반에 나열되어 있다.
- A path **is shaded** by some trees. 길 하나가 나무들에 의해서 그늘져 있다.

② 현재진행 수동태

현재진행 수동태는 사물 중심의 사진에서 주로 오답 문장의 형태로 출제됩니다. '지붕이 수리되고 있다'거나 '상자가 옮겨지고 있다'와 같이 누군가의 동작에 의해서 주어가 어떤 상태로 되고 있는 중임을 나타내는 데 쓰입니다.

주어+is[are] being+p.p.	주어가 ~되고 있다

Boxes are being moved.
상자들이 옮겨지고 있다.

- A car is being sprayed with water. 차 한 대에 물이 뿌려지고 있다.
- A presentation is being shown on a screen. 프레젠테이션이 스크린에 보여지고 있다.
- Flowers are being arranged in vases. 꽃들이 꽃병들에 꽂꽂이되고 있다.

③ 현재완료 수동태

현재완료 수동태는 사물 중심의 사진에서 주로 출제되며, '물건이 쌓여 있다'거나 '창문이 열려 있다'와 같이 과거에 누군가에 의해 이루어진 동작의 결과가 현재까지 계속되는 것을 나타내는 데 쓰입니다.

주어+have[has] been+p.p.	주어가 ~되어 있다

Construction vehicles have been parked near the trees.
건설 차량들이 나무들 가까이에 주차되어 있다.

- A lamp has been turned on next to a bed. 침대 옆에 램프 하나가 켜져 있다.
- Some furniture has been set out on a deck. 데크에 가구가 설치되어 있다.
- Serving trays have been filled with the food. 쟁반들이 음식으로 채워져 있다.
- Some potted plants have been placed outdoors. 몇 개의 화분 식물들이 야외에 놓여 있다.

수동태 익히기 PRACTICE P1_02

각 사진을 묘사하는 문장을 듣고 빈칸을 채우세요. 음성은 두 번 들려드립니다.

1

They __________ __________ together on the steps.

사람들이 계단에 함께 **모여 있다.**

2

A flowerpot __________ __________ __________ on a stair by the wall.

화분 하나가 벽 옆의 계단에 **놓여 있다.**

3

Plants __________ __________ __________.

식물들에 **물이 주어지고 있다.**

4

The fruit __________ __________ __________ high in the vehicle.

과일이 차량에 높게 **쌓여 있다.**

정답 및 해설 p. 9

UNIT 01

사람 중심 사진

사람 중심 사진에서는 사람의 동작이나 상태를 나타내는 동사를 잘 듣는 것이 중요합니다. 아는 만큼 들린다고 하죠? 핵심 어휘를 먼저 익혀보세요.

핵심 기출 어휘

P1_03

주요 동작 표현

carrying 나르고 있다

hanging 걸고 있다

pointing at 가리키고 있다

holding 잡고 있다

putting on 입고 있다(= trying on)

handing 건네주고 있다

serving 서빙하고 있다

repairing 고치고 있다(= fixing)

pouring 따르고 있다

writing down 적고 있다

reaching for ~을 향해 손을 뻗고 있다

examining 자세히 보고 있다

sweeping 쓸고 있다

shaking hands 악수하고 있다

leaning against 기대어 있다

주요 사물/도구 표현

monitor 모니터
laptop 노트북 컴퓨터
grocery 식료품
produce 농산물
luggage 수하물, 짐
patio 테라스
cart 수레, 카트

suitcase 여행가방
tool 연장
artwork 미술품
staircase 계단(= stairs)
file 파일
supplies 사무용품
shelf 선반(= rack)

drawer 서랍
cabinet 캐비닛
pole 기둥
fencing 울타리(= fence)
(recycling) bin (재활용) 쓰레기통
meal 식사

receipt 영수증
folder 폴더
board 게시판
document 서류(= paper)
equipment 기기, 기구
merchandise 상품
plant 식물

빈출 사진과 정답 문장

P1_04

시험에 자주 나오는 사진 상황과 정답으로 제시될 수 있는 문장들을 익혀보세요.

1인 등장 사진

1. 사무/업무 보는 사진

❶ He's looking at a monitor.
남자가 모니터를 보고 있다.

❷ He's operating a computer.
남자가 컴퓨터를 작동시키고 있다.

2. 쇼핑하는 사진

❶ He's shopping for groceries.
남자가 식료품을 사고 있다.

❷ He's examining some produce.
남자가 농산물을 살펴보고 있다.

3. 수리[작업]하는 사진

❶ She's working on a bicycle.
여자가 자전거를 손보고 있다.

❷ She's repairing the bicycle.
여자가 자전거를 수리하고 있다.

2인 이상 등장 사진

4. 회의하는 사진

❶ A man is pointing at something in the book.
한 남자가 손으로 책에 있는 뭔가를 가리키고 있다

❷ One of the men is writing something down.
남자들 중 한 명이 뭔가를 적고 있다.

5. 걷거나 이동하는 사진

❶ Some people are walking on the platform.
몇몇 사람들이 승강장에서 걷고 있다.

❷ Some people are carrying their luggage.
몇몇 사람들이 짐을 들고 가고 있다.

6. 식당에 있는 사진

❶ Customers are sitting on the patio.
손님들이 테라스에 앉아 있다.

❷ A waiter is serving some patrons.
웨이터가 손님들을 시중들고 있다.

기출 문제풀이 전략

1인 사진

 P1_05

인물의 주요 동작을 먼저 파악한 후, 장소나 사물, 착용 상태 등을 살펴보세요.

(A) He's hanging up a picture.
(B) He's cleaning his desk.
(C) He's holding a cup.
(D) He's arranging some furniture.

–

(A) 남자가 그림을 걸고 있다.
(B) 남자가 책상을 청소하고 있다.
(C) 남자가 컵을 들고 있다.
(D) 남자가 가구를 배치하고 있다.

STEP 01

사진 파악

❶ 인물의 주요 동작 및 인상착의 파악
holding a cup / looking at a paper

❷ 장소와 주요 사물 파악
indoors / office / cabinet / files / bulletin board

STEP 02

오답 소거

(A) ~~hanging up a picture~~ (X)
그림이 보이지도 않으며 뭔가를 걸고 있는 동작도 아님

(B) ~~cleaning~~ his desk (X)
청소하고 있지 않음

(C) holding a cup (O)
적절한 묘사

(D) ~~arranging some furniture~~ (X)
가구를 배치하고 있지 않음

정답 (C)

| WORDS | hang up 걸다 arrange 정리하다, 배치하다

CHECK UP

오답을 소거하면서 알맞은 답을 고르세요. 그런 다음 다시 들으면서 빈칸을 채우세요. 

1

(A) She's __________ a door. (O/X)
(B) She's __________ __________ some notices. (O/X)
(C) She's __________ a pamphlet. (O/X)
(D) She's __________ her glasses. (O/X)

2

(A) He's __________ __________ a hose. (O/X)
(B) He's __________ __________ a tree. (O/X)
(C) He's __________ his hands. (O/X)
(D) He's __________ __________ some plants. (O/X)

정답 및 해설 p. 10

2인 이상 사진

P1_07

인물들의 공통 동작과 개별 동작을 파악한 후, 착용 상태 등을 살펴보세요.

(A) A woman is putting her backpack on a cart.

(B) The people are shaking hands.

(C) The people are waving good-bye.

(D) A man is handing a woman her suitcase.

–

(A) 여자가 카트 위에 배낭을 놓고 있다.

(B) 사람들이 악수를 하고 있다.

(C) 사람들이 손을 흔들며 작별하고 있다.

(D) 남자가 여자에게 여행가방을 건네주고 있다.

| WORDS | wave 손을 흔들다 hand 건네주다

STEP 01

사진 파악

❶ 공통 동작

shaking hands / greeting / talking

❷ 개별 동작

carrying a suitcase

❸ 장소와 주요 사물

airport / baggage claim / carousel

STEP 02

오답 소거

(A) putting her ~~backpack~~ on a ~~cart~~ (X)
사진에 배낭도 카트도 보이지 않음

(B) shaking hands (O)
적절한 묘사

(C) ~~waving good-bye~~ (X)
손을 흔들며 작별하는 모습이 아님

(D) ~~handing a woman her suitcase~~ (X)
가방을 건네주고 있지 않음

정답 (B)

CHECK UP 오답을 소거하면서 알맞은 답을 고르세요. 그런 다음 다시 들으면서 빈칸을 채우세요. P1_08

1

(A) They're __________ the chairs. (O/X)

(B) They're __________ __________ some books. (O/X)

(C) They're __________ the plant. (O/X)

(D) They're __________ a presentation. (O/X)

2

(A) One of the men is __________ __________ a wall. (O/X)

(B) A woman is __________ a bag. (O/X)

(C) Some people are __________ on a staircase. (O/X)

(D) Some people are __________ __________ a street. (O/X)

정답 및 해설 p. 10

장소별 빈출 표현

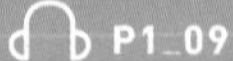

사무실

operating a computer 컴퓨터를 조작하다
arranging the chairs 의자를 배치하다
searching through some files 파일을 뒤지다
moving furniture 가구를 옮기다
typing on a keyboard 키보드를 치다
turning on a lamp 램프를 켜다
passing papers 서류를 전달하다
organizing documents 서류를 정돈하다
giving a presentation 발표하다
looking out a window 창밖을 보다
plugging[unplugging] a cord 코드를 꽂다[빼다]
facing a screen 스크린을 마주보다
picking up a laptop 노트북 컴퓨터를 집어 들다
taking notes on paper 종이에 메모하다

거리 / 공원 / 공공장소

watering the plant 식물에 물을 주다
crossing a street 길을 건너다
waiting in line 줄 서서 기다리다
drinking from a bottle 병으로 마시다
viewing some artwork 미술품을 보다
tying one's shoe 신발 끈을 묶다
removing a safety helmet 안전모를 벗다
boarding a boat 배에 타다
rowing a boat 배를 젓다
resting on a bench 벤치에서 쉬다
getting into a vehicle 차량에 타다
exiting[getting out of] a vehicle 차량에서 내리다
waiting for a train 기차를 기다리다
climbing up some steps 계단을 올라가다

상점 / 식당

shopping for groceries 식료품을 사다
paying for some books 책값을 계산하다
pulling[pushing] a cart 카트를 끌다[밀다]
placing items on a shelf 물품을 선반에 놓다
wrapping up some merchandise 상품을 포장하다
printing out a receipt 영수증을 출력하다
signing a receipt 영수증에 서명하다
setting up tables 테이블을 차리다
preparing some food 음식을 준비하다
dining 식사하다(= eating a meal)
wiping[clearing] off a table 테이블을 치우다
taking off an apron 앞치마를 벗다

작업장 / 공사장

working on a bicycle 자전거를 손보다
trimming some bushes 덤불을 다듬다
setting up a ladder 사다리를 설치하다
repairing[fixing] a roof 지붕을 고치다
installing a railing 난간을 설치하다
putting away some rope 밧줄을 치우다
polishing the floor 바닥을 문지르다
wiping some windows 창문을 닦다
emptying a recycling bin 재활용 쓰레기통을 비우다
loading[unloading] a truck
트럭에 (물건을) 싣다[내리다]

ETS 문제로 훈련하기

P1_10

사진을 가장 잘 묘사하는 문장을 고른 후, 빈칸을 채우세요.

1 

(A) (B) (C) (D)

(A) He's ________ to some ________.

(B) He's ________ a ________.

(C) He's ________ a ________.

(D) He's ________ a ________.

2 

(A) (B) (C) (D)

(A) The men are ________ a ________.

(B) The men are ________ the ________.

(C) The men are ________ ________ tables.

(D) The men are ________ ________.

3 

(A) (B) (C) (D)

(A) She's ________ ________ some files.

(B) She's ________ ________ ________ on a shelf.

(C) She's ________ a desk ________.

(D) She's ________ some ________ on the wall.

4 

(A) (B) (C) (D)

(A) The women are ________ each other.

(B) The women are ________ ________.

(C) One woman is ________ the other a ________.

(D) One woman is ________ ________.

정답 및 해설 p. 11

ETS 실전 테스트

1.

(A) (B) (C) (D)

2.

(A) (B) (C) (D)

3.

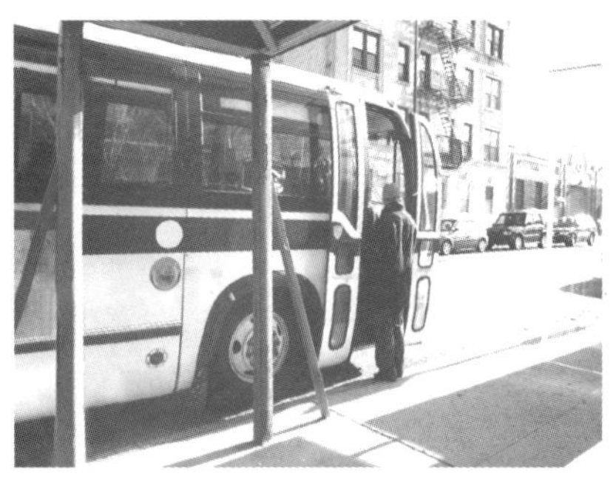

(A) (B) (C) (D)

4.

(A) (B) (C) (D)

5.

(A) (B) (C) (D)

6.

(A) (B) (C) (D)

7.

(A) (B) (C) (D)

8.

(A) (B) (C) (D)

9.

(A) (B) (C) (D)

10.

(A) (B) (C) (D)

11.

(A) (B) (C) (D)

12.

(A) (B) (C) (D)

정답 및 해설 p. 12

UNIT 02 사물·풍경 중심 사진

사물·풍경 중심 사진에서는 사물의 위치나 상태를 나타내는 표현을 잘 듣는 것이 중요합니다. 또한 사람과 사물·풍경 묘사가 혼합되어 등장하는 문제도 꼭 출제되니 같이 파악하는 연습을 하세요.

핵심 기출 어휘

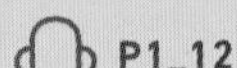

주요 위치 표현

in front of the door
문 앞에

against the wall
벽에 기대어

on the floor[ground]
바닥에

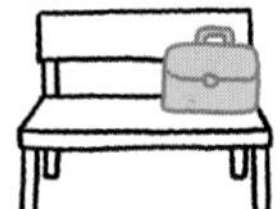

on the bench
벤치 위에

in a corner
코너에

on a windowsill
창턱에

along a trail
오솔길을 따라

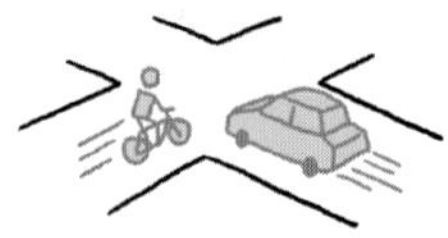

at an intersection
교차로에서

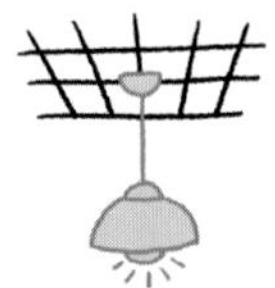

from the ceiling
천장에서

between the chairs
의자 사이에

in a row
일렬로

around the table
테이블 주위에

주요 상태 표현

be loaded[filled] with ~로 가득 차 있다
be stacked 쌓여 있다
be under construction 공사 중이다
be on display 진열되어 있다(= be being displayed)
be left open 열려 있다
be positioned along ~을 따라 놓여 있다
be occupied 자리가 차 있다
be spread out 펼쳐져 있다
be located 위치해 있다
lead to ~로 이어지다, 통하다
be divided[separated] by ~로 나뉘어져 있다
be propped up against ~에 기대어 있다
be scattered 흩어져 있다
be stocked with ~로 채워져 있다

빈출 사진과 정답 문장

P1_13

시험에 자주 나오는 사진 상황과 정답으로 제시될 수 있는 문장들을 익혀보세요.

사물·풍경 사진

1. 가구가 배치된 사진

❶ There is a rug in front of the door.
문 앞에 깔개 하나가 있다.

❷ The chairs are positioned against the wall.
의자들이 벽에 기대어 놓여 있다.

2. 차가 주차된 거리 사진

❶ A vehicle is parked on the street.
차량 한 대가 도로에 주차되어 있다.

❷ A line is painted on the road.
도로에 선 하나가 페인트칠 되어 있다.

3. 풍경 사진

❶ Some boats are floating in the water.
보트 몇 척이 물에 떠 있다.

❷ Lampposts are lined up in a row.
가로등 기둥들이 일렬로 세워져 있다.

사람/사물·풍경 혼합 사진

4. 카페·식당 사진

❶ The waitress is serving a customer some food.
웨이트리스가 손님에게 음식을 제공하고 있다.

❷ The table is covered with a cloth.
탁자가 천으로 덮여 있다.

5. 야외·공원 사진

❶ The bike is loaded with bags.
자전거에 가방들이 실려 있다.

❷ A man is resting on the bench.
한 남자가 벤치에서 쉬고 있다.

6. 작업하는 사진

❶ The men are doing some work on the house.
남자들이 집 공사를 하고 있다.

❷ There is a ladder leaning against the building.
건물에 기대어 있는 사다리가 있다.

기출 문제풀이 전략

사물·풍경 사진

P1_14

사진에서 두드러지는 사물이나 풍경에 주목하고, 주변 사물의 위치나 상태도 파악하세요.

(A) A laptop computer is being repaired.
(B) Office equipment is being unpacked.
(C) Some chairs are stacked in a corner.
(D) A plant has been placed on a windowsill.

–

(A) 노트북 컴퓨터가 수리되고 있다.
(B) 사무기기의 포장이 풀어지고 있다.
(C) 의자 몇 개가 구석에 쌓여 있다.
(D) 창문턱에 식물이 놓여 있다.

STEP 01

사진 파악

❶ **핵심 사물 파악**
a desk next to a window / a laptop on a desk / a plant on a windowsill

❷ **주변 사물 파악**
a lamp on a desk / a chair / some paper

STEP 02

오답 소거

(A) A laptop computer ~~is being repaired~~. (X)
수리하고 있는 사람이 없음

(B) Office equipment ~~is being unpacked~~. (X)
포장을 풀고 있는 사람이 없음

(C) ~~Some chairs are stacked~~ in a corner. (X)
의자가 쌓여 있지 않음

(D) A plant has been placed on a windowsill. (O)
창문턱에 화분이 있음 　　정답 (D)

| WORDS | equipment 장비, 기구 unpack 풀다, 꺼내다 stack 쌓다 windowsill 창문턱

CHECK UP 오답을 소거하면서 알맞은 답을 고르세요. 그런 다음 다시 들으면서 빈칸을 채우세요. P1_15

1

(A) A building is ___________ ___________. (O/X)
(B) A street is being ___________. (O/X)
(C) Some cars are ___________ at a traffic light. (O/X)
(D) Some cars are ___________ side by side. (O/X)

2

(A) Chairs are ___________ ___________ against a ___________. (O/X)
(B) A coffee pot is being ___________. (O/X)
(C) A café window ___________ a street. (O/X)
(D) Tables have been ___________ for a ___________. (O/X)

정답 및 해설 p. 16

사람/사물·풍경 혼합 사진

P1_16

사람이 크게 부각되지 않은 경우, 두드러진 사물이나 전반적인 풍경에 주목하세요.

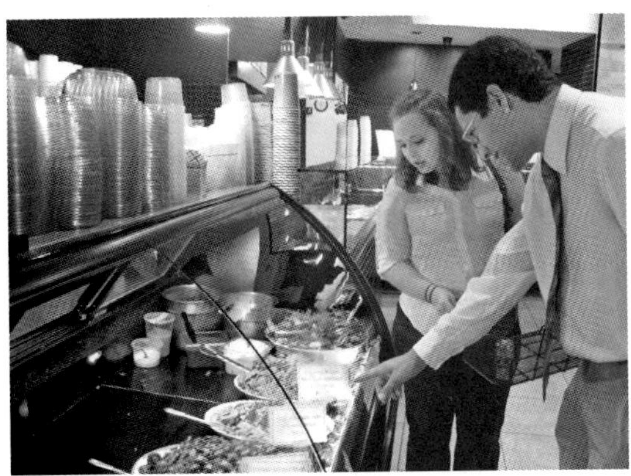

(A) The man is paying for his dinner.
(B) A server is taking food out of a container.
(C) Some windows are being cleaned.
(D) Some food is on display.

–

(A) 남자가 저녁값을 계산하고 있다.
(B) 종업원이 용기에서 음식을 꺼내고 있다.
(C) 일부 창문이 청소되고 있다.
(D) 몇 가지 음식이 진열되어 있다.

| WORDS | container 용기, 그릇

STEP 01

사진 파악

❶ **핵심 사물 파악**
food on display / a display case / plastic containers

❷ **사람 동작 파악**
pointing at a dish / choosing some food

STEP 02

오답 소거

(A) The man is ~~paying for~~ his dinner. (X)
돈을 지불하는 모습이 아님

(B) ~~A server is taking food out of~~ a container. (X)
종업원도 보이지 않으며 음식을 꺼내고 있지 않음

(C) ~~Some windows are being cleaned.~~ (X)
사진에 창문이 없으며 청소하고 있는 사람도 없음

(D) Some food is on display. (O)
음식이 진열되어 있음 　정답 (D)

CHECK UP 오답을 소거하면서 알맞은 답을 고르세요. 그런 다음 다시 들으면서 빈칸을 채우세요. P1_17

1

(A) Dishes are ________ on the table. (O/X)
(B) Customers are ________ food on their ________. (O/X)
(C) Some pans are being ________. (O/X)
(D) Restaurant workers are ________ some ________. (O/X)

2

(A) People are ________ suitcases in a ________. (O/X)
(B) People are ________ ________ in a park. (O/X)
(C) Cars are being ________ down a road. (O/X)
(D) Tents are being ________ ________ in a field. (O/X)

정답 및 해설 p. 17

장소별 빈출 표현

집/사무실/회의실

left in a sink 싱크대 안에 놓여 있는
blocked by boxes 박스로 막힌
posted to a bulletin board 게시판에 게시된
be being put away 치워지고 있다
be being replaced 교체되고 있다
be being vacuumed 진공청소기로 청소되고 있다
placed on top of a desk 책상 위에 놓여진
be being installed 설치되고 있다
scattered on a rug 깔개 위에 흩어져 있는
be being unrolled 펼쳐지고 있다
parked in a garage 차고에 주차된
pushed under a desk 책상 아래로 밀어 넣어진
pushed against a wall 벽에 밀어진
stored inside a cabinet 캐비닛 안에 보관된

공원/물가

have fallen on the ground 땅에 떨어져 있다
have been swept[raked] into a pile 쓸어서[갈퀴로 쓸어서] 한 무더기로 모여 있다
chained to a pole 기둥에 쇠사슬로 매어져 있는
be leaning against a column 기둥에 기대어 있다
be lying on the ground 땅바닥에 놓여 있다
overlook a lake 호수를 내려다보다
hanging from a tree 나무에 매달린
have been cut down 베어져 쓰러져 있다
be crowded with tourists 관광객들로 붐비다
be sailing in the ocean 바다에서 항해 중이다
be moving toward a bridge 다리 쪽으로 움직이다
be being cleared from a street 길에서 치워지고 있다

거리/교통/공공시설

be being towed by a truck 트럭에 의해 견인되고 있다
mounted on a bus 버스에 실린[올려진]
be raised 올려지다
stuck in traffic 교통체증에 갇힌
suspended from a window 창문에 매달린
hung up 걸려 있는
parked in a row 일렬로 주차된
traveling in the same[opposite] direction 같은[반대] 방향으로 가는
decorated with flowers 꽃으로 장식된

주방/식당/상점

be hanging from the ceiling 천장에 달려 있다
piled on the floor 바닥에 쌓여 있는
stacked in a pile 무더기로 쌓여 있는
organized in a display case 진열장에 정리되어 있는
separated into containers 용기에 따로 담긴
lined up on a shelf 선반에 줄지어 있는
be wide open 활짝 열려 있다
displayed on shelves 선반에 진열된
be being rolled up 말려 올라가고 있다
be being mopped 대걸레로 닦여지고 있다
has been closed 닫혀 있다
stored in a freezer 냉동실에 보관된

ETS 문제로 훈련하기

P1_19

사진을 가장 잘 묘사하는 문장을 고른 후, 빈칸을 채우세요.

1

(A) (B) (C) (D)

(A) A ________ has been ________ in a cabinet.

(B) Some appliances are being ________.

(C) A kitchen ________ has been ________ ________.

(D) Some items are ________ ________ a microwave oven.

2

(A) (B) (C) (D)

(A) A highway is ________ for ________.

(B) Cars are ________ in ________ ________.

(C) ________ are being ________ on a highway.

(D) Vehicles are ________ onto a ________ ________.

3

(A) (B) (C) (D)

(A) The man is ________ a shopping ________.

(B) Merchandise has been ________ on ________.

(C) ________ have been ________ near a cash register.

(D) The ________ is being ________.

4

(A) (B) (C) (D)

(A) She's ________ water from a ________.

(B) She's ________ ________ from a file.

(C) ________ ________ are ________ on a desk.

(D) Some ________ have been ________ next to a ________.

정답 및 해설 p. 18

ETS 실전 테스트

1.

(A) (B) (C) (D)

2.

(A) (B) (C) (D)

3.

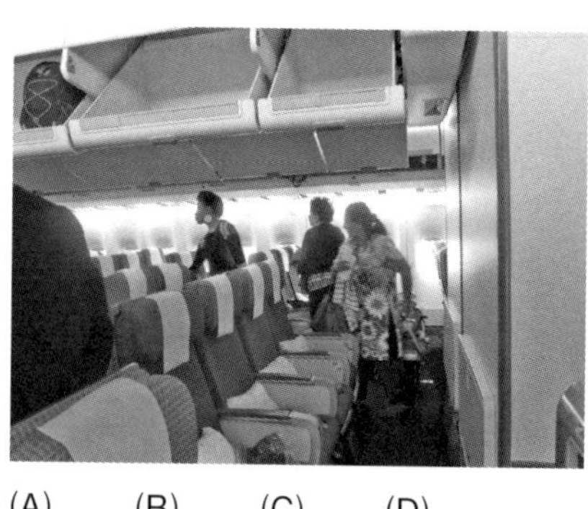

(A) (B) (C) (D)

4.

(A) (B) (C) (D)

5.

(A) (B) (C) (D)

6.

(A) (B) (C) (D)

7.

(A) (B) (C) (D)

8.

(A) (B) (C) (D)

9.

(A) (B) (C) (D)

10.

(A) (B) (C) (D)

11.

(A) (B) (C) (D)

12.

(A) (B) (C) (D)

정답 및 해설 p. 19

LISTENING TEST

In the Listening test, you will be asked to demonstrate how well you understand spoken English. The entire Listening test will last approximately 45 minutes. There are four parts, and directions are given for each part. You must mark your answers on the separate answer sheet. Do not write your answers in your test book.

PART 1

Directions: For each question in this part, you will hear four statements about a picture in your test book. When you hear the statements, you must select the one statement that best describes what you see in the picture. Then find the number of the question on your answer sheet and mark your answer. The statements will not be printed in your test book and will be spoken only one time.

Statement (C), "They're sitting at a table," is the best description of the picture, so you should select answer (C) and mark it on your answer sheet.

1.

2.

Go on to the next page

3.

4.

5.

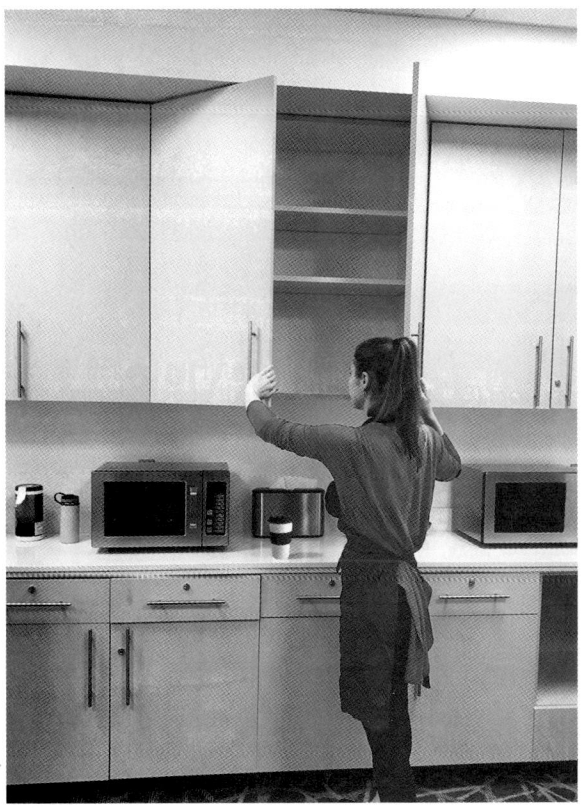

6.

LC

PART 02

질의 응답

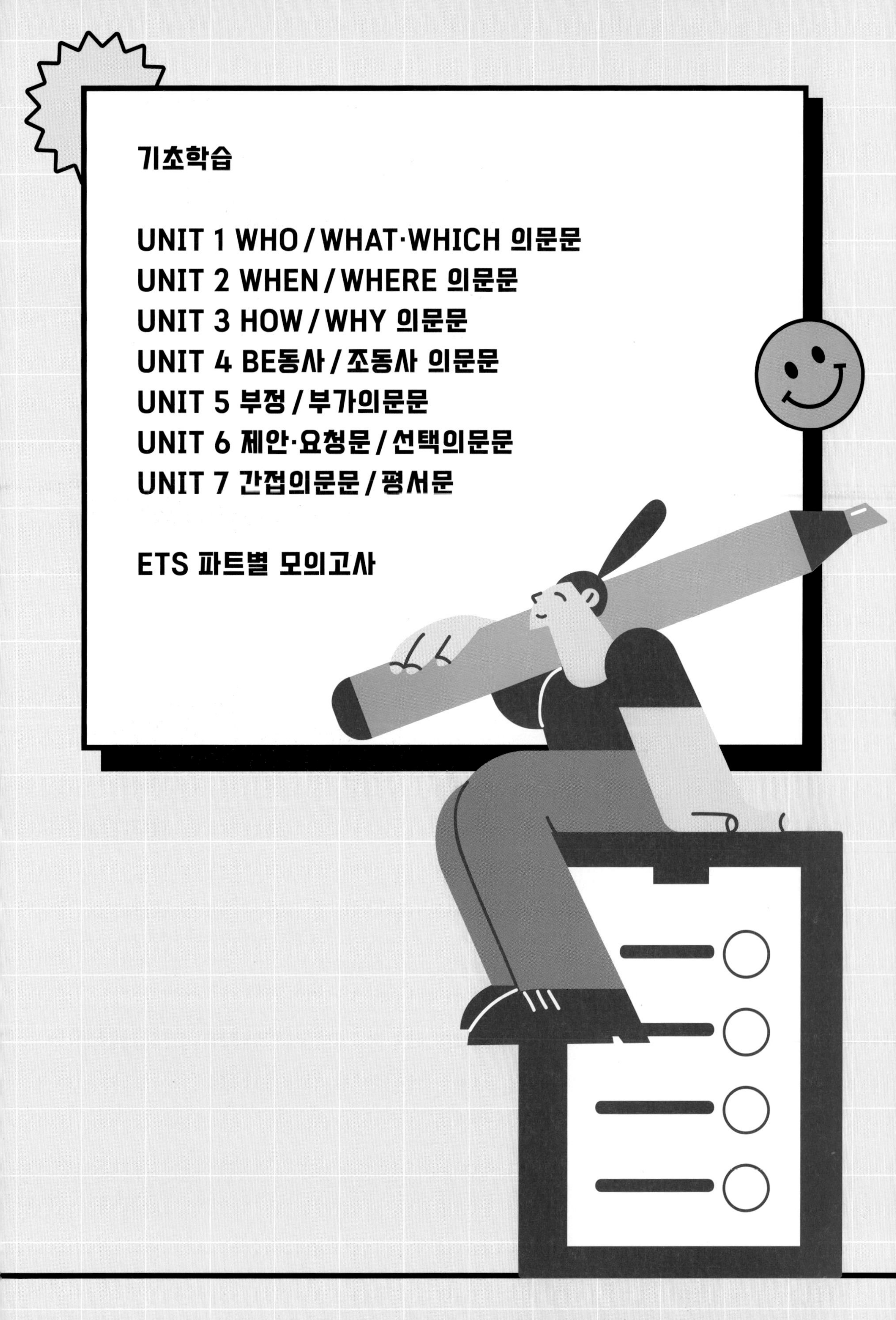
기초학습

UNIT 1 WHO / WHAT·WHICH 의문문
UNIT 2 WHEN / WHERE 의문문
UNIT 3 HOW / WHY 의문문
UNIT 4 BE동사 / 조동사 의문문
UNIT 5 부정 / 부가의문문
UNIT 6 제안·요청문 / 선택의문문
UNIT 7 간접의문문 / 평서문

ETS 파트별 모의고사

PART 2 | 질의 응답

25문항

Part 2 시험은 이렇게 나와요

시험지에 보여지는 것 없이 듣고만 푸는 문제입니다. 하나의 질문에 대한 답변 세 개를 듣고, 질문에 가장 적절한 응답 하나를 고르면 됩니다.

문제지

7. Mark your answer on your answer sheet.

8. Mark your answer on your answer sheet.

문제지에는
이것만 보여요.
오로지 듣기에만
집중하세요.

음원

Number 7.

M-Au What was the planning meeting about?
W-Br **(A) The upcoming product launch.**
(B) At the next meeting.
(C) No, Sandra is working on the floor plan.

Number 8.

W-Br When do you start your internship?
M-Cn (A) Yes, I really enjoy it.
(B) A computer software company.
(C) At the beginning of the summer.

이런 음원이 들려요.

ETS가 제안하는 꿀팁!

1 질문의 앞 부분이 중요해요.

질문 앞 부분의 3-4단어를 들으면 거의 질문의 요지를 알 수 있답니다. 특히 의문사가 있는 의문문은 의문사를 놓치면 안되겠죠? 질문의 앞 부분에 집중하세요.

Do you usually work during lunch? 보통 점심 시간에 일을 하나요?
Where did you get your laptop fixed? 노트북 컴퓨터는 어디에서 고쳤나요?

2 의문사 의문문에 Yes/No 대답은 무조건 오답이에요.

의문사 의문문에는 Yes / No로 답할 수가 없죠. 의문사에 해당하는 대답을 해야 하니까요. 의문사가 들린 질문에서 Yes / No기 들리면 바로 오답 처리하세요.

Q. **Who**'s teaching this afternoon's cooking class? 오늘 오후의 요리 수업은 누가 가르치나요?	A1 Robert's scheduled for today. (O) 로버트가 오늘로 예정되어 있어요. A2 ~~No~~, I couldn't reach him on the phone. (X) 아니요, 그와 전화로 연락할 수 없었어요.

3 유사 발음을 사용하거나 어휘를 반복한 오답에 주의하세요.

질문 속에 들린 단어와 비슷한 발음의 단어나 똑같은 어휘가 나오는 경우는 오답일 경우가 많답니다.

Q. I'm going to get a cup of **coffee**. 커피를 한 잔 마실 거예요.	A1 Would you get me one, too? (O) 저도 한 잔 가져다 주실래요? A2 No, I already made ~~copies~~. (X) 아니요, 이미 복사를 했어요.

4 연상되는 어휘를 사용한 오답에 주의하세요.

질문 속의 어떤 단어 때문에 연상되는 상황을 오답으로 제시하는 경우가 많아요.

Q. **Why** did Louise decide to retire this year? 루이스는 왜 올해 은퇴하기로 결정했나요?	A1 I have no idea. (O) 잘 모르겠어요. A2 These are very good reasons. (X) 이것들은 아주 좋은 이유들이에요.

기초학습

1 질문 잘 듣기

P2_01

Part 2는 질문의 앞부분을 특히 잘 듣는 것이 중요합니다. 질문 듣기 연습을 집중적으로 해보세요.

의문사 있는 질문 듣기 연습

질문을 잘 듣고 빈칸에 알맞은 의문사를 써 넣으세요.

1 __________ called while I was out?

2 __________ did they put the new copier?

3 __________ would be a good time to meet?

4 __________ on the schedule for this afternoon?

5 __________ do you like the new software?

6 __________ did you decide to move?

7 __________ __________ should I use?

8 __________ __________ __________ applied for the position?

9 __________ you tell me __________ __________ I should buy?

10 __________ __________ do the attendants check the parking meters?

의문사 없는 질문 듣기 연습

질문을 잘 듣고 빈칸에 알맞은 말을 써 넣으세요.

11 ________ ________ the bus to Liverpool?

12 ________ ________ need any help moving these boxes?

13 ________ ________ joining us for the concert?

14 ________ ________ of the company policies changed this year?

15 ________ ________ consider applying for a job at the hotel?

16 ________ ________ like to take a short break?

17 ________ ________ ________ more expensive yesterday?

18 ________ ________ take notes at tomorrow's meeting?

19 ________ ________ order you plastic cups, or paper ones?

20 ________ finish the rest of the painting tomorrow.

정답 및 해설 p. 26

답변 잘 고르기

P2_02

Part 2는 질문도 잘 들어야 하지만 질문에 적절한 응답을 고르는 것 또한 중요합니다. 질문에 어울리는 응답 고르는 연습도 해보세요.

질문을 잘 듣고 빈칸에 알맞은 말을 넣은 다음 알맞은 응답을 고르세요.

1 ________ should we leave?

(A) Yes, I like to read. (B) At four, I think.

2 ________ leading the budget workshop?

(A) At three o'clock. (B) Natasha is.

3 ________ do you commute to work?

(A) By train. (B) Yes, every day.

4 ________ the weather like today?

(A) On the weather report. (B) Well, it was snowing earlier.

5 ________ the cafeteria ________ after eight?

(A) No, I already ate it. (B) No, only until seven.

6 ________ did you ________ those programs for the performance?

(A) Not until eight P.M. (B) At the entrance.

7 ________ did you call me earlier?

(A) From my office phone. (B) Because I need some advice.

8 ________ you finish the paperwork?

(A) No, not yet. (B) Oh, I have one.

9 ________ ________ ________ ________ join us for the jazz concert on Friday?

(A) I'd like to, but I have plans. (B) More than fifty members.

10 ________ ________ ________ did you reorganize?

(A) The one by the window. (B) In numerical order.

정답 및 해설 p. 27

UNIT 01

Who/What·Which 의문문

기출 문제풀이 전략 | Who 의문문 P2_03

Who 의문문은 행위의 주체나 대상을 묻는 질문입니다. 사람 이름이나 인칭대명사, 직책/직업, 부서명/회사명 등으로 답변할 수 있으며, Yes/No로는 대답할 수 없으니 유의하세요.

Q. Who's chairing the committee?
(A) Near the table.
(B) The marketing director.
(C) Every other month.

–
위원회는 누가 주재하죠?
(A) 테이블 근처에요.
(B) 마케팅 이사님이요.
(C) 격월로요.

| WORDS | chair 주재하다

STEP 01

질문 유형 파악

Who 의문문 – 누가 주재하는가?

STEP 02

오답 소거

(A) ~~Near the table.~~ (X)
장소를 묻는 Where 의문문에 대한 답변

(B) The marketing director. (O)
직책명

(C) ~~Every other month.~~ (X)
빈도를 묻는 How often 의문문에 대한 답변

정답 (B)

CHECK UP 질문을 듣고 오답을 소거하면서 알맞은 응답을 고르세요. P2_04

1
(A) Ninety centimeters. (O/X)
(B) On Thursday. (O/X)
(C) Mr. Lopez will. (O/X)

2
(A) Not me. (O/X)
(B) From the office. (O/X)
(C) In the afternoon. (O/X)

3
(A) My previous supervisor. (O/X)
(B) Sixteen Maple Street. (O/X)
(C) Two years ago. (O/X)

| WORDS | previous 이전의 supervisor 관리자, 감독

정답 및 해설 p. 28

빈출 질문 및 응답 패턴 | Who 의문문

유형 1 사람 이름 / 대명사로 답변하는 경우

Kate, Sam 같은 사람 이름이나 we, you 같은 인칭대명사가 정답으로 제시됩니다.

Q. Who is the man standing next to your manager?
당신의 관리자 옆에 서 있는 남자가 누구죠?

A1 Mr. Chang from Marketing. 마케팅부 장 씨요.
A2 He's one of the new employees. 신입사원들 중 한 명이에요.
A3 Someone from the sales department. 영업부의 누군가예요.
✕ It is Jason's. 그것은 제이슨 거예요.
→ 이름이 언급되었지만 사물의 주인에 대한 답변을 제시한 오답

유형 2 직책 / 직업 / 부서명 / 조직명으로 답변하는 경우

manager(관리자) 같은 직책명, receptionist(접수담당자) 같은 직업, sales department(영업부) 같은 부서명, committee(위원회) 같은 조직명이 정답으로 제시됩니다.

Q. Who sent us this package?
누가 이 소포를 우리에게 보냈나요?

A1 The manager did, I suppose.
[직책명] 제 생각에는 관리자가 한 것 같아요.
A2 It's probably from our production department.
[부서명] 우리 생산부에서 왔을 거예요.
✕ I'll ship it tomorrow. 제가 그것을 내일 보낼게요.
→ I로 시작하지만 질문과 다른 시제로 혼동을 유발하는 오답

유형 3 장소 / 위치로 답변하는 경우

Who 의문문에 '장소'나 '위치'로 대답하는 경우도 있습니다.

Q. Who has the training schedule?
누가 교육일정표를 가지고 있죠?

A1 There is one on my desk. 제 책상 위에 하나 있어요.
A2 I have it right here. 제가 바로 여기 가지고 있어요.
✕ He made it. 그가 그것을 만들었어요.
→ He로 시작하지만 질문의 동사와 상관없는 내용을 제시한 오답

유형 4 우회적 답변

'모른다'는 의미의 다양한 응답 또는 제3의 답변 등 간접적으로 달리 대답하는 경우도 있습니다.

Q. Who can assist me with the project?
누가 프로젝트와 관련해서 저를 도와줄 수 있나요?

A1 It hasn't been decided yet. 아직 결정되지 않았어요.
A2 I'll ask George. 조지한테 물어볼게요.

기출 문제풀이 전략 | What·Which 의문문

P2_06

What 의문문은 시간, 가격, 주제, 의견, 방법 등 다양한 정보를 묻는 질문으로, What 뒤에 오는 명사 키워드와 동사를 잘 듣는 것이 중요합니다. Which 의문문은 'Which+명사'의 형태로 나오므로 Which 뒤의 명사를 놓치지 않고 들어야 합니다.

Q. What size vehicle would you like to rent?
(A) Yes, I like it.
(B) The small parking area.
(C) I need a large one.

–

어떤 크기의 차량을 빌리고 싶으세요?
(A) 네, 마음에 들어요.
(B) 작은 주차구역이요.
(C) 큰 것이 필요해요.

| WORDS | vehicle 차량

STEP 01

질문 유형 파악

'What+ 명사' 의문문 – 어떤 크기의 차량?

STEP 02

오답 소거

(A) ~~Yes, I like it.~~ (X)
의문사 의문문 Yes/No 답변 불가
like 중복 사용하여 혼동을 유도한 답변

(B) ~~The small parking area.~~ (X)
vehicle(차량) 단어에서 연상하도록 유도한 답변

(C) I need a large one. (O)
차량 크기 설명

정답 (C)

CHECK UP 질문을 듣고 오답을 소거하면서 알맞은 응답을 고르세요. P2_07

1 (A) A table for five people. (O/X)
(B) Chocolate, please. (O/X)
(C) At the retirement party. (O/X)

2 (A) The one on the right. (O/X)
(B) The office closes at six. (O/X)
(C) Yes, it's official. (O/X)

3 (A) At twelve fifteen. (O/X)
(B) The budget report. (O/X)
(C) Yes, it's up to date. (O/X)

| WORDS | retirement 은퇴, 퇴직 official 공식적인 budget 예산 up to date 최신의

정답 및 해설 p. 28

빈출 질문 및 응답 패턴 | What·Which 의문문

P2_08

유형 1 〈What·Which+명사〉 형태의 질문

〈What+명사 ~?〉 형식으로는 시간, 종류, 색상 등의 정보를 묻고, 〈Which+명사/Which of+명사〉 형식으로는 선택사항을 묻습니다. 〈What·Which+명사〉 의문문에서는 질문에서 언급한 명사를 대명사 one으로 받아 대답하는 경우가 많습니다.

Q. What papers need to be forwarded to you?
어떤 서류들이 당신에게 보내져야 하나요?

A1 The ones Ms. Wang gave you the other day.
지난번에 왕 씨가 당신에게 준 것들이요.

A2 The construction project files. 건설 프로젝트 파일들이요.

Q. Which room is the seminar taking place in?
어느 방에서 세미나가 열릴 건가요?

A1 The one on your right. 당신 오른쪽에 있는 거요.

A2 In room 506. 506호에서요.

유형 2 〈What+동사/What+be동사+명사〉 형태의 질문

〈What+동사 ~?〉 형식으로 행위나 의견 등을 묻는 경우가 많고, 〈What+be동사+명사 ~?〉 형식으로는 비용, 방법 등을 주로 묻습니다.

Q. What are you **planning** to do this weekend?
이번 주말에 무엇을 할 계획인가요?

A1 I'll be visiting my family in Hong Kong.
홍콩에 있는 가족을 방문할 거예요.

A2 I'll just stay home and relax. 그냥 집에서 쉴 거예요.

✕ No, I don't have time this Saturday.
아니요, 이번 주 토요일에는 시간이 없어요.
→ 의문사 의문문에 Yes/No로 답변한 오답

Q. What is the fastest **way** to the airport?
공항으로 가는 가장 빠른 길은 무엇이죠?

A1 Take the subway. 지하철을 타세요.

A2 I'll drive you there. 제가 거기까지 태워다 드릴게요.

✕ I'll do it right away. 당장 그것을 할게요.
→ 유사발음어(way–away)로 혼동을 유발하는 오답

유형 3 둘 다 가능/둘 다 아니다 답변

Which 의문문은 하나를 택하여 답하는 경우가 대부분이지만, 둘 다 좋다거나 둘 다 아니라는 응답도 나올 수 있습니다.

Q. Which desk do you want to buy for your office?
어떤 책상을 사무실용으로 구입하고 싶으세요?

A1 Both would be good. 둘 다 좋겠어요.

A2 Either is fine with me. 둘 중 어느 것이든 좋아요.

A3 None of them. 둘 다 싫어요.

Who/What·Which 의문문 빈출 표현

P2_09

직위/직책

supervisor 관리자, 감독(= director, manager)
new employee 신입 사원
entire staff 전 직원
receptionist 접수담당자
accountant 경리, 회계사
client 고객
keynote speaker 기조 연설자
guest lecturer 초빙 강사
attendee 참석자
security guard 경비원
assistant 조수, 보조원
property manager 건물 관리자
technician 기술자
caterer 출장연회업자[업체]
representative 직원, 대리인
editor 편집자

조직/부서

corporation 회사(= firm, company)
committee 위원회
head office 본사(= headquarters)
branch office 지점, 지사
sales department 영업부
production department 생산부
maintenance 유지보수
public relations 홍보
accounting department 회계부
personnel department 인사부(= human resources department)
warehouse (물류) 창고(= stockroom, storage room)

What + 명사 / Which + 명사

What time 몇 시
What size vehicle 어떤 크기의 차량
What kind of food 어떤 종류의 음식
What flavor of ice cream 어떤 맛 아이스크림
What ingredients 어떤 성분들
Which room 어느 방
Which pair of sunglasses 어느 선글라스
Which restaurant 어느 식당
Which stores 어느 가게들
Which of + 복수 명사 ~중 어느 것

What + 명사키워드 / What + 동사

[가격] **What's the price[cost] of A?** A의 가격[비용]은 얼마인가요?
[주제] **What was the topic of A?** A의 주제는 무엇이었나요?
[방법] **What's the best[fastest] way to ~?** ~하는 가장 좋은[빠른] 방법은 무엇인가요?
[상태] **What is A like?** A는 어떠한가요?
[행동] **What should I do with A?** A를 어떻게 할까요?
[사건] **What happened at A?** A에서 무슨 일이 있었나요?
[의견] **What do you think of[about] A?** A에 대해 어떻게 생각합니까?

ETS 문제로 훈련하기

P2_10

STEP 01

문장의 핵심 파악하기

질문을 듣고 알맞은 응답을 고른 후, 빈칸을 채우세요.

1 (A) (B) (C)

Q. _______ _______ the _______ to the supply closet?

(A) I'm _______ tonight.

(B) I _______ it to Jane.

(C) It's actually quite _______.

2 (A) (B) (C)

Q. _______ did you _______ of our proposal?

(A) _______ hours.

(B) I was _______.

(C) No, I didn't _______ I did.

3 (A) (B) (C)

Q. _______ planning the client _______?

(A) It was _______.

(B) At a French _______.

(C) A _______ of entrees.

4 (A) (B) (C)

Q. _______ _______ makes color copies?

(A) These copies aren't very _______.

(B) Yes, I like that _______.

(C) The _______ in Mr. Moro's office.

STEP 02

실전에 가깝게 훈련하기

질문에 알맞은 응답을 고르세요.

5 Mark your answer. (A) (B) (C)

6 Mark your answer. (A) (B) (C)

7 Mark your answer. (A) (B) (C)

8 Mark your answer. (A) (B) (C)

9 Mark your answer. (A) (B) (C)

10 Mark your answer. (A) (B) (C)

| WORDS | charge 요금; 충전하다 lock up 문단속을 하다 annual 연례의 nondairy 유제품을 함유하지 않은

정답 및 해설 p. 29

ETS 실전 테스트

1. Mark your answer on your answer sheet. (A) (B) (C)

2. Mark your answer on your answer sheet. (A) (B) (C)

3. Mark your answer on your answer sheet. (A) (B) (C)

4. Mark your answer on your answer sheet. (A) (B) (C)

5. Mark your answer on your answer sheet. (A) (B) (C)

6. Mark your answer on your answer sheet. (A) (B) (C)

7. Mark your answer on your answer sheet. (A) (B) (C)

8. Mark your answer on your answer sheet. (A) (B) (C)

9. Mark your answer on your answer sheet. (A) (B) (C)

10. Mark your answer on your answer sheet. (A) (B) (C)

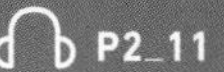
P2_11

11. Mark your answer on your answer sheet. (A) (B) (C)

12. Mark your answer on your answer sheet. (A) (B) (C)

13. Mark your answer on your answer sheet. (A) (B) (C)

14. Mark your answer on your answer sheet. (A) (B) (C)

15. Mark your answer on your answer sheet. (A) (B) (C)

16. Mark your answer on your answer sheet. (A) (B) (C)

17. Mark your answer on your answer sheet. (A) (B) (C)

18. Mark your answer on your answer sheet. (A) (B) (C)

19. Mark your answer on your answer sheet. (A) (B) (C)

20. Mark your answer on your answer sheet. (A) (B) (C)

정답 및 해설 p. 32

UNIT 02

When / Where 의문문

기출 문제풀이 전략 | When 의문문

P2_12

When 의문문은 시점을 묻는 질문으로, When 뒤의 시제를 표현하는 동사를 특히 유의하여 들어야 합니다. 오답에도 시제 관련 표현이 제시되는 경우가 많으므로 주의하세요.

Q. When is your next available appointment?
(A) I met Dr. Jones.
(B) Sorry, that item is not available.
(C) This Thursday at ten A.M.

–
다음에 예약 가능한 시간이 언제인가요?
(A) 존스 박사를 만났어요.
(B) 죄송합니다, 그 물품은 없습니다.
(C) 이번 주 목요일 오전 10시에요.

| WORDS | appointment 약속

STEP 01
질문 유형 파악

When 의문문 – 예약 가능한 시간이 언제인가?

STEP 02
오답 소거

(A) I met ~~Dr. Jones~~. (X)
appointment(약속, 예약)에서 의사를 연상하도록 유도한 답변

(B) Sorry, that item is not ~~available~~. (X)
available을 반복 사용한 오답

(C) This Thursday at ten A.M. (O)
시간 답변

정답 (C)

CHECK UP 질문을 듣고 오답을 소거하면서 알맞은 응답을 고르세요. P2_13

1 (A) Maybe four times. (O/X)
(B) About two hours ago. (O/X)
(C) At her office. (O/X)

2 (A) No, I haven't seen him. (O/X)
(B) They're quite expensive. (O/X)
(C) Later this afternoon. (O/X)

3 (A) On Saturday evening. (O/X)
(B) To celebrate Mariko's birthday. (O/X)
(C) Yes, and he's bringing his brother. (O/X)

| WORDS | times 배, 번 celebrate 기념하다, 축하하다

정답 및 해설 p. 38

빈출 질문 및 응답 패턴 | When 의문문

P2_14

유형 1 미래 표현으로 답변하는 경우

tomorrow(내일)나 soon(곧)과 같은 간단한 표현뿐만 아니라, in a day(하루 후에)나 not until Friday(금요일이 되어서야)와 같이 조금 어려운 표현들도 함께 익혀두세요.

Q. **When** is **the deadline** for the budget report? 예산 보고서 마감은 언제인가요?	A1 Next Tuesday. 다음 주 화요일이요. A2 In a week. 1주일 후에요. × For three days. 3일 동안이요. → 'for+기간'은 how long 의문문에 대한 답변을 제시한 오답

유형 2 과거 표현으로 답변하는 경우

yesterday(어제)나 last week(지난주)과 같은 과거 표현이 답변으로 나오는 경우입니다.

Q. **When** did you **get tickets** for the concert? 언제 콘서트 표를 샀나요?	A1 Just yesterday. 바로 어제요. A2 A few days ago. 며칠 전에요. × Yes, I want to buy them. 네, 그것들을 사고 싶어요. → 의문사 의문문에 Yes/No로 답변한 오답

유형 3 시간 부사절로 답하는 경우

as soon as(~하자마자)나 before / after(~하기 전에 / ~한 후에) 등의 시간 접속사가 이끄는 부사절이 이끄는 답변이 나오는 경우입니다.

Q. **When** did you **leave** the office? 언제 사무실에서 나갔나요?	A1 **As soon as** the meeting ended. 회의 끝나자마자요. A2 Right **after** the rain stopped. 비가 그친 직후에요.

유형 4 우회적 답변

의문사의 종류에 상관 없이 정답으로 자주 등장하는 유형입니다. '모른다'는 의미의 표현이나 기타 간접적인 응답으로 답변할 수 있습니다.

Q. **When** is the art museum scheduled to **reopen**? 그 미술관은 언제 다시 개관할 예정인가요?	A1 It's not certain yet. 아직 확실하지 않아요. A2 Let me check the schedule. 일정표를 확인해볼게요.

기출 문제풀이 전략 | Where 의문문

P2_15

Where 의문문은 주로 장소를 묻는 질문입니다. 대부분 장소나 위치를 나타내는 직접적인 답변이 가능하지지만 우회적인 답변에도 유의해야 합니다.

Q. Where are the spare tools?
(A) David had them this morning.
(B) Sure, you can take a break.
(C) A ride-sharing service.

–

여분의 연장은 어디에 있나요?
(A) 데이빗이 오늘 아침에 갖고 있었어요.
(B) 물론이에요, 휴식을 취하셔도 되요.
(C) 승차공유 서비스예요.

| WORDS | spare 여분의 tool 연장, 도구 ride-sharing 함께 타는, 함께 타기

STEP 01

질문 유형 파악

Where 의문문 – 어디 있는가?

STEP 02

오답 소거

(A) David had them this morning. (O)
어디에 있는지 답변

(B) ~~Sure~~, you can take a break. (X)
의문사 의문문에 Yes/No, Sure 답변 불가

(C) ~~A ride-sharing service.~~ (X)
질문과 상관없는 답변

정답 (A)

CHECK UP 질문을 듣고 오답을 소거하면서 알맞은 응답을 고르세요. P2_16

1 (A) At the corner of Pine Street and Seventh Avenue. (O/X)
(B) Please lock the door. (O/X)
(C) The new invention. (O/X)

2 (A) Earlier than that. (O/X)
(B) Karen probably knows. (O/X)
(C) I don't think we can. (O/X)

3 (A) She's making a phone call. (O/X)
(B) They charge more. (O/X)
(C) I have an extra one. (O/X)

| WORDS | lock 잠그다 invention 발명(품) charge (요금을) 청구하다

정답 및 해설 p. 39

빈출 질문 및 응답 패턴 | Where 의문문

P2_17

Where 의문문에서는 대부분 사람이나 사물이 있는 장소 및 위치가 답변으로 제시되며, 가끔 사람이나 출처가 정답으로 제시되기도 합니다.

유형 1 장소/위치로 답변하는 경우

at the hotel이나 on the desk처럼 〈전치사+위치/장소〉 형태의 답변이 정답으로 가장 많이 등장합니다.

Q. Where is the quarterly sales **report**?
분기별 매출 보고서는 어디에 있나요?

A1 It's in the file cabinet. 그것은 서류 캐비닛 안에 있어요.

A2 I put it on the table. 제가 탁자 위에 두었어요.

× At the stadium. 경기장에서요.
→ 장소 관련 표현으로 자주 등장하는 전치사 **At**으로 시작했지만, 매출 보고서와 상관없는 장소를 제시한 오답

유형 2 사람/출처 표현으로 답변하는 경우

사람 또는 출처를 나타내는 표현이 포함된 답변은 응용된 유형으로, 난이도는 높지만 출제빈도는 낮은 편입니다.

Q. Where did you **put** the calculator?
계산기를 어디에 두셨나요?

A1 Mr. Morgan borrowed it a while ago.
조금 전에 모건 씨가 빌려갔어요.

A2 I saw Jerry using it at the meeting.
제리가 회의에서 쓰고 있는 것을 봤어요.

× For the staff meeting. 직원 회의를 위해서요.
→ 이유를 묻는 **Why** 의문문에 대한 답변을 제시한 오답

유형 3 우회적 답변

'모른다'는 의미의 다양한 응답 또는 제3의 답변은 의문사의 종류에 상관없이 정답으로 자주 등장하는 유형입니다.

Q. Where has Lisa Martino **worked** for the last three years?
리사 마르티노는 지난 3년간 어디에서 근무했나요?

A1 I'll find out for you. 제가 알아볼게요.

A2 She didn't mention it. 그녀가 말하지 않았어요.

A3 I have no idea. 잘 모르겠네요.

When/Where 의문문 빈출 표현

P2_18

시간 표현

[시점]

at two o'clock 2시에
at noon 정오에
before noon 정오 전에
until he comes 그가 올 때
within 90 days 90일 이내에
earlier than ~보다 일찍
as soon as the meeting ends 회의가 끝나자마자
right after lunch 점심 직후에
on September first 9월 1일에
since last winter 지난 겨울 이후로 죽

[과거]

already 이미
two hours ago 2시간 전에
a few days ago 며칠 전에
a while ago 조금 전에
at that time 그때에
last week 지난주

[현재]

right now 지금 당장(= right away)
for now 지금은
sometimes 때때로(= occasionally)
this year 올해
every month 매달
on weekdays 주중에

[미래]

soon 곧(= shortly)
later 나중에
in a minute 잠시 후에
this Thursday 이번 주 목요일
no later than Friday 늦어도 금요일까지
at the latest 늦어도
sometime next week 다음 주 중에
by the end of the week 이번 주 말까지

장소/위치 표현

[in/at/on]

in the new office 새 사무실에서
in the Franklin theater 프랭클린 극장에서
in New York 뉴욕에서
in front of the lobby 로비 앞에서
in the lower left corner 왼쪽 아래 구석에
at Gate four 4번 게이트에서
at the conference 회의에서
at the back of the room 방 뒤쪽에
at a bus stop[station] 버스 정류장[역]에서
at the corner of the street 길모퉁이에
on the bottom[top] shelf 맨 아래[위] 선반에
on the table 테이블 위에
on Fourth Street 4번 가에서
on the right[left] 오른[왼]쪽에
on the Web site 웹사이트에
on the fifth floor 5층에

[기타 전치사]

next to the printer 프린터 옆에
near Fifth Avenue 5번 가 근처에
across the street 길 건너에
over there 저쪽에
all over the world 전 세계에
opposite side of the road 도로 건너편에
around the city 도시 주변에, 도시에
down the hall 복도 끝에

ETS 문제로 훈련하기

P2_19

STEP 01 문장의 핵심 파악하기

질문을 듣고 알맞은 응답을 고른 후, 빈칸을 채우세요.

1 (A) (B) (C)

Q. ______ is the cargo plane ______?

(A) ______ ten minutes.

(B) Some auto ______.

(C) At ______ four.

2 (A) (B) (C)

Q. ______ did you ______ this digital camera?

(A) The old one ______ ______.

(B) I paid in ______.

(C) From our ______.

3 (A) (B) (C)

Q. ______ did you ______ the sales department?

(A) Yes, I'm ______ it here.

(B) About three years ______.

(C) In my new ______.

4 (A) (B) (C)

Q. ______ should I ______ this page?

(A) ______ your name.

(B) Two ______, please.

(C) In the lower ______ ______.

STEP 02 실전에 가깝게 훈련하기

질문에 알맞은 응답을 고르세요.

5 Mark your answer. (A) (B) (C)

6 Mark your answer. (A) (B) (C)

7 Mark your answer. (A) (B) (C)

8 Mark your answer. (A) (B) (C)

9 Mark your answer. (A) (B) (C)

10 Mark your answer. (A) (B) (C)

| WORDS | cargo plane 화물 수송기 lower 아래쪽의 storage 저장, 보관 laundry 세탁 qualifications 자격 요건

정답 및 해설 p. 39

ETS 실전 테스트

1. Mark your answer on your answer sheet. (A) (B) (C)

2. Mark your answer on your answer sheet. (A) (B) (C)

3. Mark your answer on your answer sheet. (A) (B) (C)

4. Mark your answer on your answer sheet. (A) (B) (C)

5. Mark your answer on your answer sheet. (A) (B) (C)

6. Mark your answer on your answer sheet. (A) (B) (C)

7. Mark your answer on your answer sheet. (A) (B) (C)

8. Mark your answer on your answer sheet. (A) (B) (C)

9. Mark your answer on your answer sheet. (A) (B) (C)

10. Mark your answer on your answer sheet. (A) (B) (C)

11. Mark your answer on your answer sheet. (A) (B) (C)

12. Mark your answer on your answer sheet. (A) (B) (C)

13. Mark your answer on your answer sheet. (A) (B) (C)

14. Mark your answer on your answer sheet. (A) (B) (C)

15. Mark your answer on your answer sheet. (A) (B) (C)

16. Mark your answer on your answer sheet. (A) (B) (C)

17. Mark your answer on your answer sheet. (A) (B) (C)

18. Mark your answer on your answer sheet. (A) (B) (C)

19. Mark your answer on your answer sheet. (A) (B) (C)

20. Mark your answer on your answer sheet. (A) (B) (C)

정답 및 해설 p. 42

UNIT 03

How / Why 의문문

기출 문제풀이 전략 | How 의문문

P2_21

How 의문문은 How 단독으로 쓰일 때는 수단/방법, 의견/상태 등을 묻지만, How 뒤에 연결되는 형용사나 부사에 따라 수량, 가격, 기간, 빈도 등을 묻는 질문입니다. 따라서 뒤에 어떤 단어가 오는지 주의 깊게 들어야 합니다.

Q. How should I ship this package to the client?
(A) No, I forgot to deliver it.
(B) Please use the express service.
(C) In the manual.

–
이 소포를 고객에게 어떻게 배송해야 하나요?
(A) 아니요, 배달하는 걸 깜박했어요.
(B) 빠른 배송을 이용하세요.
(C) 매뉴얼에요.

| WORDS | ship 배송하다 client 고객 manual 매뉴얼, 안내서

STEP 01
질문 유형 파악

How 의문문 – 어떻게 배송하나요?

STEP 02
오답 소거

(A) ~~No~~, I forgot to deliver it. (X)
의문사 의문문 Yes/No 답변 불가

(B) Please use the express service. (O)
방법을 제시한 적절한 답변

(C) ~~In the manual.~~ (X)
Where 의문문에 어울리는 답변

정답 (B)

CHECK UP 질문을 듣고 오답을 소거하면서 알맞은 응답을 고르세요. P2_22

1
(A) Four months ago. (O/X)
(B) In the capital. (O/X)
(C) About six years. (O/X)

2
(A) I'll look for it. (O/X)
(B) Pretty well, I think. (O/X)
(C) About two months ago. (O/X)

3
(A) Usually to meet with clients. (O/X)
(B) They're on vacation. (O/X)
(C) Three or four times a year. (O/X)

| WORDS | capital 수도 client 고객, 의뢰인

정답 및 해설 p. 48

빈출 질문 및 응답 패턴 | How 의문문

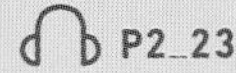

P2_23

유형 1 수단/방법을 묻는 질문과 답변

〈How+조동사+주어+동사+(목적어) ~?〉 형식의 질문은 특정 행위를 위한 수단이나 방법을 묻습니다. 이 유형에 대한 답변은 〈by[through]+명사〉 또는 명령문이나 평서문 형식으로 제시됩니다.

Q. How will the shipment be transported? 배송품은 어떻게 운반될 건가요?	A1 It'll go by air. 항공편으로 갈 거예요. A2 We're still looking for the cheapest way. 가장 싼 방법을 아직 찾고 있어요. ✕ Sometime next week. 다음 주쯤에요. → When 의문문에 대한 답변을 제시한 오답

유형 2 수량/가격/기간/빈도를 묻는 질문과 답변

〈How+형용사[부사]〉 형식의 질문에는 대개 숫자가 정답으로 제시됩니다.

Q. How many people will attend the seminar? 몇 사람이 세미나에 참석할 건가요? (수량)	A1 Probably ten or so. 아마 10명쯤이요. A2 Only a few in the division. 부서에서 몇 명만이요.
Q. How much will it cost to have my shirts cleaned? 제 셔츠들을 세탁하는 데 얼마가 드나요? (가격)	A1 Five dollars per shirt. 셔츠당 5달러입니다. A2 It comes to thirty euros. 금액은 30유로입니다.
Q. How long have you been studying Spanish? 스페인어를 공부한 지 얼마나 됐나요? (기간)	A1 For almost a year. 거의 1년이요. A2 Since I graduated from college. 대학 졸업 이후로 죽요.
Q. How often is the company newsletter published? 사보가 얼마나 자주 발행되나요? (빈도)	A1 Once a month. 한 달에 한 번이요. A2 It comes out biannually. 반 년마다 나와요.

유형 3 의견/상태를 묻는 질문과 답변

〈How+be동사+명사?〉나 〈How do[would] you like+명사?〉의 형식으로 의견이나 상태를 물을 수 있습니다.

Q. How do you like your coffee? 커피를 어떻게 해 드릴까요?	A1 With sugar and cream, please. 설탕과 크림을 넣어주세요. A2 I'll have mine black. 저는 블랙으로 할게요. ✕ Thanks, I'd like that. 고마워요, 그거 좋겠네요. → 커피를 주겠다는 제안(offer)에 대한 답변을 제시한 오답

기출 문제풀이 전략 | Why 의문문 P2_24

Why 의문문은 이유나 원인, 목적을 묻는 질문으로 뒤에 이어지는 동사와 시제에도 유의하여 들어야 합니다.

Q. Why did he return the battery charger?
(A) Because it's not the right model.
(B) Earlier this morning.
(C) At the electronics store.

–

그는 왜 배터리 충전기를 반품했나요?
(A) 적절한 모델이 아니기 때문이에요.
(B) 오늘 아침 일찍이요.
(C) 전자제품 매장에서요.

| WORDS | charger 충전기

STEP 01

질문 유형 파악

Why 의문문 – 왜 반품했는가?

STEP 02

오답 소거

(A) Because it's not the right model. (O)
반품한 이유 설명

(B) ~~Earlier this morning.~~ (X)
When 의문문에 대한 답변

(C) ~~At the electronics store.~~ (X)
Where 의문문에 대한 답변이며, battery charger에서 연상하도록 유도한 답변

정답 (A)

CHECK UP 질문을 듣고 오답을 소거하면서 알맞은 응답을 고르세요. P2_25

1 (A) It's near the office. (O/X)
(B) No, it hasn't. (O/X)
(C) Because we're expecting bad weather. (O/X)

2 (A) Yes, that's her name. (O/X)
(B) She needed directions. (O/X)
(C) About ten minutes ago. (O/X)

3 (A) You'll have to ask Ms. Park. (O/X)
(B) Yes, please come in. (O/X)
(C) In the next building. (O/X)

| WORDS | direction 지시, 안내

정답 및 해설 p. 49

빈출 질문 및 응답 패턴 | Why 의문문 P2_26

Why 의문문은 이유, 원인, 목적을 묻는 질문으로, 답변 맨 앞에 Because가 나오기도 하며 생략되는 경우도 많습니다. 그 외 역으로 되묻는 답변이나 우회적 답변도 가끔 등장합니다.

유형 1 이유/원인을 나타내는 답변

〈Because+주어+동사〉나 〈Because of+명사〉 구조의 답변이 제시되기도 하고, Because가 생략되어 나오기도 합니다. 이때는 답변이 질문에 논리적으로 어울리는지 정확하게 의미를 파악해야 합니다.

Q. Why did you **contact** the warehouse?
창고에 왜 연락했나요?

A1 Because I needed to check the product availability.
제품이 있는지 확인해야 했기 때문에요.

A2 Because of a missing item. 없어진 물품 때문에요.

✕ Because it was new. 새것이기 때문이었어요.
→ **Because로 시작하지만 상관없는 내용이 이어진 오답**

Q. Why were you **late** to the party?
파티에 왜 늦었나요?

A1 My car broke down. 제 차가 고장 났어요.

A2 I was really busy doing some paperwork.
서류 작업을 하느라 너무 바빴어요.

✕ I'm late for an appointment. 약속에 늦었어요.
→ **late를 반복 사용한 오답**

유형 2 목적을 나타내는 답변

〈to+동사원형(~하기 위해서)〉, 〈in order to+동사원형(~하기 위해서)〉과 같은 to부정사나 〈for+명사(~을 위하여)〉와 같은 전치사구, so (that)(~하기 위해서)과 같은 접속사로 답변이 제시됩니다.

Q. Why was the meeting **canceled**?
회의가 왜 취소되었나요?

A1 For personal business. 개인적인 용무 때문에요.

A2 So (that) I could meet an important client.
중요한 고객을 만나기 위해서요.

✕ You can go up to the second floor. 2층으로 올라가시면 됩니다.
→ **'to+위치/장소'는 Where 의문문에 대한 답변이므로 오답**

유형 3 역질문 및 우회적 답변

질문에는 평서문으로 답을 해야 한다는 편견을 버리세요. 도리어 역질문으로 답하는 경우도 있습니다.

Q. Why did you **call** Peter this morning?
오늘 아침 피터에게 왜 전화했나요?

A1 Didn't Peter tell you? 피터가 말 안 했나요?

A2 Why do you ask? 왜 물어 보세요?

How/Why 의문문 빈출 표현

수단/방법

express service[shipping] 빠른 배송
by overnight delivery 익일 배송으로
by air 항공으로
by bus[subway] 버스[지하철]로
take a taxi 택시를 타다
ride a bike 자전거를 타다
My friend dropped me off. 친구가 내려줬어요.
by cash[credit card] 현금[신용카드]으로
in writing 서면으로
press[push] the green button 초록 버튼을 누르다
by using social media 소셜미디어를 이용해서
by advertising more 더 홍보해서

의견/상태

I had a great time. 즐거웠어요.
look great 좋아 보이다
go well 잘되다, 잘 진행되다
increase by ten percent 10% 증가하다
It was very successful. 매우 성공적이었어요.
nearly done 거의 다 된

수량/가격/기간/빈도

[수량/가격]
only a few 몇 안 되는
five dollars per shirt 셔츠 하나당 5달러
a dozen people 12명의 사람들
twenty dollars each 각각 20달러
approximately 대략(= about)
not enough 충분하지 않은

[기간/빈도]
for two days 이틀간
for almost a year 거의 1년간
during a break 쉬는 시간에
once/twice 한 번 / 두 번
every morning 아침마다
biannually 반년마다
once in a while 가끔
at least once a month 최소 한 달에 한 번

이유/목적

[이유]
due to bad weather 악천후 때문에
due to road construction 도로 공사 때문에
because of the power failure 정전 때문에
because my car broke down
차가 고장 났기 때문에
because our client's flight is late
고객의 비행기가 늦었기 때문에
because I got stuck in traffic
교통 체증에 갇혀 있었기 때문에

[목적]
for a business trip 출장으로
for personal business 개인 용무 차
to fill a special order
특별 주문을 처리하기 위해
to expand our customer base
고객층을 넓히기 위해
so (that) I can check 확인할 수 있도록
so (that) they can meet the deadline
그들이 마감일을 맞출 수 있도록

ETS 문제로 훈련하기

P2_28

STEP 01 문장의 핵심 파악하기

질문을 듣고 알맞은 응답을 고른 후, 빈칸을 채우세요.

1 (A) (B) (C)

Q. _______ _______ are the tickets?

(A) Only fifty _______!

(B) About _______ _______.

(C) I didn't _______ it.

2 (A) (B) (C)

Q. _______ did you _______ a sweater?

(A) In the _______.

(B) Should I _______ Mr. Liao?

(C) It's usually _______ in here.

3 (A) (B) (C)

Q. _______ can we _______ _______ for a tour of the castle?

(A) _______ you very much.

(B) I can _______ you with that.

(C) No, we _______ three.

4 (A) (B) (C)

Q. _______ did the Citro Food Market _______?

(A) Yes, just _______ _______ days ago.

(B) I'll _______ some healthy snacks.

(C) Because it needed _______ _______.

STEP 02 실전에 가깝게 훈련하기

질문에 알맞은 응답을 고르세요.

5 Mark your answer. (A) (B) (C)

6 Mark your answer. (A) (B) (C)

7 Mark your answer. (A) (B) (C)

8 Mark your answer. (A) (B) (C)

9 Mark your answer. (A) (B) (C)

10 Mark your answer. (A) (B) (C)

| WORDS | castle 성 manufacturing 제조 fill an order 주문에 응하다, 주문을 이행하다

정답 및 해설 p. 49

ETS 실전 테스트

1. Mark your answer on your answer sheet. (A) (B) (C)

2. Mark your answer on your answer sheet. (A) (B) (C)

3. Mark your answer on your answer sheet. (A) (B) (C)

4. Mark your answer on your answer sheet. (A) (B) (C)

5. Mark your answer on your answer sheet. (A) (B) (C)

6. Mark your answer on your answer sheet. (A) (B) (C)

7. Mark your answer on your answer sheet. (A) (B) (C)

8. Mark your answer on your answer sheet. (A) (B) (C)

9. Mark your answer on your answer sheet. (A) (B) (C)

10. Mark your answer on your answer sheet. (A) (B) (C)

11. Mark your answer on your answer sheet. (A) (B) (C)

12. Mark your answer on your answer sheet. (A) (B) (C)

13. Mark your answer on your answer sheet. (A) (B) (C)

14. Mark your answer on your answer sheet. (A) (B) (C)

15. Mark your answer on your answer sheet. (A) (B) (C)

16. Mark your answer on your answer sheet. (A) (B) (C)

17. Mark your answer on your answer sheet. (A) (B) (C)

18. Mark your answer on your answer sheet. (A) (B) (C)

19. Mark your answer on your answer sheet. (A) (B) (C)

20. Mark your answer on your answer sheet. (A) (B) (C)

정답 및 해설 p. 52

UNIT 04

Be동사/조동사 의문문

기출 문제풀이 전략 | Be동사 의문문

P2_30

Be동사 의문문은 의문사가 없으므로 주어 동사를 특히 잘 들어야 합니다. 주로 사실 확인이나 미래의 계획을 묻는 경우가 많으며 Yes/No 답변이 가능합니다.

Q. Is Higgins Publishing Company a British firm?
(A) No, his books are sold out.
(B) Yes, but it has offices worldwide.
(C) It's a firm offer.

–

히긴스 출판사는 영국 회사인가요?
(A) 아니요, 그의 책은 매진이에요.
(B) 네, 하지만 전 세계에 사무실이 있습니다.
(C) 그것은 확정 주문이에요.

| WORDS | firm 회사; 확실한, 확고한

STEP 01

질문 유형 파악

Be동사 의문문 - 영국 회사인가요?

STEP 02

오답 소거

(A) No, ~~his books~~ are sold out. (X)
Publishing(출판)이라는 단어에서 books(책)를 연상하도록 유도한 답변

(B) Yes, but it has offices worldwide. (O)
Yes로 답하고 부연 설명을 덧붙인 답변

(C) It's a ~~firm~~ offer. (X)
firm(회사)과 firm(확실한)을 혼동하도록 유도한 답변

정답 (B)

CHECK UP 질문을 듣고 오답을 소거하면서 알맞은 응답을 고르세요. P2_31

1
(A) It's a textile plant. (O/X)
(B) No, I have to work. (O/X)
(C) Yes, I heard that too. (O/X)

2
(A) Oh, you're right; it is. (O/X)
(B) He called the office today. (O/X)
(C) No, I don't like to sing. (O/X)

3
(A) No, the part hasn't arrived. (O/X)
(B) The label is on the back. (O/X)
(C) Let me check that for you. (O/X)

| WORDS | textile 섬유, 직물 plant 공장 label 라벨, 상표

정답 및 해설 p. 58

빈출 질문 및 응답 패턴 | Be동사 의문문

P2_32

유형 1 〈Yes/No+부연 설명〉으로 답변하는 경우

Yes/No 뒤의 부연 설명이 중요합니다. Yes/No와 어울리는지, 질문의 내용과 맞는지 잘 들어야 합니다.

Q. Is Ms. Saito out of the office today? 사이토 씨가 오늘은 외근인가요?	A1 Yes, but she'll be in tomorrow. 네, 하지만 내일은 사무실에 있을 거예요. A2 No, she's in. 아니요, 사무실에 있어요. ✕ She left it at home. 그녀는 그것을 집에 두고 왔어요. → out of the office(사무실 밖에)라는 표현에서 at home(집에)을 연상하도록 유도한 답변

유형 2 Yes/No 없이 부연 설명으로만 답변하는 경우

Yes/No가 생략된 경우이므로, 답변 내용이 적절한지 잘 판단해야 합니다.

Q. Was there heavy traffic on the highway this morning? 오늘 아침 고속도로에 교통 체증이 심했나요?	A1 It was not that bad. 그다지 나쁘지는 않았어요. A2 It was better than yesterday. 어제보다는 나았어요. ✕ OK, I'll take the train. 좋아요, 기차를 탈게요. → traffic(교통)에서 train을 연상하도록 유도한 답변

유형 3 우회적 답변

'모른다'는 의미의 표현이나 기타 간접적인 응답으로 답변할 수 있습니다.

Q. Are we still going to pick up the clients at the airport tomorrow? 우리가 내일 공항으로 고객들을 데리러 가는 거 맞나요?	A1 I've already arranged a car. 제가 차를 이미 준비해 놓았어요. A2 Let me check with the team manager. 팀장님께 확인해 볼게요.

기출 문제풀이 전략 | 조동사 의문문 P2_33

조동사 의문문은 Do나 Have, Will 등의 조동사로 시작하는 질문으로, Be동사 의문문과 마찬가지로 의문사가 없으므로 주어, 동사를 특별히 잘 들어야 하며, Yes / No 답변이 가능합니다.

Q. Do you use the public library?
(A) Turn right on Main Street.
(B) Because I returned the books.
(C) Yes, I go there every week.

–
당신은 공공도서관을 이용하나요?
(A) 메인 가에서 우회전하세요.
(B) 책을 반납했기 때문이에요.
(C) 네, 매주 그곳에 갑니다.

| WORDS | public library 공공도서관 return 반납하다

STEP 01

질문 유형 파악

조동사 의문문 - 이용하나요?

STEP 02

오답 소거

(A) ~~Turn right on Main Street.~~ (X)
질문과 상관없는 답변

(B) ~~Because I returned the books.~~ (X)
Why 의문문에 대한 응답이며, library에서 책을 반납한다는 내용이 연상되도록 유도한 답변

(C) Yes, I go there every week. (O)
적절한 답변 정답 (C)

CHECK UP 질문을 듣고 오답을 소거하면서 알맞은 응답을 고르세요. P2_34

1 (A) OK, I'll ask later. (O/X)
(B) No, it was canceled. (O/X)
(C) Oh, is it ready? (O/X)

2 (A) It takes longer now. (O/X)
(B) No, I haven't. (O/X)
(C) Near the city center. (O/X)

3 (A) Thanks for your help. (O/X)
(B) Yes, they will be. (O/X)
(C) It was beautiful. (O/X)

정답 및 해설 p. 59

빈출 질문 및 응답 패턴 | 조동사 의문문

P2_35

유형 1 Do 조동사 의문문

〈Do[Does / Did] + 주어 + 동사원형 ~?〉과 〈Do you think + (that) + 주어 + 동사 ~?〉의 형식으로 주로 출제됩니다.

Q. **Do you** have the keys to the conference room?
회의실 열쇠를 가지고 있나요?

A1 Oh no, they're back in my office.
이런, 제 사무실에 있어요.

A2 Jane has them.
제인이 가지고 있어요.

× I tried, but it was locked. 시도는 했지만, 그것은 잠겨 있었어요.
→ **keys**(열쇠)에서 **locked**(잠긴)를 연상하도록 유도한 오답

유형 2 Have 조동사 의문문

〈Have + 주어 + 과거분사(p.p.) ~?〉의 형식으로 자주 출제됩니다.

Q. **Have** you **hired** a new accountant?
새 회계사를 채용했나요?

A1 Yes, he will start work next week.
네, 그는 다음 주에 일을 시작할 거예요.

A2 Not that I know of.
제가 알기로는 아니에요.

× To introduce a new assistant. 새 비서를 소개하기 위해서요.
→ **to**부정사(~하기 위해서)는 **Why** 의문문에 대한 답변이므로 오답

유형 3 Will / Should 등 기타 조동사 의문문

〈Will / Should + 주어 + 동사 ~?〉의 형식으로 출제됩니다.

Q. **Will you help** me with this new program?
이 새 프로그램 좀 도와주실래요?

A Sure, I'll be right with you.
네, 금방 갈게요.

× It was very helpful.
매우 도움이 됐어요.
→ 유사 발음어(**help-helpful**)로 혼동을 유발하는 오답

Q. **Should we change** shipping companies?
배송 업체를 바꿔야 할까요?

A Yes, that might be more efficient.
네, 그게 더 효율적일 수도 있겠네요.

× I didn't ship them.
제가 발송하지 않았어요.
→ 질문에 쓰인 **ship**을 그대로 사용하여 혼동을 유발한 오답

Be동사/조동사 의문문 필수 혼동 어휘

P2_36

유사발음어

apartment 아파트	rent an **apartment** 아파트를 임대하다
department 부서	the shipping **department** 선적부, 발송부
part 부분, 부품	the difficult **part** 어려운 부분
party 파티, 일행	a retirement **party** 은퇴 파티
movie 영화	go to the **movies** 영화 보러 가다
move 이사하다, 움직이다	**move** to a new office 새 사무실로 이사하다
show 박람회, 프로그램	go to the trade **show** 무역박람회에 가다
shoe 신발	**shoe** store 신발 가게
charity 자선	a **charity** dinner 자선 만찬
chair 의자	adjust the **chair** height 의자 높이를 조정하다
prepare 준비하다	**prepare** the food 음식을 준비하다
repair 수리하다; 수리	**repair** the printer 프린터를 수리하다
leave 두고 오다[가다], 떠나다	**leave** a book on the desk 책을 책상 위에 두다
live 살다	**live** two blocks away 두 블록 떨어진 곳에 살다
learn 알다, 배우다	**learn** about the company 그 회사에 대해 알게 되다
run (차량 등이) 운행하다, 다니다	The bus **runs** every hour. 그 버스는 매 시간 운행한다.

동음이의어

here 여기에, 여기서	a subway station around **here** 이 근방의 지하철역
hear 듣다, 들리다	I can't **hear** anything. 아무것도 안 들리는데요.
weather 날씨	due to bad **weather** 나쁜 날씨 때문에
whether ~인지 아닌지	I don't know **whether** he will come. 그가 올지 안 올지 모르겠어요.

다의어

firm	회사	a law **firm** 법률회사
	확고한, 확실한	**firm** about the deadline 마감일에 대해 확고한
plant	심다	**plant** the flowers 꽃을 심다
	공장	visit the **plant** in Detroit 디트로이트에 있는 공장을 방문하다
store	상점	go to the **store** 상점에 가다
	저장하다	**store** products in the warehouse 창고에 상품을 저장하다

ETS 문제로 훈련하기

P2_37

STEP 01

문장의 핵심 파악하기

질문을 듣고 알맞은 응답을 고른 후, 빈칸을 채우세요.

1 (A) (B) (C)

Q. _______ David's _______ party on Friday?

(A) Yes, are you _______?

(B) We had a _______ time.

(C) No, it's _______ Monday.

2 (A) (B) (C)

Q. ______ ______ deliver the letter personally?

(A) No, I sent it ______ ______.

(B) Several people were ______.

(C) No, I didn't ______ ______.

3 (A) (B) (C)

Q. ______ ______ any extra tea cups?

(A) In the _______ over the sink.

(B) Just ______ ______, thanks.

(C) I ______ ______ this morning.

4 (A) (B) (C)

Q. ______ ______ read our annual sales report?

(A) Yes, it's quite _______.

(B) It was ______ ______ euros.

(C) I'll come to the ______ ______.

STEP 02

실전에 가깝게 훈련하기

질문에 알맞은 응답을 고르세요.

5 Mark your answer. (A) (B) (C)

6 Mark your answer. (A) (B) (C)

7 Mark your answer. (A) (B) (C)

8 Mark your answer. (A) (B) (C)

9 Mark your answer. (A) (B) (C)

10 Mark your answer. (A) (B) (C)

| WORDS | annual 연례의, 연간의 landlord 주인 leaky 새는 tap 수도꼭지 overseas 해외에 attendance list 참석자 명단

정답 및 해설 p. 59

ETS 실전 테스트

1. Mark your answer on your answer sheet. (A) (B) (C)

2. Mark your answer on your answer sheet. (A) (B) (C)

3. Mark your answer on your answer sheet. (A) (B) (C)

4. Mark your answer on your answer sheet. (A) (B) (C)

5. Mark your answer on your answer sheet. (A) (B) (C)

6. Mark your answer on your answer sheet. (A) (B) (C)

7. Mark your answer on your answer sheet. (A) (B) (C)

8. Mark your answer on your answer sheet. (A) (B) (C)

9. Mark your answer on your answer sheet. (A) (B) (C)

10. Mark your answer on your answer sheet. (A) (B) (C)

11. Mark your answer on your answer sheet. (A) (B) (C)

12. Mark your answer on your answer sheet. (A) (B) (C)

13. Mark your answer on your answer sheet. (A) (B) (C)

14. Mark your answer on your answer sheet. (A) (B) (C)

15. Mark your answer on your answer sheet. (A) (B) (C)

16. Mark your answer on your answer sheet. (A) (B) (C)

17. Mark your answer on your answer sheet. (A) (B) (C)

18. Mark your answer on your answer sheet. (A) (B) (C)

19. Mark your answer on your answer sheet. (A) (B) (C)

20. Mark your answer on your answer sheet. (A) (B) (C)

정답 및 해설 p. 62

UNIT 05

부정/부가의문문

기출 문제풀이 전략 | 부정의문문 P2_39

부정의문문은 Be동사 및 조동사의 부정형으로 시작하는 의문문입니다. 부정의문문의 not은 '부정'의 의미가 아니라, 자신의 생각을 '확인'하거나 상대방의 '동의'를 구하는 역할을 합니다. not이 붙었지만 긍정의문문과 똑같이 생각하세요.

Q. Didn't you get a copy of the schedule for the workshop?
(A) No, not the revised one.
(B) I can reschedule.
(C) The speaker was quite good.

–

워크숍 일정 사본 못 받았나요?
(A) 아니오, 수정본은 못 받았어요.
(B) 일정을 다시 잡을게요.
(C) 발표자가 꽤 훌륭했어요.

| WORDS | revised 수정된, 개정된 reschedule 일정을 다시 잡다

STEP 01

질문 유형 파악

부정의문문 - 못 받았나요?

STEP 02

오답 소거

(A) No, not the revised one. (O)
적절한 답변

(B) I can ~~reschedule~~. (X)
schedule과 발음이 비슷한 reschedule을 사용하여 혼동을 유도한 답변

(C) ~~The speaker~~ was quite good. (X)
workshop에서 speaker(발표자)를 연상하도록 유도한 답변

정답 (A)

CHECK UP 질문을 듣고 오답을 소거하면서 알맞은 응답을 고르세요. P2_40

1
(A) No, it's open every day. (O/X)
(B) I live close by. (O/X)
(C) From the top shelf. (O/X)

2
(A) No, it's not broken. (O/X)
(B) Yes, usually around ten. (O/X)
(C) Take your time. (O/X)

3
(A) It's hard to open. (O/X)
(B) I just did yesterday. (O/X)
(C) Yes, it was a surprise! (O/X)

정답 및 해설 p. 68

빈출 질문 및 응답 패턴 | 부정의문문

P2_41

유형 1 긍정으로 답변하는 경우

부정의문문은 긍정의문문과 똑같다고 생각하면 됩니다. 긍정이면 Yes입니다. 우리말로 번역하여 혼동하지 않도록 하세요.

Q. Isn't Sam coming today?
샘 오늘 오지 않나요?
→ 샘 오늘 오죠?

A Yes, he'll be here soon. 네, 곧 여기 올 거예요.
✕ I can't go there today. 저는 오늘 거기 갈 수 없어요.
→ 3인칭의 Sam으로 묻는 질문에 I로 답변한 주어 불일치 오답

Q. Didn't you want to buy a new jacket?
새 재킷을 사고 싶지 않았니요?
→ 새 재킷 사고 싶었죠?

A Yes, my old one is too small. 네, 예전 것은 너무 작아요.
✕ You've been to this store before.
당신은 전에 이 가게에 와 본 적이 있어요.
→ buy a new jacket에서 store를 연상하도록 유도한 오답

유형 2 부정으로 답변하는 경우

질문에 대해 아니라면 No입니다. 긍정의문문으로 질문하는 경우와 똑같습니다.

Q. Aren't the cabinets supposed to be installed today?
캐비닛이 오늘 설치되기로 하지 않았나요?

A No, they're behind schedule. 아니요, 일정이 늦어지고 있어요.
✕ From the warehouse. 창고에서요.
→ cabinets에서 warehouse를 연상하도록 유도한 오답

Q. Won't Lisa attend the time management workshop?
리사가 시간 관리 워크숍에 참석하지 않을까요? → 리사가 시간 관리 워크숍에 참석하겠죠?

A No, she has been sick all week.
아니요, 그녀는 일주일 내내 아팠어요.
✕ I've never been to that shop. 그 가게에 가 본 적이 없어요.
→ 유사발음어(workshop-shop)로 혼동을 유발하는 오답

유형 3 우회적으로 답변하는 경우

의문문 유형에 상관 없이 정답으로 자주 등장하는 유형입니다. '모른다'는 의미의 표현이나 기타 간접적인 응답으로 답변할 수 있습니다.

Q. Didn't Mr. Johnson call for an appointment yesterday?
어제 존슨 씨가 예약 때문에 전화하지 않았나요?

A1 Actually, it was Mr. Thompson.
사실 그건 톰슨 씨였어요.
A2 Let me check. 알아볼게요.

기출 문제풀이 전략 | 부가의문문

P2_42

부가의문문은 평서문 끝에 'be동사/조동사+주어의 대명사' 형식의 꼬리 질문, 또는 right이나 correct가 붙는 유형입니다. 부정의문문과 마찬가지로, 부가의문문 또한 어떤 사실에 대해 '확인' 또는 '동의'를 구하려는 의도로 붙입니다. 앞의 평서문이 긍정이면 꼬리 질문은 부정, 앞의 평서문이 부정이면 꼬리 질문은 긍정의 형태가 됩니다.

Q. Your suitcase is new, isn't it?
(A) The baggage counter.
(B) Just a suit and tie.
(C) No, it's not.

–

당신 여행가방은 새것이죠, 그렇지 않나요?
(A) 수하물 카운터에요.
(B) 양복과 넥타이만요.
(C) 아니요, 그렇지 않아요.

| WORDS | baggage 수하물 suit 양복, 정장

STEP 01

질문 유형 파악

부가의문문 - 그렇지 않나요?

STEP 02

오답 소거

(A) ~~The baggage counter.~~ (X)
suitcase(여행가방)에서 공항의 baggage counter(수하물 카운터)를 연상하도록 유도한 답변

(B) Just ~~a suit~~ and tie. (X)
suitcase와 발음이 유사한 suit를 사용하여 혼동하도록 유도한 답변

(C) No, it's not. (O)
적절한 답변

정답 (C)

CHECK UP 질문을 듣고 오답을 소거하면서 알맞은 응답을 고르세요. P2_43

1 (A) Yes, very much. (O/X)
(B) He didn't eat there. (O/X)
(C) Next to the stove. (O/X)

2 (A) No, not yet. (O/X)
(B) We need two more pairs. (O/X)
(C) Yes, it does. (O/X)

3 (A) Three o'clock on Monday. (O/X)
(B) Actually, we need three bedrooms. (O/X)
(C) It overlooks the river. (O/X)

| WORDS | stove 가스레인지, 난로 overlook 내려다보다

정답 및 해설 p. 69

빈출 질문 및 응답 패턴 | 부가의문문

P2_44

유형 1 〈긍정 평서문+부정 부가의문문〉 형식의 질문

앞에 나온 평서문이 긍정이면 꼬리 질문은 부정 형태가 됩니다. '~해요. 그렇지 않나요?'라는 의미로 사실을 확인하거나 동의를 구하는 질문입니다. 부정의문문과 마찬가지로 긍정/부정에 구애 없이 긍정의 답이면 Yes, 부정의 답이면 No로 답합니다.

Q. These watches are waterproof, **aren't they?**
이 시계들은 방수가 되죠, 그렇지 않나요?

A1 Yes, and they're durable, too. 네, 그리고 내구성도 있어요.
A2 No, they're not. 아니요, 그것들은 아니에요.
× The water is too cold. 이 물은 너무 차가워요.
→ 일부 발음이 같은 두 단어(waterproof-water)를 사용하여 혼동을 유도한 오답

Q. You can work late tonight, **can't you?**
오늘 밤에 야근할 수 있죠, 그렇지 않나요?

A1 Yes, I'm available. 네, 전 시간 돼요.
A2 No, not tonight. Sorry. 아니요, 오늘 밤은 안 돼요. 죄송해요.
A3 I wish I could. 할 수 있으면 좋겠네요.
× Yes, this morning. 네, 오늘 아침에요.
→ Yes 뒤에 어울리지 않는 내용이 이어진 오답

유형 2 〈부정 평서문+긍정 부가의문문〉 형식의 질문

앞에 나온 평서문이 부정이면 꼬리 질문은 긍정 형태가 됩니다. '~하지 않죠. 그렇죠?'라는 의미로 사실을 확인하거나 동의를 구하는 질문입니다. 긍정/부정에 구애 없이 긍정의 답이면 Yes, 부정의 답이면 No로 답합니다.

Q. This isn't your coat, **is it?**
이것은 당신의 코트 아니죠, 그렇죠?
→ 이것은 당신의 코트죠?

A1 Yes, I bought it yesterday. 네, 어제 샀어요.
A2 No, mine is here. 아니요, 제 것은 여기에 있어요.
× The women's section is downstairs. 여성복 매장은 아래층이에요.
→ 의미상 연결이 가능한 두 표현(coat 코트-women's section 여성복 매장)을 사용해서 혼동을 유발하는 오답

Q. You didn't finish the financial report, **did you?**
재정 보고서를 끝내지 않았죠, 그렇죠?
→ 보고서를 끝냈죠?

A1 Yes, I put it on your desk. 네, 당신 책상 위에 올려 놓았어요.
A2 No, I need two more days. 아니요, 이틀 정도 더 필요해요.
A3 Can you wait until tomorrow? 내일까지 기다릴 수 있으신가요?
× Yes, I had fish for dinner. 네, 저는 저녁으로 생선을 먹었어요.
→ 유사발음어(finished-fish)로 혼동을 유발하는 오답

부정/부가의문문 필수 혼동 어휘

유사발음어

schedule 일정을 잡다 **reschedule** 일정을 다시 잡다, 재조정하다	**scheduled** for next week 다음 주로 예정된 **reschedule** our appointment 약속을 재조정하다
supplies 물품, 용품 **surprise** 놀람; 놀라다	office **supplies** 사무용품 a **surprise** party 깜짝 파티
workshop 워크숍 **shop** 가게	lead the accounting **workshop** 회계 워크숍을 이끌다 a gift **shop** 선물가게
suitcase 여행가방 **suit** 정장	pack a **suitcase** 여행가방을 꾸리다 a **suit** and tie 정장과 넥타이
repair 수리하다; 수리 **pair** 한 쌍, 한 벌	**repair** the photocopier 복사기를 수리하다 a nice **pair** of shoes 멋진 신발 한 켤레
instruction 교육, 지시 **construction** 건설, 건축	**instruction** manual 사용안내서 a road **construction** project 도로 건설 프로젝트
assign 부여하다, 할당하다 **sign** 서명하다	**assign** a task 업무를 부여하다 **sign** the agreement 계약서에 서명하다
ferry 여객선 **free** 무료인, 자유로운	the **ferry** to the island 섬으로 가는 여객선 The shipping is **free**. 배송은 무료다.
factory 공장 **satisfactory** 만족스러운	a tour of the **factory** 공장 견학 The result is **satisfactory**. 결과는 만족스럽다.
presentation 발표 **present** 제시하다, 제출하다	make a **presentation** 발표하다 **present** the financial plan 재무계획서를 제출하다

다의어

park	공원 주차하다	go to the **park** 공원에 가다 **park** a bike 자전거를 주차하다
book	책 예약하다	borrow a **book** 책을 빌리다 **book** a flight 항공편을 예약하다
order	순서, 질서 주문하다	be out of **order** 고장 나다 **order** some equipment 몇 가지 장비를 주문하다
issue	문제 (정기 간행물의) 호 발부하다	have some **issues** 문제가 좀 있다 the latest **issue** 최신호 **issue** the library card 도서관 대출 카드를 발급하다

ETS 문제로 훈련하기

P2_46

STEP 01 문장의 핵심 파악하기

질문을 듣고 알맞은 응답을 고른 후, 빈칸을 채우세요.

1 (A) (B) (C)

Q. _____ _____ _____ your new office?

(A) Yes, it's a lot _______.

(B) I can _____ _____ _____.

(C) No, it _______ yesterday.

2 (A) (B) (C)

Q. The printer's still _______, isn't it?

(A) It was _______ this morning.

(B) He hasn't _______ yet.

(C) I'll go _______.

3 (A) (B) (C)

Q. I _____ _____ anything important, did I?

(A) It was _______ yesterday.

(B) She _______ a part of it.

(C) No, we just _______.

4 (A) (B) (C)

Q. _____ _____ admission free for children under five?

(A) Yes, you can _______ here.

(B) No, but their tickets are _____ _____

(C) It's at the south _______.

STEP 02 실전에 가깝게 훈련하기

질문에 알맞은 응답을 고르세요.

5 Mark your answer. (A) (B) (C)

6 Mark your answer. (A) (B) (C)

7 Mark your answer. (A) (B) (C)

8 Mark your answer. (A) (B) (C)

9 Mark your answer. (A) (B) (C)

10 Mark your answer. (A) (B) (C)

| WORDS | turn off 끄다 admission 입장 available 이용 가능한 entertaining 재미있는 maintenance 유지보수 instruction 지시사항 confusing 혼란스러운 work out 운동하다

정답 및 해설 p. 69

ETS 실전 테스트

1. Mark your answer on your answer sheet. (A) (B) (C)

2. Mark your answer on your answer sheet. (A) (B) (C)

3. Mark your answer on your answer sheet. (A) (B) (C)

4. Mark your answer on your answer sheet. (A) (B) (C)

5. Mark your answer on your answer sheet. (A) (B) (C)

6. Mark your answer on your answer sheet. (A) (B) (C)

7. Mark your answer on your answer sheet. (A) (B) (C)

8. Mark your answer on your answer sheet. (A) (B) (C)

9. Mark your answer on your answer sheet. (A) (B) (C)

10. Mark your answer on your answer sheet. (A) (B) (C)

11. Mark your answer on your answer sheet. (A) (B) (C)

12. Mark your answer on your answer sheet. (A) (B) (C)

13. Mark your answer on your answer sheet. (A) (B) (C)

14. Mark your answer on your answer sheet. (A) (B) (C)

15. Mark your answer on your answer sheet. (A) (B) (C)

16. Mark your answer on your answer sheet. (A) (B) (C)

17. Mark your answer on your answer sheet. (A) (B) (C)

18. Mark your answer on your answer sheet. (A) (B) (C)

19. Mark your answer on your answer sheet. (A) (B) (C)

20. Mark your answer on your answer sheet. (A) (B) (C)

정답 및 해설 p. 72

UNIT 06

제안·요청문/선택의문문

기출 문제풀이 전략 | 제안·요청문 P2_48

제안문은 상대방에게 의견을 제안하거나 권유할 때, 요청문은 상대방에게 도움을 요청하거나 허락을 구할 때 쓰는 문장입니다. 수락하거나 거절하는 등의 답변이 주로 나옵니다.

Q. Why don't you join us for a bike ride next Saturday?
(A) We're open Monday through Friday.
(B) The one next in line.
(C) Thanks, I'd like that.

–

다음 주 토요일에 우리와 같이 자전거 타는 게 어때요?
(A) 저희는 월요일부터 금요일까지 영업합니다.
(B) 다음 분이요.
(C) 고마워요, 좋아요.

STEP 01

질문 유형 파악

Why don't you 제안문 – 같이 타는 게 어때요?

STEP 02

오답 소거

(A) We're open ~~Monday through Friday~~. (X)
Saturday에서 연상하여 요일을 언급한 오답

(B) ~~The one next in line~~. (X)
질문과 상관없는 오답

(C) Thanks, I'd like that. (O)
제안에 대한 적절한 답변

정답 (C)

CHECK UP 질문을 듣고 오답을 소거하면서 알맞은 응답을 고르세요. P2_49

1
(A) What's your confirmation number? (O/X)
(B) That's a good idea. (O/X)
(C) I didn't bring a manual. (O/X)

2
(A) I'll just have water. (O/X)
(B) We already paid last week. (O/X)
(C) It was really delicious. (O/X)

3
(A) Sorry, I dropped it. (O/X)
(B) Yesterday afternoon. (O/X)
(C) No problem. (O/X)

| WORDS | confirmation 확인, 확정 drop 떨어뜨리다

정답 및 해설 p. 78

빈출 질문 및 응답 패턴 | 제안·요청문

P2_50

유형 1 제안문 ❶

상대방에게 의견을 제안하거나 권유하는 문장입니다.

Why don't you[we] ~? ~하는 게 어때요? **How about ~?** ~하는 게 어때요? **Let's ~.** ~합시다.

Q. **Why don't we** get tickets for the play first?
How about getting tickets for the play first?
Let's get tickets for the play first.
연극 표를 먼저 사는 게 어때요?
(연극 표를 먼저 삽시다.)

A1 That's a good idea.
그거 좋은 생각이네요.

A2 OK, let me call the theater now.
네, 제가 지금 극장에 전화할게요.

유형 2 제안문 ❷

상대방에게 무엇을 하고 싶은지 묻거나 무엇을 제공해주길 원하는지 묻는 문장입니다.

Would you like ~? ~ 좋으세요? **Would you like to ~?** ~하실래요?
Would you like me to ~? ~해 드릴까요? **Do you want me to ~?** ~해 드릴까요?

Q. **Would you like me to** get you anything at the supermarket?
슈퍼마켓에서 뭐 사다 드릴까요?

A1 Yes, I could use some milk.
네, 우유가 필요해요.

A2 I'm OK, thanks.
괜찮아요, 고마워요.

유형 3 요청문

상대방에게 뭔가를 부탁·요청하는 질문입니다. 수락과 거절의 표현을 같이 기억해두세요.

Can[Could] you ~? ~해 주시겠어요? **Please ~.** ~해 주세요.
Would you mind -ing? ~해도 괜찮을까요? **May[Can, Could] I ~?** ~해도 될까요?

Q. **Could[Can] you** mail this contract to Kalmar Incorporated?
Would you mind mail**ing** this contract to Kalmar Incorporated?
칼마 사에 이 계약서를 우편으로 보내 주시겠어요?

A1 OK, no problem.
네, 문제 없어요.

A2 I'd love to, but I'm busy today.
그러고 싶지만, 오늘은 바빠요.

기출 문제풀이 전략 | 선택의문문

선택의문문은 'A or B'의 두 가지 사항 중에 어느 것을 고를 것인지 묻는 질문입니다. or 앞뒤의 A, B 자리에는 동일한 구조의 단어, 구, 문장이 옵니다. 둘 중 하나를 선택하는 답변이 가장 많지만, 둘 다 선택한다든가 제3의 답변이 나오기도 합니다.

Q. Do we need to take a number, or can we just get in line?

(A) We can get in line.

(B) I didn't count them.

(C) Sure, I'll buy it for you.

–

번호표를 뽑아야 하나요, 아니면 그냥 줄 서면 되나요?

(A) 줄을 서면 돼요.

(B) 세지 않았어요.

(C) 물론이죠, 제가 사드릴게요.

| WORDS | take a number 번호표를 뽑다 count 세다

STEP 01

질문 유형 파악

선택의문문 – 번호표 아니면 줄 서기?

STEP 02

오답 소거

(A) We can get in line. (O)

둘 중 하나를 말한 적절한 답변

(B) I didn't ~~count~~ them. (X)

number에서 count(세다)를 연상하도록 유도한 오답

(C) ~~Sure, I'll buy it for you.~~ (X)

질문과 상관없는 오답

정답 (A)

CHECK UP 질문을 듣고 오답을 소거하면서 알맞은 응답을 고르세요. P2_52

1
(A) To see my friend. (O/X)
(B) He already took it. (O/X)
(C) I chose July this year. (O/X)

2
(A) I enjoy both. (O/X)
(B) No, I won't be home. (O/X)
(C) At around five o'clock. (O/X)

3
(A) It is a nice day. (O/X)
(B) Try shaking it first. (O/X)
(C) Write your name on the inside cover. (O/X)

| WORDS | shake 흔들다

정답 및 해설 p. 79

빈출 질문 및 응답 패턴 | 선택의문문

P2_53

유형 1 둘 중 하나 선택

두 개의 선택 사항 중에서 하나를 선택하는 답변으로, 가장 많이 출제되는 정답 유형입니다. 선택의문문은 기본적으로 Yes / No 답변이 불가능하지만, 문장 전체를 선택하는 유형의 질문에 대해서는 Yes / No로 답변할 수 있다는 점을 기억해 두세요.

Q. Can you help me, **or** are you busy?
저를 도와줄 수 있나요, 아니면 바쁜가요?

A1 Yes, I'll be with you shortly.
네, 곧 갈게요. (= 도와주겠다)

A2 Sorry, I can't right now.
미안하지만, 지금은 안 돼요. (= 바쁘다)

✕ To meet a client. 고객을 만나기 위해서요.
→ 이유를 묻는 **Why** 의문문에 대한 답변을 **'to+동사원형(~하기 위해서)'**으로 제시한 오답

유형 2 둘 다 선택/둘 다 거절

두 개 중 어느 것이든 괜찮다는 답변이나 두 개 모두 선택하지 않는 답변도 가끔 나옵니다.

Q. Would you like cream **or** milk in your coffee?
커피에 크림을 넣으시겠어요, 아니면 우유를 넣으시겠어요?

A1 Either is fine with me.
어느 것이든 괜찮습니다. (둘 다 선택)

A2 It doesn't matter.
상관없어요. (둘 다 선택)

A3 Neither, thanks.
고맙지만, 둘 다 됐습니다. (둘 다 거절)

✕ Yes, I'd love to. 네, 그러고 싶어요.
→ 문장 선택의문문만 **Yes/No**로 대답 가능하므로 오답

유형 3 제3의 선택

제시된 두 개의 선택 사항이 아닌 제3의 것을 선택하는 답변으로, 선택 사항의 내용을 정확히 파악해야 정답을 고를 수 있습니다.

Q. Is the planning meeting scheduled for Monday **or** Tuesday?
기획회의가 월요일인가요, 화요일인가요?

A1 Actually, it will take place on Thursday.
사실 목요일에 열려요.

A2 Which day would be better for you?
어느 요일이 더 좋으세요?

✕ She didn't attend the meeting.
그녀는 회의에 참석하지 않았어요.
→ 질문의 **meeting**을 그대로 반복하여 혼동을 유도한 오답

제안·요청문/선택의문문 빈출 표현

P2_54

제안/요청 추가 표현

Shall I[we] ~? 제가[우리] ~할까요?

Why don't I ~? 제가 ~하면 어떨까요?

Let me ~. 제가 ~할게요.

Would[Do] you mind if ~?
~해도 괜찮으세요?

Would you be interested in ~?
~하는 거 어떠세요?

Do you need help ~?
~하는 거 도와드릴까요?

Shall we repaint the lobby?
로비를 다시 칠할까요?

Why don't I print out a map for you?
제가 지도를 출력해드리면 어떨까요?

Let me pay for dinner. 저녁은 제가 낼게요.

Do you mind if I leave early?
제가 일찍 나가도 괜찮으세요?

Would you be interested in joining our tour? 우리 투어에 합류하는 거 어떠세요?

수락/동의

Certainly. / Sure. 물론이죠.(= Absolutely. Definitely. Why not? Of course.)

Yes, please. 네, 그렇게 해 주세요.

No problem. 문제 없어요.

Not at all. 전혀요.

That should help. 도움이 되겠네요.

That sounds good to me. 저는 좋아요.

If you don't mind. 괜찮으시다면요.

I'd love to. 그러고 싶어요.(= I'd be happy to.)

I really should. 꼭 그래야죠.

Go ahead. 그렇게 하세요.(= Be my guest.)

That's a good idea. 좋은 생각이에요.

That would be great. 그럼 아주 좋겠네요.

If it's not too much trouble.
그게 너무 수고스럽지 않다면요.

I think we'd better. 네, 그게 낫겠어요.

It's my pleasure. 제가 좋아서 한 걸요.

I appreciate it. 감사히 생각해요.

Thanks for inviting me.
초대해 주셔서 감사합니다.

거절/부정

I'm sorry, but I'll do that next time.
미안하지만, 다음에 할게요.

Thanks, but I can handle it.
감사합니다만, 제가 처리할 수 있어요.

I'd love to, but I am busy today.
그러고 싶지만, 오늘은 바빠요.

I'm afraid I can't.
유감이지만 그럴 수 없어요.(= I'm afraid not.)

I can manage, thanks.
내가 혼자 할 수 있어요, 고마워요.

I'd rather not. 하지 않는 게 낫겠어요.

I have other plans. 다른 일이 있어요.

I'll consider it. 고려해 보죠.

Let me think about it. 생각해 보죠.

I'm afraid I won't have time.
유감스럽게도 시간이 없을 것 같아요.

Sorry, I have an appointment then.
미안하지만 그때 약속이 있어요.

I'm not sure I can help you.
제가 도와줄 수 있을지 잘 모르겠네요.

I'm OK, thanks. 괜찮아요, 감사합니다.

Sorry, it's all booked.
죄송하지만, 예약이 다 찼습니다.

I'm sorry, they're sold out. 죄송하지만, 매진입니다.

ETS 문제로 훈련하기

P2_55

STEP 01 문장의 핵심 파악하기

질문을 듣고 알맞은 응답을 고른 후, 빈칸을 채우세요.

1 (A) (B) (C)

Q. _______ _______ _______ take Broad Street?

(A) About five _______.

(B) I'll _______ it with me.

(C) It's _______ for repairs.

2 (A) (B) (C)

Q. Would you like to _______ in the _______ or my office?

(A) I _______ with you.

(B) Let's _______ in the cafeteria.

(C) I _______ it off.

3 (A) (B) (C)

Q. _______ _______ _______ by credit card?

(A) He can go _______ _______.

(B) More than _______ days.

(C) You _______ can.

4 (A) (B) (C)

Q. Do you want the _______ or paperback version of the _______?

(A) Yes, it's _______.

(B) _______ is fine.

(C) On _______ fifty-seven.

STEP 02 실전에 가깝게 훈련하기

질문에 알맞은 응답을 고르세요.

5 Mark your answer. (A) (B) (C)

6 Mark your answer. (A) (B) (C)

7 Mark your answer. (A) (B) (C)

8 Mark your answer. (A) (B) (C)

9 Mark your answer. (A) (B) (C)

10 Mark your answer. (A) (B) (C)

| WORDS | hardcover 양장본(의) paperback 문고판 receipt 영수증 directory 안내 책자, 건물 안내도

정답 및 해설 p. 79

ETS 실전 테스트

1. Mark your answer on your answer sheet. (A) (B) (C)

2. Mark your answer on your answer sheet. (A) (B) (C)

3. Mark your answer on your answer sheet. (A) (B) (C)

4. Mark your answer on your answer sheet. (A) (B) (C)

5. Mark your answer on your answer sheet. (A) (B) (C)

6. Mark your answer on your answer sheet. (A) (B) (C)

7. Mark your answer on your answer sheet. (A) (B) (C)

8. Mark your answer on your answer sheet. (A) (B) (C)

9. Mark your answer on your answer sheet. (A) (B) (C)

10. Mark your answer on your answer sheet. (A) (B) (C)

P2_56

11. Mark your answer on your answer sheet. (A) (B) (C)

12. Mark your answer on your answer sheet. (A) (B) (C)

13. Mark your answer on your answer sheet. (A) (B) (C)

14. Mark your answer on your answer sheet. (A) (B) (C)

15. Mark your answer on your answer sheet. (A) (B) (C)

16. Mark your answer on your answer sheet. (A) (B) (C)

17. Mark your answer on your answer sheet. (A) (B) (C)

18. Mark your answer on your answer sheet. (A) (B) (C)

19. Mark your answer on your answer sheet. (A) (B) (C)

20. Mark your answer on your answer sheet. (A) (B) (C)

정답 및 해설 p. 82

UNIT 07

간접의문문/평서문

기출 문제풀이 전략 | 간접의문문 P2_57

간접의문문은 일반 의문문 안에 의문사 의문문이 포함된 형태의 의문문입니다. 간접의문문에서 의문사 이하는 평서문의 어순(주어+동사)이 되며, 중간에 나오는 의문사를 잘 듣는 것이 중요합니다.

Q. Do you know why Insoo's moving?
(A) With Evanton Moving.
(B) He's accepted a job in Austin.
(C) Another two years.

–
인수 씨가 왜 이사 가는지 아세요?
(A) 에반톤 이사업체로요.
(B) 오스틴에 있는 일자리를 수락했어요.
(C) 2년 더요.

STEP 01

질문 유형 파악

간접의문문 - 왜인지 아세요?

STEP 02

오답 소거

(A) With Evanton ~~Moving~~. (X)
질문의 moving을 그대로 사용한 오답

(B) He's accepted a job in Austin. (O)
이유를 설명한 적절한 답변

(C) ~~Another two years.~~ (X)
질문과 상관없는 오답

정답 (B)

CHECK UP 질문을 듣고 오답을 소거하면서 알맞은 응답을 고르세요. P2_58

1
(A) Try the gift shop. (O/X)
(B) On the television. (O/X)
(C) Tomorrow morning. (O/X)

2
(A) How about another time? (O/X)
(B) It begins at eight. (O/X)
(C) She started at a young age. (O/X)

3
(A) I believe it was an engineer from Japan. (O/X)
(B) Actually, we're heading East. (O/X)
(C) To improve traffic conditions. (O/X)

| WORDS | head ~로 향하다 improve 개선하다

정답 및 해설 p. 88

빈출 질문 및 응답 패턴 | 간접의문문

P2_59

유형 1 〈Do you know+의문사〉 형식의 질문

간접의문문은 대부분 〈Do you know+의문사 ~?〉 구조의 질문입니다. 질문 내용의 핵심은 의문사 이하에 있으므로, 의문사를 반드시 들어야 정답을 찾을 수 있습니다.

꿀팁 의문사 의문문은 Yes/No로 답변할 수 없지만, 간접의문문은 처음에 의문사가 아닌 조동사로 시작하므로 Yes/No로 답변이 가능하다는 것을 명심하세요.

Q. Do you know when Susan can finish editing the article?
수잔이 언제 기사 편집을 마칠지 아세요?

A1 Yes, next Monday.
네, 다음 주 월요일이요.

A2 She'll call and let me know.
그녀가 전화해서 알려줄 거예요.

Q. Do you know who posted this notice on the bulletin board?
누가 게시판에 이 공지를 게시했는지 아세요?

A1 Ask Tom, the marketing manager.
마케팅 팀장인 톰에게 물어보세요.

A2 I believe it was Ms. Han's assistant.
한 씨의 비서였을 거예요.

Q. Do you know why Tom hasn't come yet?
톰이 아직 오지 않은 이유를 아세요?

A1 Because of heavy traffic.
교통 체증 때문이에요.

A2 Yes, he needs to meet a client this afternoon.
네, 그는 오늘 오후에 고객을 만나야 해요.

유형 2 기타 형식의 질문

〈Can[Could] you tell me+의문사 ~?〉, 〈Can[May] I ask+의문사 ~?〉 등의 다른 형식의 질문도 출제됩니다.

Q. Can you tell me how to operate this machine?
이 기계의 작동법을 제게 알려주실 수 있나요?

A1 Sorry, I don't know.
미안해요, 모르겠네요.

A2 Okay, I'll be right there.
좋아요, 곧 그쪽으로 갈게요.

Q. May I ask which room I should go to for the computer training?
컴퓨터 교육을 받으려면 어느 방으로 가야 하는지 여쭤 봐도 될까요?

A1 It's just next door.
바로 옆방이에요.

A2 It'll be held in the auditorium.
강당에서 열릴 거예요.

기출 문제풀이 전략 | 평서문

P2_60

〈주어+동사〉의 구조를 취하는 평서문은 어떤 사실이나 정보의 전달, 의견 제시, 요청 등 여러 가지 목적으로 사용됩니다. 평서문은 정해진 답변 유형이 따로 없고, 답변이 다양하게 나올 수 있어 난이도가 높은 편입니다.

Q. I wasn't able to open the e-mail attachment.

(A) OK, I'll send it again.

(B) They closed early today.

(C) By express delivery.

–

이메일 첨부파일을 열 수가 없었어요.

(A) 네, 다시 보내드릴게요.

(B) 그들은 오늘 일찍 문을 닫았어요.

(C) 빠른 배송으로요.

| WORDS | attachment 첨부(파일)

STEP 01

질문 유형 파악

평서문 – 열 수가 없었어요.

STEP 02

오답 소거

(A) OK, I'll send it again. (O)
다시 보내주겠다는 적절한 답변

(B) They ~~closed~~ early today. (X)
질문의 open에서 closed를 연상하도록 유도한 오답

(C) ~~By express delivery.~~ (X)
e-mail에서 mail(우편; 부치다)만 듣고 연상하도록 유도한 오답

정답 (A)

CHECK UP 질문을 듣고 오답을 소거하면서 알맞은 응답을 고르세요. P2_61

1 (A) Oh, I didn't know that. (O/X)
(B) It's quieter with the door closed. (O/X)
(C) Here, borrow mine. (O/X)

2 (A) Satoko is traveling in September. (O/X)
(B) It's where I take all of my clients. (O/X)
(C) Pasta and a salad. (O/X)

3 (A) She intended to order some. (O/X)
(B) I'll be there in ten minutes. (O/X)
(C) Yes, they're very similar. (O/X)

| WORDS | intend 의도하다, 계획하다 similar 비슷한

정답 및 해설 p. 88

빈출 질문 및 응답 패턴 | 평서문

P2_62

유형 1 사실/정보 전달이나 상황을 설명하는 평서문

'나는 다음 주에 세미나에 간다'와 같은 정보나 '복사기가 고장 났다'와 같은 문제 상황을 설명하는 유형입니다.

Q. The furniture for the meeting room has finally arrived.
회의실에 놓을 가구가 마침내 도착했네요.

A1 Let's move them.
그것들을 옮깁시다.

A2 It's about time.
그럴 때가 되었네요.

✕ Yes, he arrived today.
네, 그는 오늘 도착했어요.
→ 질문의 주어가 3인칭 사물(The furniture)이므로, 정답의 주어도 같은 3인칭 사물(it)이 되어야 한다.

Q. The fax machine stopped working.
팩스기 작동이 멈췄어요.

A1 I'll have a look at it for you.
제가 한번 볼게요.

A2 I'll call a repair person.
제가 수리 기사에게 전화할게요.

유형 2 의견 제시 및 제안의 평서문

'그것은 정말 아름다운 그림이네요'와 같이 의견을 제시하는 유형으로, 다양한 답변이 나올 수 있습니다.

Q. I think this program is very great.
이 프로그램이 매우 좋다고 생각해요.

A1 Yes, it's quite helpful.
네, 상당히 도움이 되네요.

A2 I agree with you. 동의해요.

Q. Maybe we should call to make a reservation first.
전화해서 예약부터 해야 할 거예요.

A1 Yes, that's a good idea.
네, 그거 좋은 생각이네요.

A2 OK, I'll call right now.
좋아요, 당장 전화할게요.

유형 3 요청 또는 희망 사항을 나타내는 평서문

'예약하고 싶다' 또는 '누구와 통화하고 싶다' 등의 요청이나 희망 사항을 평서문으로 표현하기도 합니다.

Q. I'd like to make a reservation.
예약하고 싶은데요.

A1 For how many people?
몇 분이시죠?

A2 May I have your name, please?
성함을 말씀해 주시겠어요?

간접의문문/평서문 빈출 표현

P2_63

사실/상황 전달

James was promoted to personnel manager.	제임스는 인사부장으로 승진했어요.
We have not decided yet.	우리는 아직 결정을 못했어요.
It's almost finished.	거의 끝났어요.
It's been quite a while.	꽤 오래 되었어요.
I heard all the tickets are sold out.	모든 표가 매진이라고 들었어요.
I can't figure out our new computer system.	새 컴퓨터 시스템을 이해 못 하겠어요.
I can't seem to locate my key.	열쇠를 찾을 수 있을 것 같지 않아요.
I didn't realize the museum was closed.	박물관이 닫은 줄 몰랐어요.
I'm sorry, but this model is out of stock.	죄송하지만, 이 모델은 재고가 없어요.

의견 제시

I'd like to get a new one.	새것을 하나 갖고 싶어요.
I'll have to consider it.	그걸 고려해 봐야겠어요.
You should try the new one.	새것을 시도해 보세요.
He will be better soon.	그는 곧 나아질 거예요.
It depends.	상황에 따라 달라요.
Not at this point.	이 시점에서는 아니에요.
Either one is fine.	아무거나 괜찮아요.
I don't mind at all.	전혀 상관없어요.
I really enjoyed the jazz festival.	재즈 페스티벌은 정말 즐거웠어요.

제안/요청

Don't forget to bring the budget report.	예산 보고서 가져오는 것 잊지 마세요.
I was planning to borrow them.	그것들을 빌릴 계획이었어요.
Try the IT department.	IT 부서에 연락해 보세요.
Let me show you what we have.	우리가 갖고 있는 것을 보여 드릴게요.
Make sure to finish by Monday.	월요일까지 꼭 끝내세요.
Remember to update your contact information.	연락처 업데이트 하는 것을 기억하세요.
I would like to cancel my hotel reservations.	호텔 예약을 취소하고 싶습니다.
I'd like you to leave soon.	당신은 곧 출발하는 게 좋겠어요.
I think you should ask Kevin.	케빈에게 물어 보는 게 좋겠어요.
We need to register for the online workshop.	온라인 워크숍에 등록해야 해요.
I'd be happy to send you a sample of our magazine.	저희 잡지의 견본 한 권을 보내드리겠습니다.

ETS 문제로 훈련하기

P2_64

STEP 01 문장의 핵심 파악하기

질문을 듣고 알맞은 응답을 고른 후, 빈칸을 채우세요.

1 (A) (B) (C)

Q. Eric wants to ______ ______ before you leave.

(A) I'll ______ ______ him at four.

(B) Yes, I have a ______.

(C) How many should I ______?

2 (A) (B) (C)

Q. Can you tell me ______ the nearest ______ ______ is?

(A) It's just around the ______.

(B) ______ 20 minutes.

(C) No, I'm sorry, you ______.

3 (A) (B) (C)

Q. ______ ______ your ______ on our new advertisement.

(A) ______ ______ the back door.

(B) I can ______ it tomorrow.

(C) Let's ______ some.

4 (A) (B) (C)

Q. Do you know ______ the journal article is ______?

(A) No more than three thousand ______.

(B) He ______ it in a magazine.

(C) Early ______ ______.

STEP 02 실전에 가깝게 훈련하기

질문에 알맞은 응답을 고르세요.

5 Mark your answer. (A) (B) (C)

6 Mark your answer. (A) (B) (C)

7 Mark your answer. (A) (B) (C)

8 Mark your answer. (A) (B) (C)

9 Mark your answer. (A) (B) (C)

10 Mark your answer. (A) (B) (C)

| WORDS | advertisement 광고 article 기사 ought to ~해야 한다 shipment 선적, 배송 warehouse 물류 창고 subscription 구독 effective 효과적인 turn up 높이다, 올리다 expire 만료되다 routine inspection 정기 점검

정답 및 해설 p. 89

ETS 실전 테스트

P2_65

1. Mark your answer on your answer sheet. (A) (B) (C)

2. Mark your answer on your answer sheet. (A) (B) (C)

3. Mark your answer on your answer sheet. (A) (B) (C)

4. Mark your answer on your answer sheet. (A) (B) (C)

5. Mark your answer on your answer sheet. (A) (B) (C)

6. Mark your answer on your answer sheet. (A) (B) (C)

7. Mark your answer on your answer sheet. (A) (B) (C)

8. Mark your answer on your answer sheet. (A) (B) (C)

9. Mark your answer on your answer sheet. (A) (B) (C)

10. Mark your answer on your answer sheet. (A) (B) (C)

11. Mark your answer on your answer sheet. (A) (B) (C)

12. Mark your answer on your answer sheet. (A) (B) (C)

13. Mark your answer on your answer sheet. (A) (B) (C)

14. Mark your answer on your answer sheet. (A) (B) (C)

15. Mark your answer on your answer sheet. (A) (B) (C)

16. Mark your answer on your answer sheet. (A) (B) (C)

17. Mark your answer on your answer sheet. (A) (B) (C)

18. Mark your answer on your answer sheet. (A) (B) (C)

19. Mark your answer on your answer sheet. (A) (B) (C)

20. Mark your answer on your answer sheet. (A) (B) (C)

정답 및 해설 p. 92

PART 2

Directions: You will hear a question or statement and three responses spoken in English. They will not be printed in your test book and will be spoken only one time. Select the best response to the question or statement and mark the letter (A), (B), or (C) on your answer sheet.

7. Mark your answer on your answer sheet.
8. Mark your answer on your answer sheet.
9. Mark your answer on your answer sheet.
10. Mark your answer on your answer sheet.
11. Mark your answer on your answer sheet.
12. Mark your answer on your answer sheet.
13. Mark your answer on your answer sheet.
14. Mark your answer on your answer sheet.
15. Mark your answer on your answer sheet.
16. Mark your answer on your answer sheet.
17. Mark your answer on your answer sheet.
18. Mark your answer on your answer sheet.
19. Mark your answer on your answer sheet.
20. Mark your answer on your answer sheet.
21. Mark your answer on your answer sheet.
22. Mark your answer on your answer sheet.
23. Mark your answer on your answer sheet.
24. Mark your answer on your answer sheet.
25. Mark your answer on your answer sheet.
26. Mark your answer on your answer sheet.
27. Mark your answer on your answer sheet.
28. Mark your answer on your answer sheet.
29. Mark your answer on your answer sheet.
30. Mark your answer on your answer sheet.
31. Mark your answer on your answer sheet.

LC

PART 03

짧은 대화

기초학습
문제 유형
UNIT 01 직장 내 업무
UNIT 02 인사
UNIT 03 회의 / 행사
UNIT 04 기타 사무실 대화
UNIT 05 여가 / 여행
UNIT 06 교통 / 주거
UNIT 07 쇼핑 / 주문
UNIT 08 식당 / 호텔
UNIT 09 각종 편의시설
ETS 파트별 모의고사

PART 3 | 짧은 대화

39문항

Part 3 시험은 이렇게 나와요

짧은 대화문을 듣고, 이에 딸린 문제 3개를 풀게 됩니다. 대화당 3문제씩 푸는 패턴이 13번 반복되어 총 39문제 (32번~70번)로 구성됩니다.

문제지

32. Why is the woman calling?

(A) To invite a friend to dinner
(B) To make a reservation
(C) To place an order
(D) To change an appointment

33. What is the problem?

(A) No tables are available at the requested time.
(B) The business closes at six o'clock.
(C) An item is out of stock.
(D) An order was canceled.

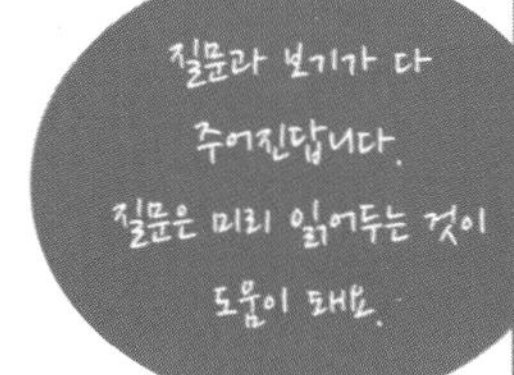

질문과 보기가 다
주어진답니다.
질문은 미리 읽어두는 것이
도움이 돼요.

34. What does the man suggest?

(A) Meeting earlier
(B) Checking for cancellations later
(C) Trying another location
(D) Coming another day

음원

Questions 32 through 34 refer to the following conversation.

W Hi, [32] I'd like to make a reservation for dinner at the Blue Moon Grill for tomorrow night.
M Certainly. How many people will be in your party?
W There will be eight of us. We'd prefer 6:30 if there's a table available then.
M Hmm. [33] We may have a problem fitting you in at 6:30... It looks as if we're all booked then. I'll put you down for seven o'clock, and, if you want, [34] you can call back tomorrow to see if there've been any cancellations.

32. Why is the woman calling?
33. What is the problem?
34. What does the man suggest?

이런 음원이 들려요.

ETS가 제안하는 꿀팁!

Part 3은 대화를 들으면서 질문과 보기를 읽기도 해야 하는 고난도의 파트입니다. 다음과 같은 사항에 주의하세요.

1 대화문을 듣기 전에 미리 질문을 읽으며 키워드를 파악하세요.

대화를 듣기 전에 문제의 의도를 잘 파악해야 정답을 찾기가 쉽답니다.

32. Why is the woman calling?	여자가 전화한 이유?
33. What is the problem?	문제점?
34. What does the man suggest?	남자가 제안하는 것?

2 남자와 여자가 하는 말을 구분하세요.

문제에 남자와 여자가 제시된 경우, 누가 말할 때 단서가 나올지 미리 파악하고 기다리세요.

Why is the woman calling? → **여자가 말할 때 단서가 나오겠죠?**	여자가 전화한 이유?
What does the man suggest? → **남자가 말할 때 단서가 나오겠죠?**	남자가 제안하는 것?

3 문제 순서대로 답이 들립니다!

대화가 전개되는 순서에 따라 대부분 답이 나와요.

전반부	W Hi, [32] I'd like to make a reservation for dinner at the Blue Moon Grill for tomorrow night.	**32.** Why is the woman calling? → **To make a reservation**
중반부	M Certainly. How many people will be in your party? W There will be eight of us. We'd prefer 6:30 if there's a table available then. M Hmm. [33] We may have a problem fitting you in at 6:30... It looks as if we're all booked then.	**33.** What is the problem? → **No tables are available at the requested time.**
후반부	I'll put you down for seven o'clock, and, if you want, [34] you can call back tomorrow to see if there've been any cancellations.	**34.** What does the man suggest? → **Checking for cancellations later**

기초학습

Paraphrasing(바꿔 표현하기) 익히기

Part 3에서는 대화에 나온 단어나 구를 정답에 그대로 제시하는 경우보다 같은 의미를 가진 다른 말로 바꿔 표현하는 경우가 많습니다. 이를 paraphrasing(패러프레이징)이라고 하는데, Part 3에서 자주 출제되는 paraphrasing 유형을 배워봅시다.

① 동의어/유사 표현 의미가 같지만 다른 표현을 사용하는 경우입니다.

대화 내 단서	질문 및 정답
I asked the company if they would pay for my relocation expenses. 제 이사비를 내줄 건지 회사에 물어봤어요.	**Q. 남자가 요청한 것?** **A.** A moving allowance 이주 보조금
Actually, I just canceled them. We had to cut part of our travel budget because sales have been down the past three months. 사실 방금 취소했어요. 지난 3개월 동안 판매가 감소했기 때문에 출장 예산 일부를 삭감해야 했거든요.	**Q. 남자가 계획을 취소한 이유?** **A.** His budget has been reduced. 예산이 삭감되었다.

② 포괄적 상위어 표현 상위 개념의 어휘를 사용하는 경우입니다.

대화 내 단서	질문 및 정답
I'm looking for a present for my brother. 남동생을 위한 선물을 찾고 있습니다.	**Q. 남자가 찾고 있는 것?** **A.** A gift for a relative 친지를 위한 선물
She called to update her home address and telephone number. 그녀는 자신의 새로운 집주소와 전화번호를 알려주려고 전화했어요.	**Q. 스코트 씨가 전화한 이유?** **A.** To provide new contact information 새로운 연락처를 제공하기 위해

③ 축약 표현 길게 풀어 쓴 표현을 간단히 요약하여 말하는 경우입니다.

대화 내 단서	질문 및 정답
I'd like to reserve that —how much do you need for a deposit? 그 방을 예약하고 싶습니다. 예약금이 얼마죠?	**Q. 남자가 요청하는 정보?** **A.** The amount of a deposit 예약금 액수
This year we plan to open twelve regional offices in Canada, South America, and Europe. 올해 우리는 캐나다와 남미, 유럽에 12개의 지사를 열 계획입니다.	**Q. 여자의 회사에서 계획 중인 것?** **A.** Set up offices in other countries 다른 나라에 사무실 열기

CHECK UP

1-5. 다음 밑줄 친 부분을 가장 잘 바꾸어 표현한 것을 고르세요.

1. Do you want to go over some last-minute notes before we meet with the client?
   (A) find (B) review

2. I'm calling to see if we can reschedule your appointment for this Friday.
   (A) change (B) request

3. What did the focus group think of our new frying pan?
   (A) cookware (B) furniture

4. Since the service was great I'd like to leave some extra money for the server, but I don't have any cash.
   (A) deposit (B) tip

5. Because this was our mistake, I'll include some free bags of our new flavored coffee for you to try.
   (A) coffee coupons (B) free samples

6-10. 다음 음원을 듣고 질문에 알맞은 말을 고르세요. 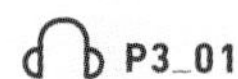

6. Why does the man ask the woman to arrive early?
   (A) To complete some paperwork (B) To meet a colleague

7. What complaint did customers have about some merchandise?
   (A) It is heavy. (B) It is not durable.

8. What does the man say he wants to do in the future?
   (A) Expand his business (B) Retire from his company

9. What is the woman talking about?
   (A) A new client (B) A coworker's new job

10. What does the man say he will do?
   (A) Send information to colleagues (B) Assist some customers

정답 및 해설 p. 104

문제 유형

기본 문제 유형 알아보기

① 전체 내용을 묻는 문제

대화의 주제나 장소, 화자의 신분 등 전체적인 내용을 묻는 질문은 주로 대화의 시작 부분에서 답을 알 수 있습니다. 질문의 주요 키워드를 먼저 파악한 후, 대화의 앞 부분을 잘 들으며 단서를 잡으세요.

1. 주제/목적 문제

• What is the topic of the conversation?	대화의 주제는?
• What are the speakers discussing?	무엇에 대해 논의하고 있는가?
• What is the woman calling about?	여자는 무엇에 관해 전화하고 있는가?
• Why does the woman call[contact] the man?	여자가 남자에게 전화[연락]한 이유는?

정답이 들리는 단서 표현

소식 전달	**Have you heard** back yet about the accounting job you applied for? 당신이 지원한 회계 관련 일자리에 대한 소식을 다시 들었나요?
관심 표명	**I'm interested in** renting a small office in the city. 시내에 작은 사무실 한 곳을 임대하고 싶은데요.
전화·방문 목적	**I'm calling about** my order for coffee beans. 제가 주문한 커피 콩 때문에 전화 드렸어요. **I'm here to** see Mr. Mitra. I'm supposed to interview him at eleven thirty. 미트라 씨를 만나러 왔어요. 11시 30분에 그분을 인터뷰하기로 되어 있습니다.

2. 화자/장소 문제

직업/신분	• Who most likely is the man?	남자는 누구일 것 같은가?
	• What is the woman's occupation?	여자의 직업은?
장소/근무지	• Where most likely are the speakers?	화자들이 있는 곳은?
	• Where do the speakers probably work?	화자들이 일하는 곳은?
	• Where is the conversation most likely taking place?	대화가 일어나고 있는 곳은?

정답이 들리는 단서 표현

장소명/직업명	I'm trying to find a floor plan of the **museum**. It's my first time here. 박물관의 평면도를 찾고 있어요. 이곳이 처음이라서요. They told me how pleased they were with **our catering service**'s healthy food options. 그들은 우리 출장 연회 서비스의 건강식에 얼마나 만족했는지 말해 줬어요.
전화·방문 목적	Hello, I have a flower delivery **here for a patient in room 212**. 안녕하세요. 여기 212호실의 한 환자분께 꽃 배달 왔습니다.

문제 유형 맛보기

P3_02

W I heard Mr. Cho is retiring from the sales department next week. Is that true?

M Yes. I can't believe it. Our overseas clients are really going to miss him. But, after 30 years in sales, I hear he plans to open up his own business next month.

W Oh really? What kind of business?

M A bookstore. He's always loved reading.

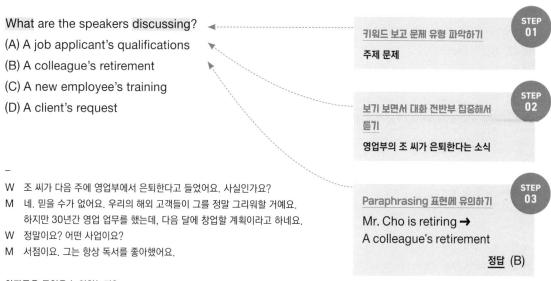

What are the speakers discussing?
(A) A job applicant's qualifications
(B) A colleague's retirement
(C) A new employee's training
(D) A client's request

STEP 01
키워드 보고 문제 유형 파악하기
주제 문제

STEP 02
보기 보면서 대화 전반부 집중해서 듣기
영업부의 조 씨가 은퇴한다는 소식

STEP 03
Paraphrasing 표현에 유의하기
Mr. Cho is retiring ➜
A colleague's retirement
정답 (B)

W 조 씨가 다음 주에 영업부에서 은퇴한다고 들었어요. 사실인가요?
M 네. 믿을 수가 없어요. 우리의 해외 고객들이 그를 정말 그리워할 거예요. 하지만 30년간 영업 업무를 했는데, 다음 달에 창업할 계획이라고 하네요.
W 정말이요? 어떤 사업이요?
M 서점이요. 그는 항상 독서를 좋아했어요.

화자들은 무엇을 논의하는가?
(A) 구직자의 자격 요건
(B) 동료의 은퇴
(C) 신입 사원 교육
(D) 고객의 요청

CHECK UP 질문의 키워드를 먼저 파악한 후 대화를 들으면서 정답을 고르세요.

P3_03

1. Where does the conversation most likely take place?
   (A) In a museum
   (B) In a hospital
   (C) In a school
   (D) In a shopping mall

2. Who most likely are the speakers?
   (A) Carpet installers
   (B) Interior designers
   (C) Cleaning staff
   (D) Office receptionists

정답 및 해설 p. 105

② 세부 사항을 묻는 문제

주로 대화의 중반부에서 나오는 질문으로, 최근에는 전체 내용을 묻는 질문이 나오지 않으면 세부 사항 묻는 문제가 두 개 나오기도 합니다. 주요 키워드 파악이 매우 중요하니, 키워드를 재빨리 파악한 후 단서를 기다리며 집중하여 들으세요.

1. 문제점/걱정거리 문제

• What is the problem?	문제점은?
• What problem does the man mention?	남자가 언급한 문제점은?
• What is the woman concerned about?	여자가 걱정하는 것은?

정답이 들리는 단서 표현

반전	but / However / Actually / Unfortunately	그러나 / 사실은/ 유감스럽게도
지체, 지연	delayed / behind schedule	지연된 / 일정이 늦은
고장	broken / out of order / not working	고장 난
부족	out of stock / run out of	품절된 / ~가 떨어진

2. 이유/원인 문제

• Why does Mr. Mitra apologize?	미트라 씨가 사과하는 이유는?
• Why does the man thank the woman?	남자가 여자에게 감사하는 이유는?
• Why does the woman need the information?	여자가 정보가 필요한 이유는?

정답이 들리는 단서 표현

사과 이유	**I'm sorry** I wasn't on time, Ms. Patel. I had a flat tire on the freeway. 늦게 와서 죄송합니다, 파텔 씨. 고속도로에서 타이어가 펑크 났어요.
놀란 이유	**I'm surprised**—I thought it would be a direct trip. 놀랍네요, 저는 직행일 거라고 생각했어요.
바쁜 이유	**I can't wait** that long because I'm interviewing for a position in New York in an hour. 1시간 후에 뉴욕에서 면접이 있기 때문에 그렇게 오래 기다릴 수 없어요.

3. 기타 세부 사항 문제

• What is the vice president working on?	부회장이 하고 있는 일은?
• What does the man want to know?	남자가 알고 싶어하는 것은?
• What event did the woman recently attend?	여자가 최근에 참석한 행사는?
• When will Simon start work?	사이먼은 언제 일을 시작하는가?

정답이 들리는 단서 표현

기타 세부 사항 문제는 다양한 정보를 묻기에, 의문사, 명사, 동사 위주의 **키워드**를 잘 파악해야 합니다.

P3_04

문제 유형 맛보기

W I'd like to ask James to make a presentation at the corporate accounts seminar.

M Sure, his presentation at last month's staff development meeting was great. But I'm worried he might not have enough time to prepare.

W Yeah, I'm worried about that, too. The seminar's in less than two weeks.

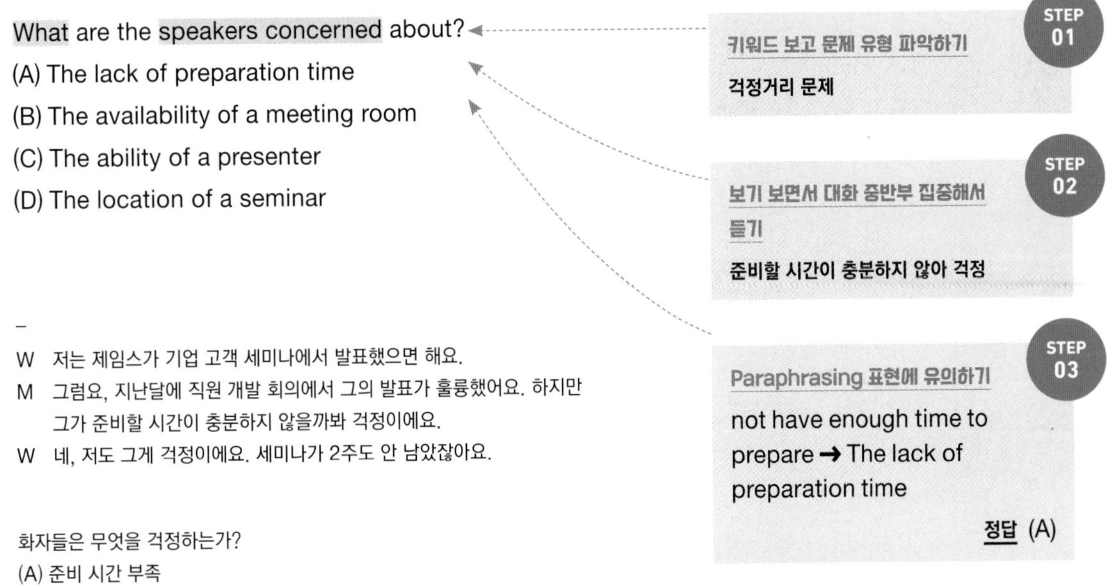

What are the speakers concerned about?

(A) The lack of preparation time

(B) The availability of a meeting room

(C) The ability of a presenter

(D) The location of a seminar

STEP 01 키워드 보고 문제 유형 파악하기

걱정거리 문제

STEP 02 보기 보면서 대화 중반부 집중해서 듣기

준비할 시간이 충분하지 않아 걱정

STEP 03 Paraphrasing 표현에 유의하기

not have enough time to prepare → The lack of preparation time

정답 (A)

–

W 저는 제임스가 기업 고객 세미나에서 발표했으면 해요.

M 그럼요, 지난달에 직원 개발 회의에서 그의 발표가 훌륭했어요. 하지만 그가 준비할 시간이 충분하지 않을까봐 걱정이에요.

W 네, 저도 그게 걱정이에요. 세미나가 2주도 안 남았잖아요.

화자들은 무엇을 걱정하는가?

(A) 준비 시간 부족

(B) 회의실 사용 가능 여부

(C) 발표자의 능력

(D) 세미나 장소

CHECK UP 질문의 키워드를 먼저 파악한 후 대화를 들으면서 정답을 고르세요.

P3_05

1. What is the woman's concern?

(A) The line for tickets is too long.

(B) There are no tickets available.

(C) The tickets are too expensive.

(D) Tickets are not available by phone.

2. What is included in the price of the apartment on Main Street?

(A) Electricity

(B) A cleaning service

(C) A fitness room

(D) Furniture

정답 및 해설 p. 106

③ 요청·제안/앞으로 일어날 일 문제

대화의 후반부에는 주로 상대방에게 요청하거나 제안하는 내용, 또는 앞으로 일어날 일에 대한 암시나 제시가 나오는 경우가 많습니다. 보기의 내용이 긴 경우가 많으므로 시간이 된다면 미리 읽어두는 편이 유리합니다.

1. 요청·제안 문제

• **What** does the **woman ask** the man to do?	여자가 남자에게 요청하는 것은?
• **What** is the **man asked** to do?	남자가 요청 받은 것은?
• **What** does the **woman suggest** doing?	여자가 제안하는 것은?
• **What** does the **woman offer** the man?	여자가 남자에게 제안하는 것은?
• **What** does the **man recommend** doing?	남자가 제안하는 것은?

2. 앞으로 일어날 일 문제

• **What** will the **woman** most likely **do next**?	여자가 다음에 할 일은?
• **What** does the **man** say he will **do next week**?	남자가 다음주에 할 일은?
• **What** is supposed to **happen tomorrow morning**?	내일 아침 일어날 일은?
• **What** does the **woman** say she will **do**?	여자가 할 일은?
• **What** does the **woman's company** plan to **do**?	여자의 회사가 계획하는 일은?

정답이 들리는 단서 표현

요청/ 앞으로 일어날 일	**Could you** fill out this form to give us a little bit more information about the problem? 이 양식을 작성해서 문제에 대해 좀 더 자세한 정보를 주시겠어요? **You should** share the customers' comments during our monthly meeting. 월례 회의에서 고객들의 의견을 공유해 주세요. **I'll just need to** see some photo ID to verify your registration. 등록 확인을 위해 사진이 부착된 신분증만 보여 주시면 됩니다.
제안/ 앞으로 일어날 일	**I'd suggest** downloading a mobile application called CarShare. 카셰어라는 모바일 앱을 다운해 보세요. **Why don't we** visit the city art museum? 시립 미술관을 방문해 보는 건 어떨까요? **Why don't you** get in touch with his assistant, Ms. Marley? 그의 비서인 말리 씨와 연락을 해 보면 어때요? **Let's** go and check how big that office really is. 가서 그 사무실의 실제 크기가 얼마인지 확인해 보죠. **I can** look it over and give you feedback. 제가 훑어보고 의견을 드릴 수 있어요. **I'll [I'm going to]** bring it back to the store this afternoon. 오늘 오후에 매장으로 가져가 봐야겠네요.

P3_06

문제 유형 맛보기

W Excuse me. I'm looking for that new book by Avani Pinto.

M I'm sorry, but we're completely sold out. However, we have more on order— the shipment'll be here sometime next week.

W Oh dear, I was hoping to buy it now—as a present for a friend who's leaving on holiday tomorrow.

M Well, what about getting Pinto's previous book, *Hillside Heights*, instead? That won a national book award, and I know we have a copy here in the store.

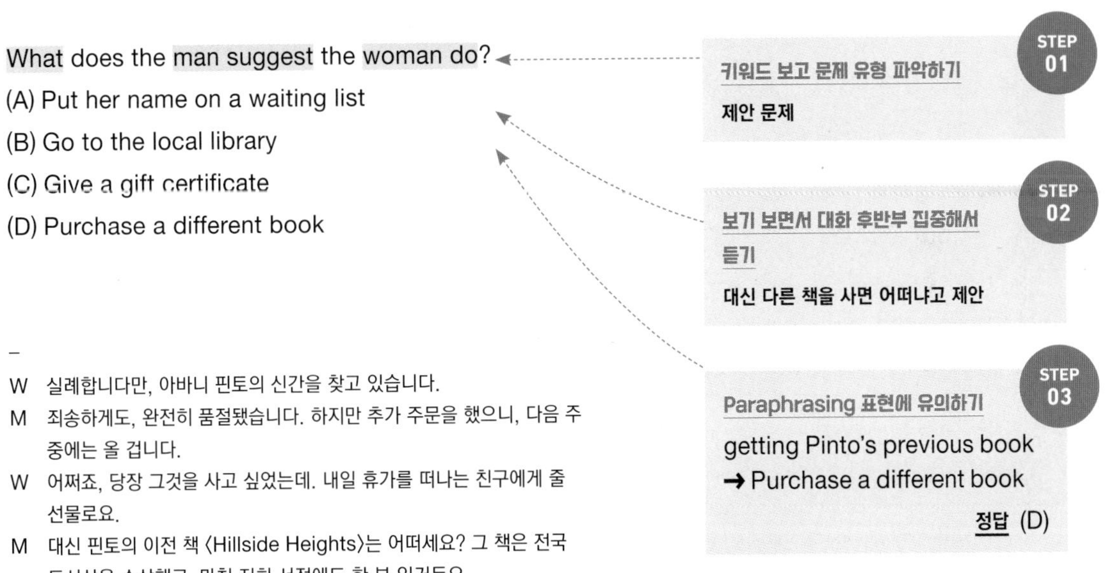

What does the man suggest the woman do?

(A) Put her name on a waiting list

(B) Go to the local library

(C) Give a gift certificate

(D) Purchase a different book

STEP 01 키워드 보고 문제 유형 파악하기

제안 문제

STEP 02 보기 보면서 대화 후반부 집중해서 듣기

대신 다른 책을 사면 어떠냐고 제안

STEP 03 Paraphrasing 표현에 유의하기

getting Pinto's previous book
→ Purchase a different book

정답 (D)

W 실례합니다만, 아바니 핀토의 신간을 찾고 있습니다.

M 죄송하게도, 완전히 품절됐습니다. 하지만 추가 주문을 했으니, 다음 주중에는 올 겁니다.

W 어쩌죠, 당장 그것을 사고 싶었는데. 내일 휴가를 떠나는 친구에게 줄 선물로요.

M 대신 핀토의 이전 책 〈Hillside Heights〉는 어떠세요? 그 책은 전국 도서상을 수상했고, 마침 저희 서점에도 한 부 있거든요.

남자는 여자에게 무엇을 하라고 제안하는가?

(A) 대기자 명단에 여자의 이름을 올린다.

(B) 지역 도서관에 간다.

(C) 상품권을 준다.

(D) 다른 책을 구매한다.

CHECK UP

질문의 키워드를 먼저 파악한 후 대화를 들으면서 정답을 고르세요. P3_07

1. What does the woman suggest the man do?

(A) Drop off his luggage

(B) Call a travel agent

(C) Look at a schedule

(D) Wait in the lobby

2. What will the man probably do next?

(A) Reschedule his trip

(B) Cancel his order

(C) Pay the mailing fee

(D) Call his supervisor

정답 및 해설 p. 107

고난도 유형 알아보기

① 3인 대화 문제

2인 대화뿐 아니라, 남1-남2-여, 여1-여2-남 등으로 구성되는 3인 대화도 등장합니다. 3인 대화는 화자들의 관계나 이름 파악에 특히 주목해야 합니다.

1 질문에 이름이 언급되거나 men(2명의 남자 화자) 또는 women(2명의 여자 화자)이 등장할 수 있으므로 질문을 잘 파악하는 것이 중요합니다.

2 해당 번호 디렉션 맨 뒤에 with three speakers라고 나오므로 3인 대화임을 미리 알 수 있습니다. 대화 도중 사람 이름이 나오면 세 번째 화자의 등장을 기대하세요.

3 3인 대화이다 보니, 대화의 길이가 다른 대화보다 길어지는 경우가 많습니다. 끝까지 집중해서 들으세요.

• **What** were the **men doing last weekend**?	남자들은 지난주에 무엇을 하고 있었는가?
• **Where** do the **women** probably **work**?	여자들이 일하는 곳은?

주의! 공통점이 있는 두 명에 대해 묻는 경우는 men, women으로 질문합니다.

• **What** does **Ms. Delaney ask for**?	딜레이니 씨가 요청하는 것은?
• **What** does the **woman suggest** doing?	여자가 제안하는 것은?

주의! 특정 한 명에 대해 묻는 경우는 사람 이름이 등장하거나 man, woman으로 질문합니다.

문제 유형 맛보기

P3_08

W Hi Ken, hi Julio! How did the art gallery opening go last weekend? Was the client happy with the marketing materials?

M¹ Alfredo? He was very pleased.

M² And it's worth checking out the gallery when you have some time.

M¹ Yes, the place is so bright and modern, with a fantastic collection of local works of art.

W You know, I'm taking a vacation in that area in February.

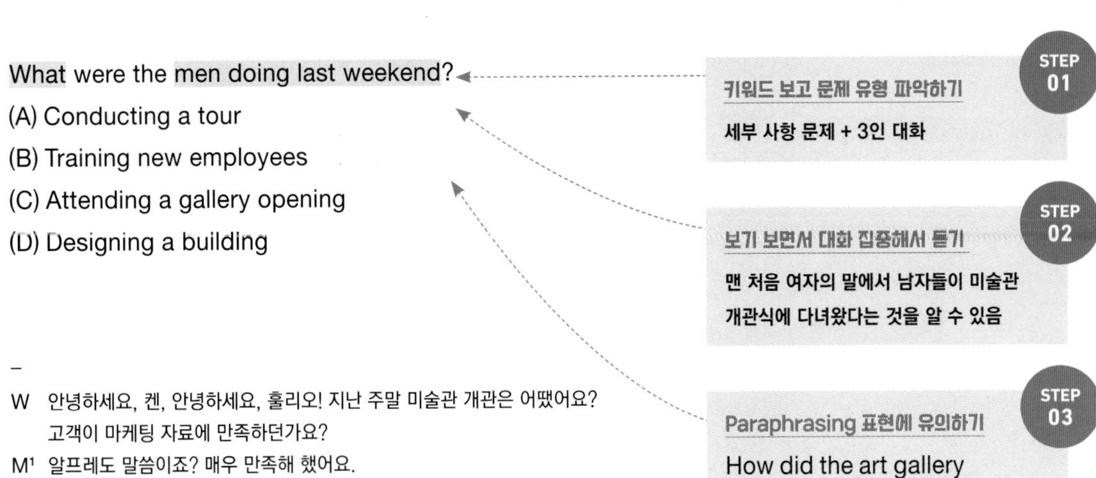

What were the men doing last weekend?
(A) Conducting a tour
(B) Training new employees
(C) Attending a gallery opening
(D) Designing a building
STEP 01
키워드 보고 문제 유형 파악하기
세부 사항 문제 + 3인 대화
STEP 02
보기 보면서 대화 집중해서 듣기
맨 처음 여자의 말에서 남자들이 미술관 개관식에 다녀왔다는 것을 알 수 있음
STEP 03
Paraphrasing 표현에 유의하기
How did the art gallery opening go → Attending a gallery opening
정답 (C)

W 안녕하세요, 켄, 안녕하세요, 훌리오! 지난 주말 미술관 개관은 어땠어요? 고객이 마케팅 자료에 만족하던가요?
M¹ 알프레도 말씀이죠? 매우 만족해 했어요.
M² 그리고 시간 있을 때 미술관에 가 보면 좋을 거예요
M¹ 맞아요, 멋진 지역 예술품을 소장하고 있는 아주 밝고 현대적인 곳이에요.
W 있잖아요, 저 2월에 그 지역으로 휴가를 갈 거예요.

남자들은 지난주에 무엇을 하고 있었는가?
(A) 견학 인솔
(B) 신입 사원 교육
(C) 미술관 개관 참석
(D) 건물 설계

CHECK UP 질문의 키워드를 먼저 파악한 후 대화를 들으면서 정답을 고르세요.

P3_09

1. What do the men imply about the company?
(A) It was recently founded.
(B) It is in a good financial situation.
(C) It has moved to a new location.
(D) It opened a new department.

2. What are the speakers planning to advertise?
(A) Evening classes
(B) An online store
(C) Design services
(D) A business event

정답 및 해설 p. 109

② 의도 파악 문제

화자의 의도 파악 문제는 제시된 문장을 말한 이유나 의미, 암시하는 바를 파악하는 문제입니다. 같은 표현이라도 문맥에 따라, 화자의 어조에 따라 의미가 달라질 수 있으므로, 제시된 문장의 앞뒤 맥락을 잘 파악해야 합니다.

1 질문에 제시된 인용 문장을 미리 읽어 두세요.

2 그 인용 문장이 언제 나올지 기다리며 앞뒤 문맥을 집중해서 잘 들어보세요.

• **Why** does the **man say, "Well, we'd like to"**?	남자는 왜 "음 그러고 싶어요"라고 말하는가?
• **What** does the **woman imply[mean]** when she says, **"A lot of people have been asking about it?"**	여자가 "많은 사람들이 그것에 대해 물었어요"라고 말할 때 암시[의미]하는 바는 무엇인가?

맥락에 따른 화자의 의도 파악하기

화자의 의도 파악 질문은 대화의 맥락과 화자들의 상황을 이해하는 것이 무엇보다 중요합니다. 다음 대화문을 통해 문장이 의미하는 바가 문맥에 따라 어떻게 달라지는지 알아보세요.

What does the man mean when he says, "That's not what we expected"? (A) He is surprised by some survey results. (B) He needs to choose other food.	남자가 "그건 예상하지 못했네요"라고 말할 때 의미하는 바는 무엇인가? (A) 조사 결과에 놀랐다. (B) 다른 음식을 선택해야 한다.

W Our diners' feedback surveys are all in. We, uh, got rather low ratings for our table service.
M I know... That's not what we expected.

여 식사 손님의 의견 설문 조사지가 모두 도착했어요. 음, 테이블 서비스에서 좀 낮은 등급을 받았어요.
남 그래요... **그건 예상하지 못했네요.**
→ '조사 결과에 놀랐다'는 의미

W Due to the holiday season, all cakes are sold. What about muffins instead?
M Oh. That's not what we expected. Let me check with my friends.

여 연휴 시기라 모든 케이크가 다 팔렸습니다. 대신에 머핀은 어떠세요?
남 아, **그건 예상하지 못했네요.** 친구들한테 확인을 해볼게요.
→ '다른 음식을 선택해야 한다'는 의미

P3_10

문제 유형 맛보기

M Wendy, guess what? Our team has finally updated all the customer lists. What a job! It lasted seven weeks and required lots of overtime.

W Congratulations. So you're all done, eh? Well … I'm sure you won't miss it.

M Phew! I'm just happy we got everything completed on time and on budget.

W Super. I'm confident the updates will help our future sales.

What does the woman mean when she says, "I'm sure you won't miss it"?

(A) The man is required to attend a staff meeting.
(B) There is an obvious error on a budget document.
(C) The man is likely pleased about finishing a project.
(D) There is an early deadline for submitting a report.

STEP 01 키워드 보고 문제 유형 파악하기

의도 파악 문제

STEP 02 제시 문장 기다리며 듣고, 전후 맥락 파악하기

앞에서 고객 명단을 모두 업데이트 했다고 하고, 뒤에서는 일을 마쳐서 기쁘다고 함

STEP 03 Paraphrasing 표현에 유의하기

happy we got everything completed → pleased about finishing a project

정답 (C)

M 웬디, 있잖아요. 우리 팀이 마침내 모든 고객 명단을 업데이트했어요. 힘든 일이었어요. 7주가 걸렸고, 야근을 많이 필요로 했어요.
W 축하해요. 그럼 다 끝난 건가요? 그럼… **절대 그립지는 않겠네요.**
M 휴, 제시간에 예산대로 모든 걸 마쳐서 좋아요.
W 멋지네요. 그 최신 정보가 앞으로의 판매에 도움이 될 거라 확신해요.

여자가 "절대 그립지는 않겠네요"라고 말할 때 의미하는 바는 무엇인가?
(A) 남자는 직원 회의에 참석하라는 요구를 받았다.
(B) 예산 문서에 명백한 오류가 있다.
(C) 남자는 프로젝트를 끝낸 것에 기뻐하는 것 같다.
(D) 보고서 제출 마감일이 이르다.

CHECK UP 질문의 키워드를 먼저 파악한 후 대화를 들으면서 정답을 고르세요.

P3_11

1. What does the man imply when he says, "In the past, perhaps"?
   (A) Previous staff events were highly successful.
   (B) An accounting error has occurred.
   (C) A firm's services are no longer affordable.
   (D) An upcoming event should be canceled.

2. What does the woman imply when she says, "We don't carry many travel guides"?
   (A) She is considering an idea.
   (B) She shares the man's interests.
   (C) She agrees with a criticism.
   (D) She needs help doing inventory.

정답 및 해설 p. 110

③ 시각정보 연계 문제

시각정보 연계 문제는 일상 생활이나 업무에서 흔히 볼 수 있는 리스트, 쿠폰, 표지판, 평면도 등 다양한 시각정보가 함께 제시되는 문제입니다.

1 시각정보는 질문 윗부분에 제시되므로 대화를 듣기 전에 미리 파악해 두세요.

2 시각정보 연계 문제는 시각정보만으로는 답을 알 수 없고, 대화 내용과 연결시켜야만 정답을 찾을 수 있다는 점에 주의하세요.

• Look at the **graphic. Which article's deadline** will be **changed**?	시각정보에 의하면, 어떤 기사의 마감일이 변경될 것인가?

시각정보 종류 알아보기

일정표/안내도

회의 같은 행사 일정표나 건물의 층별 안내도, 업무 분장 같은 표 종류의 시각정보가 많이 나온다.

Planning Meeting Schedule of Speakers	
1:00	Russ Everett
2:00	Shelly Wadsworth
3:00	David Bilke
4:00	Wanda Caroli

James Carlos	1st floor
Peter Gordon	2nd floor
Annabel Lee	Basement

지도/평면도

길 또는 교통 안내를 위한 지도나 건물/매장 등의 평면도가 등장하는 경우도 많다.

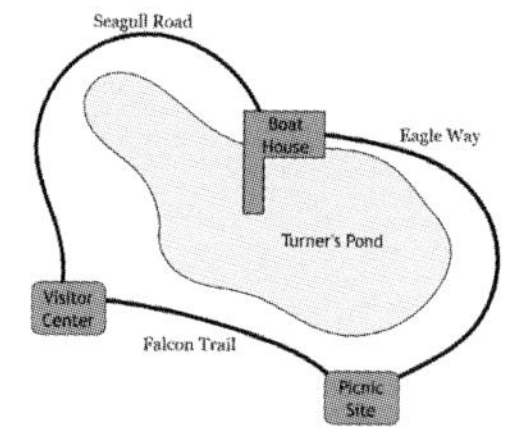

Meeting Room A
Display Area B
Lobby
Display Area D
Meeting Room C

주문서/메뉴

쇼핑이나 외식 관련 대화에서 주문이나 메뉴 등이 등장할 가능성이 높으므로 숫자 정보를 미리 파악해 두는 것이 유리하다.

Order Form of Leenoh Company 10-May-16	
Product	Quantity
Paper clips	17
Binders	10
Scissors	3
Markers	22

Japanese Lasagna	......	$19
Pita & Hummus	......	$14
Mushroom Cake	......	$9

문제 유형 맛보기

P3_12

M Good news. The Eddie Jacobs supplier just called and said the bags we ordered should arrive this morning.

W That's a relief. Customers have been asking for them for almost a week now.

M Yes, I'm sure they'll sell out very quickly. We want them to be easy to find, so where do you think we should display them?

W How about directly in front of the entrance? We want everyone that walks by to be able to see them.

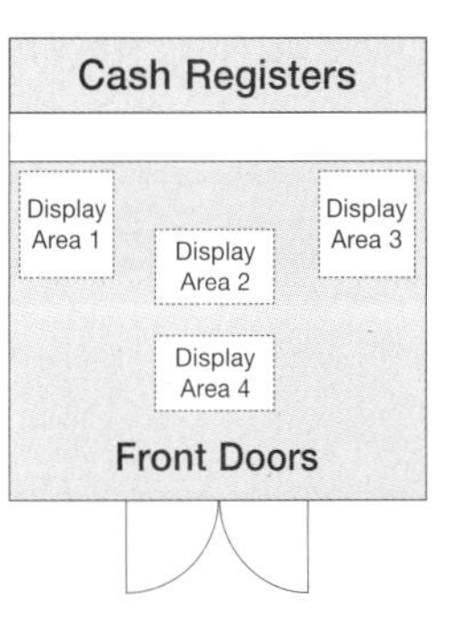

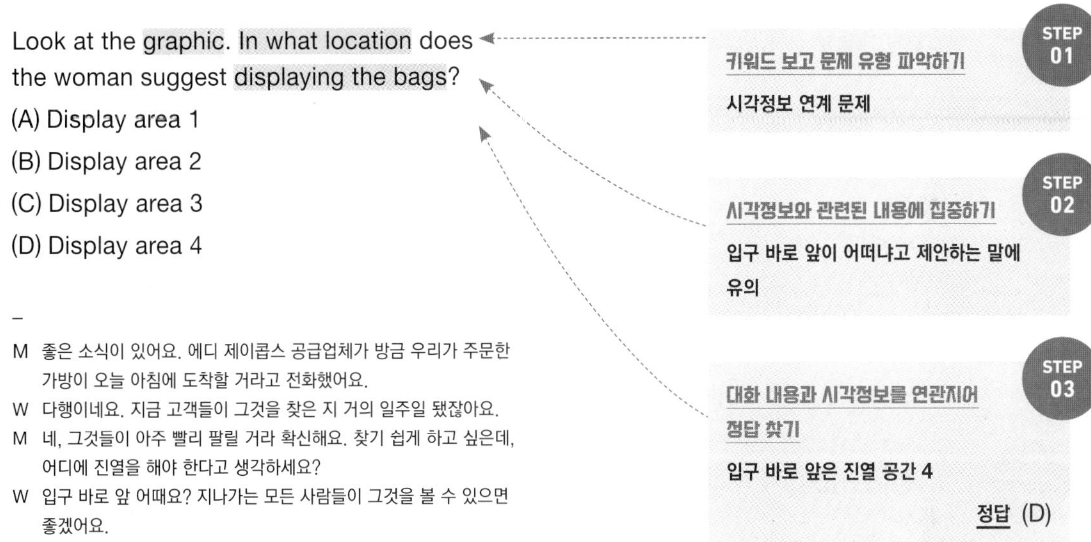

Look at the graphic. In what location does the woman suggest displaying the bags?

(A) Display area 1

(B) Display area 2

(C) Display area 3

(D) Display area 4

STEP 01 키워드 보고 문제 유형 파악하기

시각정보 연계 문제

STEP 02 시각정보와 관련된 내용에 집중하기

입구 바로 앞이 어떠냐고 제안하는 말에 유의

STEP 03 대화 내용과 시각정보를 연관지어 정답 찾기

입구 바로 앞은 진열 공간 4

정답 (D)

M 좋은 소식이 있어요. 에디 제이콥스 공급업체가 방금 우리가 주문한 가방이 오늘 아침에 도착할 거라고 전화했어요.

W 다행이네요. 지금 고객들이 그것을 찾은 지 거의 일주일 됐잖아요.

M 네, 그것들이 아주 빨리 팔릴 거라 확신해요. 찾기 쉽게 하고 싶은데, 어디에 진열을 해야 한다고 생각하세요?

W 입구 바로 앞 어때요? 지나가는 모든 사람들이 그것을 볼 수 있으면 좋겠어요.

여자는 가방을 어떤 위치에 진열할 것을 제안하는가?

(A) 진열 공간 1

(B) 진열 공간 2

(C) 진열 공간 3

(D) 진열 공간 4

CHECK UP

질문의 키워드를 먼저 파악한 후 대화를 들으면서 정답을 고르세요.

P3_13

1. Look at the graphic. Where does the woman recommend the man go?

(A) Adelaide Pizza

(B) Eckel's Cafe

(C) North Wind Sandwiches

(D) Lou's Noodles

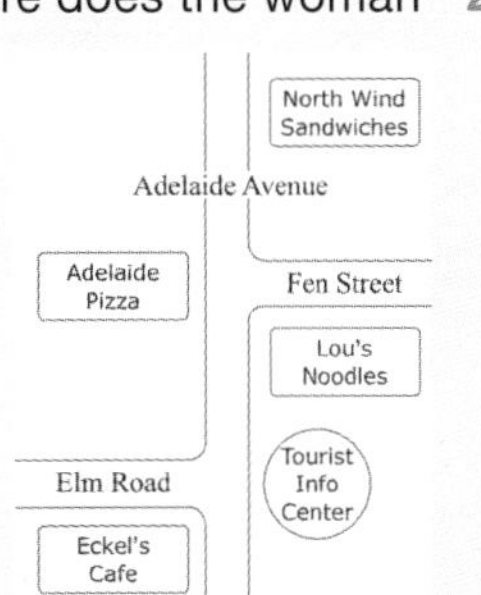

2. Look at the graphic. Which office will the woman go to?

(A) 2A

(B) 2B

(C) 2C

(D) 2D

Clayton Research Building	
Office	**Company**
2A	Stainless Security
2B	Accelerate Tech
2C	Batch Packagers
2D	Watson Chemicals

PART 3 | 기초학습

UNIT 01 직장 내 업무

직장 내 다양한 업무, 업무 협조, 일정, 교육, 마케팅 등 관련 대화로 Part 3에서 가장 많이 출제되는 주제입니다.

기출 문제풀이 전략 P3_14

STEP 01 **질문 파악** 질문을 먼저 읽으면서 키워드를 파악하세요.

1 What is being discussed?	2 What is the problem?	3 What will the woman do to solve the problem?
(A) A book cover (B) A magazine advertisement (C) A newsletter (D) A package design	(A) Some text is hard to read. (B) A page will not print. (C) Some pictures are too dark. (D) There is a spelling mistake.	(A) Buy some new ink (B) Change printer settings (C) Hire a photographer (D) Use some software

STEP 02 **정답 고르기** 대화를 들으며 키워드의 단서를 찾아 정답을 고르세요.

M Hello, Anna. 1 I'm trying to put together the newsletter for next month. I thought it would be a good idea to add some pictures of our products, but it's not working well.

W 2 Yes, I see the problem. The pictures are so dark you can't see the colors well.

M Is there some way to make them lighter? I don't know how to do that.

W 3 Let me try using my photo-editing software. I think I can easily make that change.

1. 키워드: 대화 주제
소식지를 정리하려고 한다는 말에 유의 → 정답은 (C)

2. 키워드: 문제점
사진이 너무 어두워서 색이 안 보인다는 말에 유의 → 정답은 (C)

3. 키워드: 여자의 해결 방법
사진 편집 소프트웨어를 사용해보겠다는 말에 유의 → 정답은 (D)

—

남 안녕, 애나. 다음 달 소식지를 정리하려고 해요. 우리 제품 사진을 몇 장 추가하는 게 좋을 것 같았는데 잘 안 되네요.
여 네, 문제가 있어요. 사진이 너무 어두워서 색이 잘 안 보이네요.
남 그것들을 더 밝게 만들 방법이 있나요? 어떻게 해야 할지 모르겠어요.
여 사진 편집 소프트웨어를 사용해 볼게요. 쉽게 바꿀 수 있을 것 같아요.

정답 및 해설 p. 112

CHECK UP

Step 1 다음 3개의 질문을 읽으며 키워드에 표시하세요.

Step 2 대화를 들으며 정답의 단서를 찾아 정답을 고르세요.

P3_15

1 What are the speakers discussing?

(A) Registering for a management conference

(B) Completing a course project

2 When is the deadline?

(A) On Friday

(B) On Monday

3 What will the woman probably do next?

(A) Photocopy a letter

(B) Send an e-mail

정답 및 해설 p. 113

기출로 익히는 패러프레이징

기출 문제에 등장했던 상황과 문장을 보고 정답이 어떤 식으로 패러프레이즈 되는지 확인해보세요.

대화 내 단서 포착	패러프레이징 된 정답 찾기
I'm calling because I haven't received my check for the last pay period. 지난달 급여를 받지 못해서 전화 드립니다.	**Q. 여자가 전화한 이유?** **A.** A missing paycheck 분실된 급여
Do you know what he wants to talk to us about? 그가 무엇에 대해 우리와 이야기하고 싶어 하는지 아세요?	**Q. 남자가 알고 싶어 하는 것?** **A.** The topic of an upcoming meeting 곧 있을 회의의 주제
Could you please send me an updated construction schedule immediately? 업데이트된 공사 일정을 즉시 보내 주시겠어요?	**Q. 남자가 요청하는 것?** **A.** A revised schedule 수정된 일정
I better make copies and take them over to his office right away. 복사해서 바로 그의 사무실로 갖다 주는 편이 좋겠어요.	**Q. 여자가 다음에 할 일?** **A.** Deliver some documents 서류 전달

주제별 기출 어휘

P3_16

직무/업무

management 경영, 경영진
colleague 동료(= coworker)
executive 임원, 중역
department 부서(= division, office)
marketing strategy 마케팅 전략
report to work 출근하다
confirm 확인하다, 확정하다
collaborate 협력하다
priority 우선순위
flexible working hours 탄력근무제
performance evaluation 업무 평가, 인사 고과
oversee the work 일을 감독하다
review a document 서류를 검토하다
sales associate 영업 사원
potential customer 잠재 고객
account 계좌, 계정, 고객
safety inspection 안전 검사
consult with ~와 협의하다
manufacturing process 제조 과정
submit 제출하다(= turn in)
take care of ~을 처리하다, 다루다(= deal with, handle)
be in charge of ~을 담당하다, (책임을) 맡다

일정

scheduled 예정된
schedule[set up] an appointment 약속을 잡다
reschedule 일정을 조정하다, 변경하다
postpone 미루다(= delay, put off)
cancel 취소하다(= call off)
meet a deadline 마감 기한을 맞추다
deadline extension 마감 연장
last-minute 마지막 순간의
work overtime 초과 근무하다
be due + 날짜/기간 마감일이 ~이다
launch a campaign 캠페인에 착수하다
on schedule 예정대로
behind schedule 예정보다 늦게
ahead of schedule 예정보다 빨리(= ahead of time)
schedule conflict 일정 겹침
send out a reminder 독촉장을 보내다
on short notice 촉박하게
short of staff 일손이 부족한 (= short-handed, short-staffed)

사무기기 사용

photocopy 복사하다(= make a copy)
office supplies 사무용품
maintenance 유지보수
set up 설치하다(= install)
mechanical defect 기계적 결함
feature 특색, 기능
device 기기, 장치
under warranty 보증 기간이 남은
report a malfunction 고장 신고하다
out of order 고장 난(= broken)
break down 고장 나다
run out of ~이 다 떨어지다
be jammed 끼다, 막히다
environmentally friendly 친환경적인 (= eco-friendly)
technical support 기술 지원

ETS 문제로 훈련하기

P3_17

STEP 01

문장 핵심 파악하기

먼저 질문의 키워드에 동그라미로 표시하며 질문 내용을 파악하세요. 대화를 듣고 주어진 질문에 답한 후 빈칸을 채워 보세요.

1 When did the woman order the manuals?

(A) Yesterday

(B) A month ago

> **M** The new users' manuals ___________ in the mail ___________.
> **W** It's about time! It's been _________ _________ since I placed that order!
> **M** They included a ___________ of apology — they had some ___________ with their ___________ recently.

2 What is the problem with the report?

(A) It contains misspellings.

(B) It does not include some information.

> **M** Good morning, Ms. Ericson. I finished the annual report that you asked me to prepare for tomorrow's _________ with the _________ of directors.
> **W** Thank you. I noticed that some consulting ___________ were ___________ ___________ though. Can you ___________ ___________ that information?
> **M** Sure, that's an easy change.

STEP 02

실전에 가깝게 훈련하기

질문의 키워드에 동그라미로 표시한 후, 대화를 듣고 주어진 질문에 답하세요.

3 What does the woman need help with?

(A) Organizing a seminar

(B) Contacting a customer

(C) Finding some documents

(D) Using a computer program

4 What will the speakers do next?

(A) Finish an assignment

(B) Locate some forms

(C) Send out an e-mail

(D) Speak with a coworker

정답 및 해설 p. 114

ETS 실전 테스트

1. What are the speakers discussing?
   (A) Automobiles
   (B) Computers
   (C) Televisions
   (D) Mobile phones

2. What do the speakers say about the product?
   (A) It is not selling well.
   (B) It has a mechanical defect.
   (C) It is too small.
   (D) It is overpriced.

3. What does the man suggest?
   (A) Reducing the product's price
   (B) Designing smaller models
   (C) Changing marketing strategies
   (D) Adding electronic features

---

4. What does the woman ask about?
   (A) The date of a meeting
   (B) The location of an office
   (C) The security procedures for a building
   (D) The availability of rental properties

5. What does the man offer to do?
   (A) Receive a delivery
   (B) Look up some information
   (C) Send a text message
   (D) Provide a key

6. According to the woman, what will Mr. Simpson have to do?
   (A) Confirm an address
   (B) Reserve a meeting space
   (C) Sign for some documents
   (D) Postpone a trip

7. What type of business do the speakers work at?
   (A) A consulting firm
   (B) A clothing company
   (C) A sporting goods store
   (D) A shipping company

8. Why does the man say, "your advertisements are always so good"?
   (A) To express surprise
   (B) To agree with a suggestion
   (C) To congratulate a colleague
   (D) To request help with a project

9. What does the woman suggest the man do?
   (A) Check a deadline
   (B) Give a presentation
   (C) Set up a meeting
   (D) E-mail a document

---

10. What industry do the speakers most likely work in?
    (A) Journalism
    (B) Advertising
    (C) Travel
    (D) Hospitality

11. What product do the men mention?
    (A) Airline seats
    (B) Video equipment
    (C) Electric cars
    (D) Wireless headphones

12. What would the woman like the men to do?
    (A) Read a company policy
    (B) Hire some assistants
    (C) Set up a meeting with a client
    (D) Continue working together

13. Who most likely is the man?
(A) A fitness instructor
(B) A sales associate
(C) A graphic designer
(D) A photojournalist

14. What does the woman want her brand to convey?
(A) Energy
(B) Freedom
(C) Community
(D) Relaxation

15. What does the woman say she will do tomorrow?
(A) Send some samples
(B) Choose some images
(C) Reply to an e-mail
(D) Change a price

---

16. What does the man ask the woman to do?
(A) Reschedule a presentation
(B) Arrange a banquet
(C) Train a new assistant
(D) Work on a building design

17. Why is the woman unavailable today?
(A) She has some appointments.
(B) She has a job interview.
(C) She is finishing a sales report.
(D) She is preparing for a business trip.

18. What does the man offer to do?
(A) Find some account information
(B) Submit a list of expenses
(C) Revise some sales figures
(D) Assign additional people to a project

Software version	8.2	>
Model	250–73	>
Capacity in GB	124	>
Serial Number	36998	>

19. Why is the man calling?
(A) His mobile phone is running slowly.
(B) His phone bill is incorrect.
(C) He wants to add a service.
(D) He wants to cancel an appointment.

20. Look at the graphic. Which number will the man give the woman?
(A) 8.2
(B) 250-73
(C) 124
(D) 36998

21. Why does the woman need the information?
(A) To apply a discount
(B) To check a warranty
(C) To activate some devices
(D) To recommend some software

정답 및 해설 p. 115

UNIT 02 인사

취업 면접, 신입 사원 교육, 승진, 전근, 퇴직, 인사 고과 등 직장 내 모든 인사 관련 대화가 등장합니다.

기출 문제풀이 전략

P3_19

STEP 01 **질문 파악** 질문을 먼저 읽으면서 키워드를 파악하세요.

1 What are the speakers mainly discussing?	2 What does the man say he is willing to do?	3 What most likely will happen next?
(A) A company policy (B) An advertising campaign (C) A job opportunity (D) A corporate logo	(A) Relocate overseas (B) Work overtime (C) Lead a training session (D) Meet with an executive	(A) A tour will be given. (B) Tasks will be assigned. (C) Photographs will be taken. (D) Manuals will be distributed.

STEP 02 **정답 고르기** 대화를 들으며 키워드의 단서를 찾아 정답을 고르세요.

W **1** I have one last question before we finish the interview. Could you please tell me why you believe you're the best candidate for the graphic designer position?

M Well, in addition to my six years of professional experience in the field, I'm very flexible. I know that graphic designers often have to make last minute revisions, and **2** I'm willing to work extra hours to meet deadlines.

W Good—I'm looking for someone with that kind of commitment. So, unless you have any questions, **3** why don't I show you around the office?

1. 키워드: 대화 주제
면접, 지원자, 직책 등의 어휘에 유의
→ 정답은 (C)

2. 키워드: 남자가 할 일
마감을 맞추기 위해 추가 시간 근무를 할 수 있다는 말에 유의 → 정답은 (B)
Paraphrasing work extra hours → Work overtime

3. 키워드: 다음에 일어날 일
사무실을 구경시켜 주겠다는 말에 유의 → 정답은 (A)

여 면접을 마치기 전에 마지막 질문이 하나 있습니다. 자신이 그래픽 디자이너 직에 가장 적합한 후보라고 생각하는 이유를 말씀해주시겠어요?
남 이 분야에서 6년간의 전문적 경험 외에, 저는 매우 유연합니다. 그래픽 디자이너들은 종종 마지막 순간에 수정을 해야 한다는 것을 알고 있고, 저는 마감을 맞추기 위해 초과근무를 할 용의가 있습니다.
여 좋아요. 그렇게 헌신적인 사람을 찾고 있어요. 그럼 궁금한 점이 없으시면 사무실을 구경시켜 드릴까요?

정답 및 해설 p. 123

CHECK UP **Step 1** 다음 3개의 질문을 읽으며 키워드에 표시하세요. P3_20
Step 2 대화를 들으며 정답의 단서를 찾아 정답을 고르세요.

1 What is the woman calling about?
(A) A job promotion
(B) A summer internship

2 What does the man recommend?
(A) Submitting an application
(B) Checking an online job list

3 What does the man tell the woman?
(A) She may have missed a deadline.
(B) She will have to wait several months.

정답 및 해설 p. 123

기출로 익히는 패러프레이징

기출 문제에 등장했던 상황과 문장을 보고 정답이 어떤 식으로 패러프레이즈 되는지 확인해보세요.

대화 내 단서 포착	패러프레이징 된 정답 찾기
Have you met the new programmer yet? 새 프로그래머를 만나봤나요?	**Q. 화자들이 이야기하고 있는 것?** **A.** A new colleague 새 동료
Could we talk about scheduling the interview appointments we need to do for the Web designer position? 웹디자이너 직 면접 일정을 잡아야 하는데 이야기 나눌 수 있나요?	**Q. 대화의 주제?** **A.** Coordinating some schedules 일정 조정
We'd like to give you an opportunity to move up in your career. 당신에게 승진할 기회를 주고 싶습니다.	**Q. 여자가 만나려는 이유?** **A.** To offer him a promotion 승진을 제안하기 위해
I'm scheduled to interview Janet Kelly after lunch for the new sales position. 점심 식사 후에 새 영업직에 지원한 자넷 켈리를 면접하기로 되어 있어요.	**Q. 여자가 오후에 만날 사람?** **A.** A job candidate 구직자

주제별 기출 어휘

P3_21

채용

hire 고용하다(= employy)
job opening[vacancy] 직장의 공석
résumé 이력서
apply for a job 일자리에 지원하다
job application 입사 지원서
candidate 지원자(= applicant)
interview job candidates 구직자를 면접하다
conduct an interview 면접을 실시하다
qualified 자격이 있는
qualification 자격(증)
responsibility 업무, 임무(= duty)
human resources department 인사부 (= personnel department)
temporary staff 임시 직원
benefit (급여 이외에 받는) 혜택, 수당
expert 전문가
identification card 신분증
security office 경비실
new-hire paperwork 신입 직원 서류
notify 통지하다
on the payroll 고용 상태인
complete[fill out] a form 서류를 작성하다
fill the position 공석을 채우다
look over ~을 검토하다(= review, get through)
job description 직무 기술서
accept a job offer 일자리 제안을 수락하다

승진/휴가

promotion 승진
receive a raise 임금이 인상되다
assign 임명하다
performance 실적
accomplish 성취하다
expertise 전문 지식[기술]
leave of absence 휴가, 결근
paid[unpaid] vacation 유급[무급] 휴가
be promoted to + 직책 ~으로 승진되다
deserve the promotion 승진할 자격이 있다
organize a celebration 축하 행사를 준비하다
take a vacation 휴가를 내다(= take time off)
be away on vacation 휴가 중이다
leave for vacation 휴가를 떠나다
ask for the time off 휴가를 요청하다
fill out the request form 요청서를 작성하다

은퇴/전근

retire 은퇴하다
retirement 은퇴, 퇴직
resign 사임하다
resignation 사임, 사직
transfer 전근; 전근 가다(= move, relocate)
replace (자리를) 대신하다
hard work 노고
dedication 헌신, 전념
officially 공식적으로
leave the company[job] 회사를 그만두다
move to ~으로 옮기다, 이사하다
hold a party 파티를 열다(= throw a party)
go into retirement 은퇴하다
have been with the company 회사에서 일해 왔다
hand in (one's) resignation 사직서를 제출하다
request a transfer to ~로 전근을 요청하다

ETS 문제로 훈련하기

P3_22

STEP 01

문장 핵심 파악하기

먼저 질문의 키워드에 동그라미로 표시하며 질문 내용을 파악하세요. 대화를 듣고 주어진 질문에 답한 후 빈칸을 채워 보세요.

1 What does the man confirm that he has received?

(A) An employee manual (B) A security badge

W Hi, Anton. My name's Maria and I'll be your ________ here at LW Energy Solutions. Were you able to get your ________ ________?
M Glad to be here! And yes.
W OK, great. You'll need that to ________ ________ the buildings ________.

2 How did the man find out about the job?

(A) From a friend (B) From a job recruiter

W So, from your résumé I can see you have a lot of experience with local ________ ________ in many different regions. How did you hear about the ________ ________ for an announcer?
M ________ ________ ________ ________ told me about it. His name is Bruce Akins, and he's a ________ here.
W Oh, I know Bruce.

STEP 02

실전에 가깝게 훈련하기

질문의 키워드에 동그라미로 표시한 후, 대화를 듣고 주어진 질문에 답하세요.

3 What are the speakers discussing?

(A) A vacation plan
(B) A conference schedule
(C) A coworker's new job
(D) A new client

4 What do the speakers suggest about the Sydney office?

(A) It has not opened yet.
(B) It is the company's largest branch.
(C) It houses the company headquarters.
(D) It recently won an award.

PART 3 | UNIT 02

ETS 실전 테스트

1. In what area does Tom currently work?
(A) Human resources
(B) Accounting
(C) Payroll
(D) Advertising

2. How long has Tom been working for the company?
(A) Three weeks
(B) Three months
(C) Six months
(D) Two years

3. Why is the woman meeting with Tom?
(A) To offer him a promotion
(B) To discuss an error he made
(C) To talk to him about his training
(D) To resolve a problem with his coworkers

---

4. What are the speakers discussing?
(A) Accounting procedures
(B) Hiring new employees
(C) Marketing strategies
(D) Scheduling a meeting

5. What is the man going to do next week?
(A) Interview job candidates
(B) Take a vacation
(C) Go to a conference
(D) Move to a new office

6. What is the woman concerned about?
(A) The number of meetings
(B) A change in policies
(C) The training of new employees
(D) The amount of office space

7. Why is Mr. Alvarez coming in late?
(A) He missed the train.
(B) He overslept.
(C) He got caught in traffic.
(D) He had a meeting.

8. What position is the woman applying for?
(A) Business manager
(B) Sales associate
(C) Personnel director
(D) Accounting manager

9. What is the woman asked to do?
(A) Fill out a registration form
(B) Come back the next day
(C) Wait in a seating area
(D) Submit her résumé

---

10. Where do the speakers most likely work?
(A) In a law office
(B) In an accounting firm
(C) In an employment agency
(D) In a travel company

11. What does the woman imply when she says, "Pablo is interviewing someone in the boardroom now"?
(A) A room is unavailable.
(B) A department meeting is running late.
(C) A position has not been filled.
(D) A colleague cannot help with a task.

12. What does the woman ask the man to do?
(A) Review an expense report
(B) Make a phone call
(C) Contact a supervisor
(D) Purchase some supplies

13. What was the problem with the man's performance review?
    (A) It was incomplete.
    (B) It was submitted late.
    (C) It was accidentally deleted.
    (D) It was sent to the wrong person.

14. What does the man say he will do this afternoon?
    (A) Meet with his manager
    (B) Prepare a budget
    (C) Interview a job applicant
    (D) Go on a business trip

15. What does the woman offer to do?
    (A) Make travel reservations
    (B) Revise a deadline
    (C) E-mail some guidelines
    (D) Take over a work assignment

---

16. Why does the woman congratulate the man?
    (A) He has set a sales record.
    (B) He has started his own business.
    (C) He has completed a degree program.
    (D) He has been promoted.

17. What is the topic of the seminar series?
    (A) Product design
    (B) Sales techniques
    (C) Project management
    (D) Retirement planning

18. When will the first series begin?
    (A) On April 15th
    (B) On April 30th
    (C) On May 15th
    (D) On May 30th

Company	Open Position
Circle Agency	Accounting Manager
Sakda Corporation	Web Designer
CX Incorporated	Human Resources Assistant
Totsuka Systems	Database Programmer

19. How did the woman learn about the man's company?
    (A) From a friend
    (B) From a radio show
    (C) From a Web site
    (D) From a newspaper advertisement

20. Why is the woman looking for a new job?
    (A) She wants to make a career change.
    (B) She is moving to another city.
    (C) Her former company recently closed.
    (D) Her current commute time is too long.

21. Look at the graphic. Which company does the man refer to?
    (A) Circle Agency
    (B) Sakda Corporation
    (C) CX Incorporated
    (D) Totsuka Systems

정답 및 해설 p. 126

UNIT 03 회의/행사

부서별 회의, 이사진 회의, 컨퍼런스콜 등의 회의부터 각종 기념 행사, 야유회, 박람회 등 행사 관련 대화입니다.

기출 문제풀이 전략

P3_24

STEP 01 **질문 파악** 질문을 먼저 읽으면서 키워드를 파악하세요.

1 What event did the woman recently attend?	2 What did the woman find interesting at the event?	3 What will the woman do on Wednesday?
(A) A technology seminar (B) A client dinner (C) A department celebration (D) An employee orientation	(A) A volunteer opportunity (B) A building layout (C) An accounting application (D) A guest speaker's profile	(A) Take some time off (B) Give a demonstration (C) Present an award (D) Participate in a training session

STEP 02 **정답 고르기** 대화를 들으며 키워드의 단서를 찾아 정답을 고르세요.

M Hey, Amanda. **1** How was the Business Technology Seminar?

W Oh, it was great! **2** I saw a software application for corporate accounting that was really interesting. Instead of using many different spreadsheets, this application integrates invoices, online payments, and expense tracking, all in one.

M Hmm, we'd really benefit from switching to a system like that.

W I agree. **3** I'm preparing a demonstration of the application to present at the management meeting on Wednesday. I think we should seriously consider using it.

1. 키워드: 여자가 참석한 행사
비즈니스 기술 세미나는 어땠는지 묻는 말에 유의 → 정답은 (A)

2. 키워드: 행사에서 흥미로웠던 것
흥미로운 기업 회계용 애플리케이션을 봤다는 말에 유의 → 정답은 (C)
Paraphrasing application for corporate accounting → accounting application

3. 키워드: 여자가 수요일에 할 일
경영진 회의에서 애플리케이션 시연을 한다는 말에 유의 → 정답은 (B)

—

남 안녕, 아만다. 비즈니스 기술 세미나는 어땠어요?
여 아, 좋았어요! 아주 흥미로운 기업 회계용 소프트웨어 애플리케이션을 봤어요. 이 애플리케이션은 여러 가지 스프레드시트를 사용하는 대신 송장, 온라인 결제 및 비용 추적을 모두 하나로 통합한다고 하네요.
남 흠, 그런 시스템으로 전환하면 정말 이득이 될 거예요.
여 맞아요. 수요일 경영진 회의에서 보여줄 애플리케이션 시연을 준비하고 있는데요. 그것을 사용하는 것을 진지하게 고려해야겠어요.

정답 및 해설 p. 133

CHECK UP

Step 1 다음 3개의 질문을 읽으며 키워드에 표시하세요.

Step 2 대화를 들으며 정답의 단서를 찾아 정답을 고르세요.

P3_25

1 What task is the woman in charge of?

(A) Taking inventory

(B) Planning an event

2 What does the man suggest changing?

(A) A date

(B) A supplier

3 What does the woman say she will do?

(A) Contact a business

(B) Reduce a budget

정답 및 해설 p. 133

기출로 익히는 패러프레이징

기출 문제에 등장했던 상황과 문장을 보고 정답이 어떤 식으로 패러프레이즈 되는지 확인해보세요.

대화 내 단서 포착	패러프레이징 된 정답 찾기
I leave for that banking conference in Beijing on Saturday. 토요일에 베이징에서 열리는 그 금융 컨퍼런스에 참석하기 위해 떠납니다.	**Q. 여자의 여행 목적?** **A.** To attend a conference 컨퍼런스에 참석하고자
Are you going to the company picnic this Saturday? 이번 주 토요일 회사 야유회에 갈 겁니까?	**Q. 화자들이 논의하는 것?** **A.** A work event 직장 행사
He won't be here this afternoon. 그는 오늘 오후에 여기 못 와요.	**Q. 회의가 연기된 이유?** **A.** One meeting participant cannot attend. 회의 참석자 한 명이 참석할 수 없어서
We had a farewell lunch for all the temporary workers in our department. 우리 부서의 모든 임시 직원들을 위한 송별 점심을 했어요.	**Q. 점심 식사를 한 이유?** **A.** To say good-bye to temporary staff 임시 직원들에게 작별 인사를 하기 위해

주제별 기출 어휘

P3_26

회의/발표

set up a meeting 회의를 잡다
attend a meeting 회의에 참석하다
give[make] a presentation 발표하다
staff meeting 직원 회의
client meeting 고객 회의
managers' meeting 관리자 회의
conference call 전화 회의
videoconferencing 화상회의
host a conference 회의를 주최하다
watch a demonstration 시연을 지켜보다
agenda 회의 의제
handout 인쇄물, 유인물
draft 초안
come up with ideas 아이디어를 생각해내다
hand out 나눠 주다, 배포하다
organize a meeting 회의를 준비하다

출장/행사

business trip 출장
itinerary (여행) 일정
on business 업무 차
be out of town 출장 중이다
travel expense 출장비, 여행 경비
travel reimbursement 출장 경비 환급
cover expenses 경비를 부담하다
company anniversary 창립기념일
company retreat 회사 야유회
name badge 명찰
sign 표지판, 안내판
venue 개최지, 행사장
accommodate 수용하다
post a notice 공지를 붙이다[게시하다]
awards ceremony 시상식
job fair 취업박람회(= career fair)
charity event 자선 행사
corporate event 기업 행사
fund-raiser 기금 모음 행사
grand opening 대개장
opening ceremony 개회식, 개막식
farewell party 송별회
retirement party 은퇴 파티
anniversary 기념일
raffle ticket 경품 응모권
promotional giveaways 판촉물

거래/계약

sign a(n) contract[agreement] 계약서에 서명하다
win a contract 계약을 따내다
potential[prospective] client 잠재 고객
estimate 견적(서)(= quote)
proposal 제안(서)
renew 갱신하다
expense 비용, 경비
negotiation 협상
M&A(= merger and acquisition) 합병 및 인수
take over ~을 인수하다(= acquire)
finalize the deal 협상을 마무리하다
within a budget 예산 내에
sales figures 판매 수치
exceed a budget 예산을 초과하다
go over the budget 예산을 검토하다
credit an account 계좌에 입금하다

ETS 문제로 훈련하기

P3_27

STEP 01 문장 핵심 파악하기

먼저 질문의 키워드에 동그라미로 표시하며 질문 내용을 파악하세요. 대화를 듣고 주어진 질문에 답한 후 빈칸을 채워 보세요.

1 What is the woman's profession?

(A) Journalist (B) Florist

> **W** Hi, my name is Kay Stevenson. I'm a ___________ for *Norrisville Daily*, our local ___________. I'm here to ___________ the Norrisville flower show.
>
> **M** Sure! Can I just see your ___________? Then I'll be able to give you a _________ _________ to enter the exhibit free of charge.
>
> **W** Thank you.

2 What are the speakers discussing?

(A) The dates of a career fair (B) Enrollment in an upcoming workshop

> **W** Geoff. I was making ___________ assignments for our ___________ enrichment day, and I was surprised to see that your public speaking ___________ is already ___________.
>
> **M** Yes, the ___________ filled up very quickly. In fact, I've already had to turn several people away.
>
> **W** Hmm...Maybe we should add _________ _________ to the schedule.

STEP 02 실전에 가깝게 훈련하기

질문의 키워드에 동그라미로 표시한 후, 대화를 듣고 주어진 질문에 답하세요.

3 What does the man ask the woman to do?

(A) Send out a schedule
(B) Visit a client
(C) Work at a business event
(D) Interview a job candidate

4 What will the speakers probably do on Thursday?

(A) Sign a contract
(B) Plan a trade show
(C) Purchase some jewelry
(D) Attend a meeting

정답 및 해설 p. 134

ETS 실전 테스트

1. What type of event is the woman attending?
   (A) A community festival
   (B) An industry conference
   (C) A company anniversary
   (D) A job fair

2. What does the man give the woman?
   (A) An application form
   (B) A confirmation code
   (C) A name badge
   (D) An instruction sheet

3. What does the woman ask the man to verify?
   (A) A meeting room number
   (B) A product release date
   (C) A presentation time
   (D) A booth location

---

4. Why is the man calling?
   (A) To pay an invoice
   (B) To obtain a document
   (C) To sign up for an event
   (D) To order some software

5. According to the woman, what does the man have to do?
   (A) Schedule an appointment
   (B) Complete a task online
   (C) Approve an expense
   (D) Submit a proposal

6. What does the woman request?
   (A) Some contact information
   (B) Presentation slides
   (C) Proof of attendance
   (D) Details from a bill

7. What type of event are the speakers discussing?
   (A) A company party
   (B) A business conference
   (C) A music festival
   (D) An art exhibition

8. What does the woman ask the man to do?
   (A) Reserve a banquet hall
   (B) Perform with a band
   (C) Transport some equipment
   (D) Set up a seating area

9. What does the man say he has to do Saturday afternoon?
   (A) Take his car to a repair shop
   (B) Work an additional shift
   (C) Practice music
   (D) Attend a sporting event

---

10. What will happen next month?
    (A) A venue will be renovated.
    (B) A team will go on a business trip.
    (C) A colleague will retire.
    (D) A product will launch.

11. What is the woman concerned about?
    (A) A deadline
    (B) Transportation arrangements
    (C) The number of attendees
    (D) A rental fee

12. What will the woman do next?
    (A) Send out an invitation
    (B) Purchase some tickets
    (C) Make a travel itinerary
    (D) Call a supervisor

13. Why are the speakers traveling?

(A) To audit a business
(B) To purchase some land
(C) To organize a conference
(D) To attend a ceremony

14. According to the man, what skill does the woman have?

(A) She has an excellent memory.
(B) She can speak many languages.
(C) She is able to make calculations quickly.
(D) She can repair computers easily.

15. What does the man mean when he says, "the president of the company is going to be there"?

(A) An agenda has changed.
(B) A contract will most likely be signed.
(C) They should dress formally.
(D) They will need to prepare a speech.

---

16. Where do the speakers work?

(A) At an Internet café
(B) At an office supply store
(C) At a convention center
(D) At a clothing store

17. What problem do the speakers mention?

(A) A Web site is running slowly.
(B) Some orders have not been delivered.
(C) Some staff have not reported to work.
(D) A sales report is written incorrectly.

18. What does the woman say she will do?

(A) Consult a coworker
(B) Hire some temporary workers
(C) Schedule some training
(D) Postpone an event

ANNUAL FITNESS WEEK	
Events are free for all employees!	
Monday:	Health screening
Tuesday:	Meditation training
Wednesday:	Nutrition class
Thursday:	3-kilometer walk
Friday:	Healthy picnic

19. According to the man, what is new about Fitness Week this year?

(A) Employees will watch a film.
(B) Employees will receive a gift.
(C) A celebrity will give a talk.
(D) A cooking demonstration will be held.

20. Look at the graphic. Which event will the man most likely participate in?

(A) The health screening
(B) The meditation training
(C) The nutrition class
(D) The 3-kilometer walk

21. What does the woman ask the man to do?

(A) Hand out flyers
(B) Register online
(C) Order some food
(D) Create a survey

정답 및 해설 p. 136

UNIT 04 기타 사무실 대화

직장 내에서 동료 간에 나누는 대화나 지각, 결근, 직장 이전, 사무기기 등에 관련된 대화들이 출제될 수 있습니다.

기출 문제풀이 전략

P3_29

STEP 01 **질문 파악** 질문을 먼저 읽으면서 키워드를 파악하세요.

1. Why does the man say, "I eat there a few times a week"? (A) To refuse a suggestion (B) To agree with an opinion (C) To offer an alternative (D) To reject a criticism	2. Where do the speakers work? (A) At an electronics shop (B) At a bank (C) At a warehouse (D) At an office supply store	3. Why does the woman prefer her new job to her previous job? (A) There is a greater variety of work. (B) More of the work is automated. (C) The schedule is more flexible. (D) More time is spent with clients.

STEP 02 **정답 고르기** 대화를 들으며 키워드의 단서를 찾아 정답을 고르세요.

M Hi, Lena. Have you had your lunch break yet?
W Yeah, **1** I had a sandwich from Tilly's Café. It was delicious!
M I eat there a few times a week! So, how are you adjusting to the job? **2** Are you getting acclimated to the warehouse?
W Yeah, it's going well. It's a lot easier to fill shipping orders here than at my previous job. These robots are fantastic.
M It's a good system, isn't it?
W Yes—**3** at my old job we had to do a lot of the picking and packing manually. The fact that you've automated everything makes the job much easier.

1. 키워드: 문장의 의도
샌드위치가 맛있었다고 한 말에 대한 답변임에 유의 → 정답은 (B)

2. 키워드: 화자들의 직장
물류창고에 적응이 되었는지 묻는 말에 유의 → 정답은 (C)

3. 키워드: 여자가 새 직장을 더 좋아하는 이유
자동화되어 일이 쉬워졌다는 말에 유의 → 정답은 (B)

남 안녕, 레나. 점심 먹었어요?
여 네, 틸리스 카페에서 샌드위치를 먹었어요. 맛있었어요!
남 나 일주일에 몇 번은 거기서 먹어요! 그래서, 일에 어떻게 적응하고 있나요? 물류창고에 적응되고 있어요?
여 네, 잘 되고 있어요. 이전 직장보다 여기가 배송 주문 처리하기가 훨씬 쉬워요. 이 로봇들은 환상적이에요.
남 좋은 시스템이에요, 그렇죠?
여 네, 예전 직장에서는 수작업으로 물품을 고르고 포장하는 작업을 많이 했어야 했어요. 여기는 모든 것을 자동화했기 때문에 작업이 훨씬 쉬워졌어요.

정답 및 해설 p. 144

CHECK UP

Step 1 다음 3개의 질문을 읽으며 키워드에 표시하세요.
Step 2 대화를 들으며 정답의 단서를 찾아 정답을 고르세요.

P3_30

1 What does the woman ask the man to do?

(A) Rearrange a cabinet
(B) Restock some supplies

2 Why is the man unable to help?

(A) A shipment is late.
(B) Some equipment is out of order.

3 What will happen at 1:30?

(A) The man will go to a store.
(B) The woman's colleagues will arrive.

정답 및 해설 p. 144

기출로 익히는 패러프레이징

기출 문제에 등장했던 상황과 문장을 보고 정답이 어떤 식으로 패러프레이즈 되는지 확인해보세요.

대화 내 단서 포착	패러프레이징 된 정답 찾기
I called a technician to schedule a repair appointment. 수리 약속을 하기 위해 기술자에게 전화했어요.	**Q. 남자가 전화한 사람?** **A.** A repair person 수리 기사
Do you have time to look over the quarterly income and expenditure report? 이번 분기 수입과 지출 보고서를 검토할 시간 있나요?	**Q. 화자들이 논의하는 것?** **A.** A financial report 재무 보고서
I have to leave the office in five minutes to see my dentist. 치과에 가야 해서 5분 후에 사무실에서 나가야 해요.	**Q. 남자가 사무실에서 나가는 이유?** **A.** He has a dental appointment. 치과 약속이 있다.
It's available as far as I can see on the computer calendar. I'll put you in now. 컴퓨터 달력상으로는 괜찮아요. 당신을 입력해 놓을게요.	**Q. 여자가 다음에 할 일?** **A.** Enter information in a calendar 달력에 정보 기입

주제별 기출 어휘

교육/연수

company policy 회사 정책
training session 교육
training manual 교육 자료
train an employee 직원을 교육시키다
upcoming workshop 다가오는 워크숍
required 필수의
attendant 참석자(= attendee, participant)
registration 등록(= enrollment)
certificate 증서
as scheduled 예정대로
be required to ~해야 한다
take a class 수업을 받다
register for ~에 등록하다(= sign up for, enroll in)
take part in 참석하다(= participate, attend)

사무실 대화

work overtime 초과 근무하다
deal with ~을 처리하다(= take care of, handle)
be involved in ~에 관련되다
recommendation 권고, 추천
employee handbook 직원 안내서
(employee) benefits 복리 후생
commute 통근, 통근 거리; 통근하다
detour 우회 도로; 우회하다
sick leave 병가
doctor's appointment (의사와의) 진료 약속
late for work 회사에 늦은
on the way to work 출근길에
call in sick 아파서 결근한다고 전화로 알리다
get off work 퇴근하다(= leave the office)
stop by 들르다(= drop by, come by)
have[take] a look 한번 보다
take a short break 잠시 쉬다
work extra hours 야근하다(= put in extra hours)

전화 응대/고객 서비스

contact ~에게 연락하다
connect (전화 건 사람을) 연결해 주다
reach 연락하다, 연락이 닿다
note 메모, 쪽지
extension 구내 번호, 내선 번호
exchange 교환하다; 교환
report 알리다, 전하다
complaint 불평, 불만 사항
charge 요금; 청구하다
warranty 품질 보증서
dissatisfied 불만스러운
customer service representative
고객 서비스 직원
hospitality 접대, 환대
inconvenience 불편
file a complaint 불만을 제기하다
address customer complaints
고객 불만을 해결하다
over the phone 전화로
get back to ~에게 회신 전화하다
(= return one's call)
leave a message 메시지를 남기다
get in touch with ~와 연락하다
I'll transfer you to ~으로 전화를 돌려 드릴게요
be overcharged 바가지 쓰다, 너무 많이 청구되다
report a problem 문제를 알리다

ETS 문제로 훈련하기

P3_32

STEP 01

문장 핵심 파악하기

먼저 질문의 키워드에 동그라미로 표시하며 질문 내용을 파악하세요. 대화를 듣고 주어진 질문에 답한 후 빈칸을 채워 보세요.

1 What will take place at the end of March?

(A) Computer maintenance (B) Building construction

M Hi, Julia—could you let all employees know that IT is doing ________ on our ________ the last weekend in March?
W Sure. Which ________ applications will be affected?
M This time the whole ________ will be affected.

2 Why does the man apologize to Ms. Patel?

(A) He was late for work. (B) He has to leave early tonight.

M I'm sorry I wasn't ________ ________, Ms. Patel. I had a ________ tire on the freeway.
W Oh... ________ has been very ________ this morning, so it wasn't a problem.
M Well, I'll stay late this evening to ________ ________ the time.

STEP 02

실전에 가깝게 훈련하기

질문의 키워드에 동그라미로 표시한 후, 대화를 듣고 주어진 질문에 답하세요.

3 What are the speakers discussing?

(A) A change in management
(B) A recent job promotion
(C) An increase in sales
(D) A company relocation

4 What does the man say will take place at three o'clock?

(A) A press conference
(B) An early closing
(C) A staff meeting
(D) A factory tour

정답 및 해설 p. 145

ETS 실전 테스트

1. What does the man ask the woman to do?
   (A) Buy a ticket
   (B) Edit a report
   (C) Provide some training
   (D) Visit some clients

2. When will the speakers meet?
   (A) In the morning
   (B) In the afternoon
   (C) Tomorrow
   (D) Next week

3. What will the man do next?
   (A) Check his calendar
   (B) Contact a colleague
   (C) Reserve a room
   (D) Read some instructions

---

4. Why is the woman calling?
   (A) To get driving directions
   (B) To ask about a missing item
   (C) To discuss a contract
   (D) To arrange a meeting

5. What does the man offer to do?
   (A) Order a desk
   (B) Call a client
   (C) Revise a report
   (D) Scan some documents

6. What information does the woman ask for?
   (A) Some sales figures
   (B) Some project dates
   (C) A street address
   (D) A phone number

7. What does the woman remind the man to do?
   (A) Finish a proposal
   (B) Speak with a supervisor
   (C) Update a calendar
   (D) Reserve a meeting room

8. What did the man do yesterday?
   (A) He went to a medical appointment.
   (B) He attended a technology fair.
   (C) He shopped at a department store.
   (D) He participated in a financial seminar.

9. What does the man warn the woman about?
   (A) Some sessions have been canceled.
   (B) Some products are expensive.
   (C) A building is difficult to find.
   (D) An office closes early.

---

10. Where most likely are the speakers?
    (A) At a storage facility
    (B) At an electronics factory
    (C) At a film studio
    (D) At a technology exhibition

11. What problem are the men discussing?
    (A) Some products are defective.
    (B) A container is not large enough.
    (C) There are not enough workers.
    (D) An order was canceled.

12. What does the woman say she will do?
    (A) Offer a discount
    (B) Renegotiate a contract
    (C) Inspect a shipment
    (D) Notify an engineer

13. Why does the man say, "The meeting starts soon"?
(A) To refuse an offer
(B) To ask that participants be seated
(C) To announce a schedule change
(D) To express a concern

14. What does the woman suggest that the man do?
(A) Arrange some transportation
(B) Purchase some supplies
(C) Set up a video call
(D) Take over a presentation

15. What does the man ask about?
(A) How long a meeting will be
(B) Where to find some documents
(C) How to contact a colleague
(D) When a train will depart

---

16. What are the speakers discussing?
(A) A safety requirement
(B) A shipping policy
(C) An equipment repair
(D) A production increase

17. What does the man ask about?
(A) Training for employees
(B) Adjustments to a schedule
(C) Compensation for an expense
(D) Revisions to some documents

18. What does the woman say she will provide?
(A) A sample contract
(B) A discount code
(C) A sign-up sheet
(D) A list of products

Aaron's Schedule–Tuesday

– 10:00: Intern interview
– 1:00: Marketing update
– 2:00: Marta Vargas call
– 3:00: Proposal review

19. Look at the graphic. Which meeting did the man miss?
(A) The intern interview
(B) The marketing update
(C) The Marta Vargas call
(D) The proposal review

20. Where do the speakers probably work?
(A) At a book publishing company
(B) At a travel agency
(C) At an advertising firm
(D) At a department store

21. What does the man confirm?
(A) Sales goals have increased.
(B) Every participant has arrived.
(C) A deadline will be met.
(D) A reservation will be made.

정답 및 해설 p. 147

UNIT 05

여가/여행

연극이나 영화 관람, 음악, 미술 등의 여가 활동 관련 대화와 출장, 휴가, 여행 관련 대화도 종종 출제됩니다.

기출 문제풀이 전략

P3_34

STEP 01 **질문 파악** 질문을 먼저 읽으면서 키워드를 파악하세요.

1. What are the speakers planning to attend?
   (A) A play
   (B) A concert
   (C) A lecture series
   (D) An awards ceremony

Seating Chart

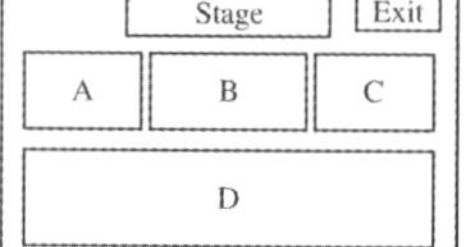

2. Look at the graphic. Where will the speakers sit?
   (A) Section A (B) Section B
   (C) Section C (D) Section D

3. What does the man suggest doing?
   (A) Printing out directions
   (B) Looking for a lower price
   (C) Inviting another colleague
   (D) Taking public transportation

STEP 02 **정답 고르기** 대화를 들으며 키워드의 단서를 찾아 정답을 고르세요.

M Hi Lin, **1** I'm ordering our tickets for the play now. Which seats would you prefer?

W Hm... **2** I always like to sit near the front, close to the stage. I can see the actors better that way.

M OK, **2** there are still seats available in the front... on the right near the exit.

W Great! Should we get there early to find a parking space?

M Actually, **3** I was thinking we should take the bus. That way we won't have to worry about parking.

1. 키워드: 화자들이 참석할 것
연극 표를 주문하려고 한다는 말에 유의 → 정답은 (A)

2. 키워드: 화자들이 앉을 곳
여자가 앞쪽에 앉는 것을 좋아한다고 하자, 남자가 출구 근처 오른쪽에 자리가 있다고 하는 말에 유의
→ 정답은 (C)

3. 키워드: 남자가 제안하는 것
버스를 타야 할 것 같다는 말에 유의
→ 정답은 (D)

남 안녕 린, 지금 우리 연극 표를 주문하고 있어요. 어느 좌석이 더 좋아요?
여 음... 나는 항상 앞쪽에 앉는 것을 좋아해요. 무대 가까이요. 그래야 배우들을 더 잘 볼 수 있어서요.
남 좋아요, 앞쪽에 아직 좌석이 있어요… 오른쪽 출구 근처에요.
여 잘됐어요! 주차 공간을 찾기 위해 일찍 도착해야 할까요?
남 사실, 버스를 타야 할 것 같아요. 그러면 주차에 대해 걱정할 필요가 없을 거예요.

정답 및 해설 p. 154

CHECK UP

Step 1 다음 3개의 질문을 읽으며 키워드에 표시하세요.

Step 2 대화를 들으며 정답의 단서를 찾아 정답을 고르세요.

P3_35

1 Why did the woman arrive late?

(A) She was stuck in traffic.

(B) She got lost along the way.

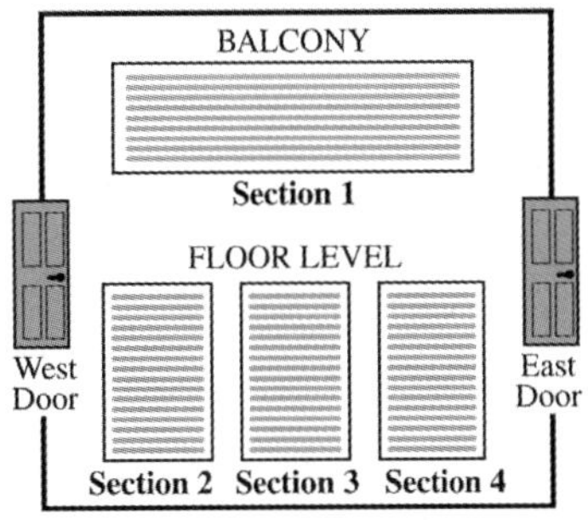

2 Look at the graphic. Which section of the theater is the man sitting in?

(A) Section 1

(B) Section 4

3 What does the woman offer to do for the man?

(A) Buy him a beverage

(B) Pay for his ticket

정답 및 해설 p. 154

기출로 익히는 패러프레이징

기출 문제에 등장했던 상황과 문장을 보고 정답이 어떤 식으로 패러프레이즈 되는지 확인해보세요.

대화 내 단서 포착	패러프레이징 된 정답 찾기
Have you seen the new film directed by Richard Nakamura? 리차드 나카무라가 감독한 새 영화 보셨어요?	**Q. 논의되고 있는 것?** **A.** A recent movie release 최신 영화 개봉
I'd actually recommend coming back on a weekday. It's usually a lot less crowded. 사실 평일에 다시 오시길 권합니다. 대체로 훨씬 덜 붐비거든요.	**Q. 여자가 하는 말?** **A.** The crowd is smaller on weekdays. 평일에는 사람이 더 적다.
I'm shocked there weren't more people here tonight. 오늘밤 여기에 사람이 더 많지 않아서 놀랐어요.	**Q. 화자가 놀란 이유?** **A.** The audience was small. 청중이 적었다.
Could you tell me how long we have to wait to enter the Mountainview Memorial Tower? 마운틴뷰 기념탑에 들어가려면 얼마나 기다려야 하는지 말씀해 주실 수 있나요?	**Q. 남자가 알고 싶어 하는 것?** **A.** The length of a delay 지연 시간

주제별 기출 어휘

영화/공연

performance 공연(= show)
balcony seat 발코니 좌석
review (공연 등에 대한) 평, 후기
usher (극장 등의) 좌석 안내원
script 대본
brochure 안내 책자(= pamphlet)
plot 구성, 줄거리
in line 줄지어 있는, 줄 서 있는
in advance 미리, 사전에
a group of ~ 명의 단체로, 한 무리의
at the box office 매표소에서
next to each other 나란히
be about to 막 ~하려고 하다
be seated 앉다
switch seats 좌석을 바꾸다
reserve tickets 표를 예약하다

여행

guided tour 가이드가 있는 여행
promote tourism 관광 홍보하다
all-day pass 1일 패스(= one day pass)
tourist 관광객
travel agency 여행사
sightseeing 관광
(tour) itinerary 여행 일정
round-trip[one-way] ticket 왕복[편도] 승차권
carry-on bag 기내 휴대용 가방
connecting flight 연결편, 갈아탈 비행기
direct flight 직항편
baggage 수하물, 짐(= luggage, suitcase)
check in (공항에서) 짐을 부치다, 탑승 수속을 하다
get to+장소 ~에 가다
car rental 자동차 대여
make a reservation 예약하다(= reserve, book)
booked up 예약이 꽉 찬(= fully booked)
confirm a reservation 예약을 확인하다
book[reserve] a flight from A to B for+날짜 ~에 A에서 B로 가는 비행기를 예약하다
take a city tour 시내 관광을 하다
extend the reservation[trip] 예약[여행]을 연장하다
adjust the itinerary 여행 일정을 조정하다
I'm staying in ~. 저는 ~에 투숙하고 있습니다.

기타 여가생활

go on vacation 휴가 가다
hiking trail 등산로
complimentary 무료의
(art) gallery 미술관(= art museum)
admission 입장(료)
exhibition 전시(회)
artwork 예술품
painting 그림(= drawing)
sculpture 조각상
worth ~할 가치가 있는
on view 전시 중인
ahead of time 시간보다 일찍, 미리
be interested in ~에 관심이 있다
be closed on Mondays 매주 월요일은 휴관이다
go through ~을 살펴보다(= view)
explore the exhibit 전시회를 둘러보다

ETS 문제로 훈련하기

P3_37

STEP 01 문장 핵심 파악하기

먼저 질문의 키워드에 동그라미로 표시하며 질문 내용을 파악하세요. 대화를 듣고 주어진 질문에 답한 후 빈칸을 채워 보세요.

1 Who is the man?

(A) A restaurant chef (B) A hotel clerk

> **M** Hello, this is the __________ __________.
> **W** Yes, I'm calling from room 508. What time does the hotel restaurant __________ for breakfast tomorrow?
> **M** Breakfast starts at 7 and ends at 10. And just a __________ that you'll need to check out of your room by 11.

2 Why is the man unable to attend tonight's show?

(A) He is out of town. (B) The show is sold out.

> **W** Slate __________, how may I help you?
> **M** I have tickets for tonight's performance, but I'm in Detroit and my __________ been __________. Can I get tickets for tomorrow's performance instead?
> **W** You can __________ __________ __________ for another event, but it looks like tomorrow night's __________ is sold out.

STEP 02 실전에 가깝게 훈련하기

질문의 키워드에 동그라미로 표시한 후, 대화를 듣고 주어진 질문에 답하세요.

3 Why is the woman unable to come at ten o'clock?

(A) She will be at work.
(B) She will be leading a tour.
(C) She will be visiting a museum.
(D) She will be taking an art class.

4 Where can the woman catch the bus?

(A) In front of the art museum
(B) At the tourist center
(C) By a historic house
(D) At the bus station

ETS 실전 테스트

1. What are the speakers discussing?
   (A) A book
   (B) A television show
   (C) A play
   (D) A musical performance

2. Who is Stephanie Peters?
   (A) A government official
   (B) A journalist
   (C) An entertainer
   (D) A store owner

3. What will the woman probably do next?
   (A) Buy a ticket for tonight's show
   (B) Turn on the radio
   (C) Watch a video
   (D) Write down some information

---

4. What would the man like to do?
   (A) Rent some bicycles
   (B) Apply for a job
   (C) Purchase some tickets
   (D) Hire a guide

5. What does the woman say will happen if the man is late?
   (A) An appointment will be rescheduled.
   (B) An item will not be available.
   (C) A notice will be mailed.
   (D) A fee will be charged.

6. What does the woman offer the man?
   (A) Some beverages
   (B) Some maps
   (C) A pen
   (D) A coupon

7. What does the woman want to do at the art gallery?
   (A) Display her paintings
   (B) Interview an artist
   (C) Apply for a job
   (D) Register for a class

8. What problem does the man mention?
   (A) A room is not big enough.
   (B) A director is not available.
   (C) A signature is missing.
   (D) A frame is broken.

9. What does the man offer to do for the woman?
   (A) Add her name to a list
   (B) Print out a schedule
   (C) Refund a deposit
   (D) Contact a repair person

---

10. Where most likely are the speakers?
    (A) At an airport
    (B) At a hotel
    (C) At a restaurant
    (D) At a travel agency

11. Why does the man say, "I've never been to this city before"?
    (A) To ask for a suggestion
    (B) To refuse a request
    (C) To confirm a date
    (D) To accept a work assignment

12. What does the man say he wants to do in the morning?
    (A) Arrange a taxi service
    (B) Book a guided tour
    (C) Exercise at a fitness center
    (D) Meet a colleague for breakfast

13. Where are the speakers?
(A) At a movie theater
(B) At a fitness center
(C) At an art museum
(D) At a research laboratory

14. What problem does the woman mention?
(A) She cannot find a supervisor.
(B) She has lost a card.
(C) A license has expired.
(D) A facility will close early.

15. What does the supervisor ask the woman to do?
(A) Check a directory
(B) Pay a service fee
(C) Come back later
(D) Fill out a form

---

16. Why did the woman arrive late to the concert?
(A) She thought the show was at a different location.
(B) She encountered a lot of traffic.
(C) Her train was delayed.
(D) A meeting ran longer than expected.

17. What does the man ask the woman for?
(A) Her signature
(B) Her credit card number
(C) Her name
(D) Her telephone number

18. According to the man, what does the woman have to wait until intermission to do?
(A) Purchase some refreshments
(B) Inquire about a membership
(C) Meet the performers
(D) Enter a concert hall

Magical Summer Cast List
Susan Lee
Lead Actress
George Ortiz
Lead Actor
Karen Smith
Supporting Actress
John Jones
Supporting Actor

19. What does the woman say is her favorite type of performance?
(A) Comedy
(B) Drama
(C) Musical
(D) Dance

20. How can employees get tickets?
(A) By ordering them online
(B) By asking a manager
(C) By going to a ticket office
(D) By completing a survey

21. Look at the graphic. According to the man, which performer is a local resident?
(A) Susan Lee
(B) George Ortiz
(C) Karen Smith
(D) John Jones

정답 및 해설 p. 157

UNIT 06 교통/주거

대중 교통이나 주차, 도로 공사 등의 교통 관련 대화나 집 구하기, 이사, 인테리어 등의 주거 관련 대화가 출제됩니다.

기출 문제풀이 전략

P3_39

STEP 01 **질문 파악** 질문을 먼저 읽으면서 키워드를 파악하세요.

1. Where is the woman? (A) At a hotel (B) At an airport (C) At a car rental office (D) At a train station	2. According to the man, what has caused a delay? (A) Road construction (B) Bad weather (C) A scheduling mistake (D) A mechanical problem	3. What does the man say he will do? (A) Contact his supervisor (B) Issue a boarding pass (C) Apply a discount (D) Print a map

STEP 02 **정답 고르기** 대화를 들으며 키워드의 단서를 찾아 정답을 고르세요.

M Hi. Thank you for calling R&M Airport Shuttle Service. How can I help you?

W Hello, my name is Sandra Johnson and **1** I'm at the Crestville Regional Airport. I had a reservation to be picked up at one o'clock, but I don't see the shuttle here.

M I'm so sorry, Ms. Johnson. I actually just spoke to the driver. **2** There's some road construction near the airport, and she had to take a detour. The shuttle should be there in about five minutes.

W Oh, great. I'll wait here then.

M OK. To apologize for the inconvenience, **3** we'll take 25 percent off your bill.

1. 키워드: 여자가 있는 장소
공항에 있다고 한 말에 유의
→ 정답은 (B)

2. 키워드: 지연된 이유
도로 공사 때문에 우회했다는 말에 유의 → 정답은 (A)

3. 키워드: 남자가 한다고 한 것
요금에서 25퍼센트 깎아준다는 말에 유의 → 정답은 (C)
Paraphrasing take 25 percent off your bill → Apply a discount

—

남 안녕하세요. R&M 공항 셔틀 서비스에 전화해 주셔서 감사합니다. 무엇을 도와드릴까요?
여 안녕하세요, 제 이름은 산드라 존슨이고 크레스트빌 지역 공항에 있는데요. 1시에 타기로 예약이 되어 있는데, 여기 셔틀이 안 보이네요.
남 정말 죄송합니다, 존슨 씨. 사실 방금 운전사와 통화했는데, 공항 근처에 도로 공사가 있어서 우회해야 했답니다. 셔틀은 약 5분 후에 도착할 겁니다.
여 아, 좋습니다. 그러면 여기서 기다릴게요.
남 좋습니다. 불편을 끼쳐드린 데 대한 사과의 표시로, 요금에서 25퍼센트를 깎아드리겠습니다.

정답 및 해설 p. 164

CHECK UP

Step 1 다음 3개의 질문을 읽으며 키워드에 표시하세요.
Step 2 대화를 들으며 정답의 단서를 찾아 정답을 고르세요.

P3_40

1 What is the problem?

(A) The car has broken down.
(B) A street is blocked.

2 Where are the speakers going?

(A) To an airport
(B) To a police station

3 What will the speakers probably do next?

(A) Call for information
(B) Talk to a police officer

정답 및 해설 p. 165

기출로 익히는 패러프레이징

기출 문제에 등장했던 상황과 문장을 보고 정답이 어떤 식으로 패러프레이즈 되는지 확인해보세요.

대화 내 단서 포착	패러프레이징 된 정답 찾기
Let's take the flight at eight o'clock. 8시 비행기를 탑시다.	**Q. 화자들의 여행 수단?** **A.** By airplane 비행기
It's just a five-minute walk. 걸어서 겨우 5분 거리예요.	**Q. 여자가 목적지에 도착하는 수단?** **A.** On foot 도보로
There was a lot of traffic on the way here. 여기 오는 길에 교통량이 많았어요.	**Q. 남자가 늦은 이유?** **A.** He was stuck in traffic. 교통 체증에 갇혀 있었다.
I can give you a rental car to use, free of charge, until you pick your car up. 차를 찾으실 때까지 렌터카를 무료 이용하도록 해드릴 수 있습니다.	**Q. 남자가 제안하는 것?** **A.** Provide a rental vehicle 대여 차량 제공하기

주제별 기출 어휘

P3_41

교통

give a ride 태워주다
bus route 버스 노선
charging station 전기차 충전소
take off 이륙하다
gate 탑승구
flight attendant 승무원
boarding pass 탑승권
baggage carousel 수하물 컨베이어
stopover 중간 기착
bound for ~행, ~으로 향하는
on board 탑승 중인
fly to + 장소 비행기로 ~에 가다
miss a flight 비행기를 놓치다
get on the flight 비행기에 타다
assign seats 좌석을 배정하다
The flight has been canceled[delayed]. 비행기가 결항[지연]되었습니다.
express train 고속 열차
depart 출발하다
final destination 종착역, 종착지
display monitor 전광판(= display board)
timetable 시간표, 일정표
train conductor 기차 승무원
take the train 기차를 타다
catch a train 기차를 잡아 타다
miss a train 기차를 놓치다
get off the train 기차에서 내리다
leave from ~에서 출발하다
transfer from A to B A에서 B로 갈아타다
go directly to ~으로 직행하다
vehicle 차량
traffic accident 교통사고
parking garage[lot, space] 주차장
rush hour traffic 출퇴근 시간대의 교통 혼잡
free of charge 무료로
be headed to ~으로 향하다
be stuck in traffic 교통 체증에 걸리다
give ~ a ride ~을 차에 태워주다
get a ride 차를 얻어 타다
get a (traffic) ticket (교통) 위반 딱지를 받다
pick ~ up ~을 차로 데리러[가지러] 가다
The traffic is heavy[light]. 교통이 혼잡하다[원활하다].

부동산/주거

real estate agent 부동산 중개인
property 부동산(= real estate)
property manager 건물 관리인
rent an apartment 아파트를 임대하다
deposit 보증금
lease 임대 계약
unit (아파트 같은 공동 주택 내의) 한 가구
garage 차고
set up a tour 집 보러 갈 약속을 잡다
furnished unit 가구가 구비된 아파트 세대
renovate 개조하다, 보수하다(= remodel)
for sale 팔려고 내놓은
resident 거주자, 주민
landlord 집주인(= property owner)
tenant 세입자
utilities (수도·전기·가스 등의) 공과금
within walking distance 걸어갈 수 있는 거리에
conveniently located 편리한 위치에 있는

ETS 문제로 훈련하기

P3_42

STEP 01 문장 핵심 파악하기

먼저 질문의 키워드에 동그라미로 표시하며 질문 내용을 파악하세요. 대화를 듣고 주어진 질문에 답한 후 빈칸을 채워 보세요.

1 What does the man tell the woman about?

(A) A closing time (B) A new regulation

M Excuse me, did you know that ____________ ____________ along this street have recently ____________? Now, you can only park here after ten P.M.
W Oh no, I didn't know that. I guess I should ____________ my car.
M There's a ____________ ____________ on the next block.

2 What is the woman planning to do?

(A) Remodel a kitchen (B) Open a restaurant

W Excuse me. I'm interested in doing some ____________ in my ____________ —can you help me with that?
M Yes, of course. And we're offering a special ____________ this month—fifteen percent off any ____________ ____________ purchases you make in our store.
W That sounds great.

STEP 02 실전에 가깝게 훈련하기

질문의 키워드에 동그라미로 표시한 후, 대화를 듣고 주어진 질문에 답하세요.

3 Look at the graphic. What time will the speakers depart?

(A) 2:15 P.M.
(B) 3:30 P.M.
(C) 4:45 P.M.
(D) 5:10 P.M.

Kassell Train Station

Destination	Departure Time
Bebra	2:15 P.M.
Giessen	3:30 P.M.
Marburg	4:45 P.M.
Frankfurt	5:10 P.M.

4 What does the man mention he would like to do?

(A) Visit an art gallery
(B) Find a hotel in Bebra
(C) Exchange some tickets
(D) Extend the length of a trip

ETS 실전 테스트

1. What are the speakers discussing?
(A) A popular book
(B) An art museum
(C) A change in plans
(D) A weather forecast

2. Who called the woman last night?
(A) A coworker
(B) A house painter
(C) An important client
(D) A building manager

3. What will the woman probably do on Friday?
(A) Go on a business trip
(B) Host a party
(C) Move to a new apartment
(D) Start a new job

---

4. What does the man want to do?
(A) Return to his hotel
(B) Attend a sports event
(C) Go to a museum
(D) Buy a bus ticket

5. What does the woman suggest that the man do?
(A) Transfer to another bus
(B) See a special exhibit
(C) Park on the street
(D) Stop at a tourist center

6. What does the woman tell the man to look for?
(A) An automated ticket machine
(B) A sports stadium
(C) A taxi stand
(D) Fourteenth Street

7. Why does the woman say, "look at all these cars"?
(A) She is surprised a garage is empty.
(B) She is worried about the traffic.
(C) She likes the designs of some cars.
(D) She wants to buy a car.

8. Who are the speakers planning to meet?
(A) Potential business partners
(B) City officials
(C) A new manager
(D) A guest speaker

9. What does the woman suggest?
(A) Taking a taxi
(B) Walking to a destination
(C) Rescheduling a workshop
(D) Canceling a project

---

10. What type of business does the man work for?
(A) An architecture firm
(B) A construction company
(C) A real estate agency
(D) A bank

11. Why is the woman pleased?
(A) An apartment is conveniently located.
(B) A job position is opening soon.
(C) Some funding has been approved.
(D) Some renovations have been completed.

12. What does the woman plan to do tomorrow afternoon?
(A) Sign some documents
(B) View a property
(C) Attend a trade show
(D) Make a presentation

13. What are the speakers mainly discussing?
(A) The status of a delayed train
(B) The features of a new train
(C) The cost of a train ticket
(D) The location of a train station

14. Why is the train agent unable to answer the woman's question?
(A) He is a new employee.
(B) He has just arrived for his shift.
(C) A computer system has stopped working.
(D) A schedule is incomplete.

15. What does the train agent suggest doing?
(A) Requesting a refund
(B) Labeling some luggage
(C) Taking a shuttle bus
(D) Checking a Web site

---

16. Where does the conversation most likely take place?
(A) At a ferry port
(B) At a train station
(C) At a bus depot
(D) At an airport

17. What does the man like about a company?
(A) It is reliable.
(B) It is conveniently located.
(C) It offers seasonal discounts.
(D) It has an online booking system.

18. What does the woman offer the man?
(A) An access code
(B) A free upgrade
(C) A meal voucher
(D) A rewards card

Leasing Options	
Rental Term	**Rent per Month**
3 months	$960
6 months	$900
9 months	$845
12 months	$795

19. What reason does the woman give for moving?
(A) She needs more space.
(B) She is beginning a new job.
(C) Her current rent is high.
(D) Her neighborhood is very noisy.

20. Look at the graphic. How much rent will the woman most likely pay?
(A) $960
(B) $900
(C) $845
(D) $795

21. What will the speakers do next?
(A) Go on a tour
(B) Revise a lease
(C) Look at a Web site
(D) Complete an application

정답 및 해설 p. 167

UNIT 07 쇼핑/주문

쇼핑, 할인 행사, 반품, 환불 등의 대화나 주문 오류 및 수정, 배송 오류 등에 관한 대화가 출제됩니다.

기출 문제풀이 전략

P3_44

STEP 01 **질문 파악** 질문을 먼저 읽으면서 키워드를 파악하세요.

1 What product are the speakers discussing? (A) Electronics (B) Footwear (C) Packing materials (D) Art supplies	2 What does the man imply when he says, "There are only fifteen boxes left"? (A) He is glad that a sale is ending. (B) He wants employees to finish a task. (C) A product is selling very well. (D) Some inventory should be relocated.	3 What does the man say that he will do? (A) Enlarge a display area (B) Extend an advertising campaign (C) Update some flyers (D) Talk to a sales representative

STEP 02 **정답 고르기** 대화를 들으며 키워드의 단서를 찾아 정답을 고르세요.

M Carlota, 1/2 I'm really pleased with how well the annual shoe clearance sale's been going.

W I've never seen anything like it. You know, 1/2 featuring the Pro X athletic sneakers was a smart idea. Just look in the storage room.

M You're right. There are only fifteen boxes left.

W It's surprising, since Pro X is such a new company. We should find a way to do more business with them.

M Good idea. 3 I'll ask the sales representative to bring more samples of their other styles.

1. 키워드: 논의하는 제품
shoe clearance sale, sneakers 등의 어휘에 유의 → 정답은 (B)
Paraphrasing shoe, sneakers → Footwear

2. 키워드: 문장의 의도
남자의 창고 정리 세일이 잘 되고 있다는 말에 유의 → 정답은 (C)

3. 키워드: 남자가 할 일
영업 담당자에게 다른 견본품을 요청하겠다는 말에 유의 → 정답은 (D)

—

남 칼로타, 연례 신발 창고 정리 세일이 얼마나 잘 진행되고 있는지 정말 만족스러워요.
여 이런 경우를 본 적이 전혀 없어요. 그러니까 프로 엑스 운동화를 내세운 것이 현명한 생각이었어요. 창고 안을 보세요.
남 맞아요. 열다섯 상자밖에 남지 않았어요.
여 놀라워요. 프로 엑스는 정말 신생 회사잖아요. 함께 더 많은 거래를 할 수 있는 방법을 찾아야겠어요.
남 좋은 생각이에요. 영업 담당자에게 다른 스타일의 견본품을 더 가져오도록 요청할게요.

정답 및 해설 p. 175

CHECK UP

Step 1 다음 3개의 질문을 읽으며 키워드에 표시하세요.

Step 2 대화를 들으며 정답의 단서를 찾아 정답을 고르세요.

P3_45

1 Where most likely are the speakers?

(A) At a plant shop

(B) At a dry-cleaning business

2 Why does the woman say, "it does require a lot of care"?

(A) To give a warning

(B) To correct some information

3 What will the man most likely do next?

(A) Go to another branch location

(B) Look at a display of products

정답 및 해설 p. 175

기출로 익히는 패러프레이징

기출 문제에 등장했던 상황과 문장을 보고 정답이 어떤 식으로 패러프레이즈 되는지 확인해보세요.

대화 내 단서 포착	패러프레이징 된 정답 찾기
I'm calling to check on our order for 10 copy machines. 우리가 주문한 복사기 10대 주문 상황을 알아보려고 전화 드렸습니다.	**Q. 여자가 묻는 것?** **A.** The status of an order 주문 처리 상황
If you spend $100 or more, you get 10 percent off your total bill. 100달러 이상 쓰시면, 총 청구 금액에서 10퍼센트 할인해 드립니다.	**Q. 남자가 할인에 대해 하는 말?** **A.** It is offering a discount. 할인을 제공한다.
Could you tell me where I'd find the bread? 빵은 어디에서 찾을 수 있나요?	**Q. 남자가 묻는 것?** **A.** The location of a product 제품의 위치
I can check the stockroom in the back. 뒤쪽 창고를 확인해 볼게요.	**Q. 여자가 다음에 할 일?** **A.** Check a storage area 창고 확인하기

PART 3 | UNIT 07

주제별 기출 어휘

P3_46

쇼핑

consumer 소비자
customer 손님, 쇼핑객(= shopper)
(sales) clerk 점원
merchandise 상품(= goods)
on sale 할인 중인
price list 가격 리스트
home appliance 가전 제품
print a receipt 영수증을 출력하다
stock shelves 물건을 진열대에 놓다
discounted rate 할인 가격
on display 진열 중인
special offer 특별 할인
sold out 매진된
in stock 재고가 있는
out of stock 재고가 없는
promotional flyer 광고 전단
name tag 가격표
covered by a warranty 보증이 되는
cutting-edge product 최첨단 상품
get[offer] a discount 할인을 받다[제공하다]
make a purchase 구매하다(= purchase, get, buy)
provide delivery service 배달 서비스를 제공하다

주문

place[make] an order 주문하다
send an invoice 청구서(송장)를 보내다
product specifications 제품 규격서
give an estimate 견적을 내다
exchange 교환하다
order status 주문 처리 상황
in bulk 대량으로
track the status 진행 상황을 추적하다
order number 주문 번호(= tracking number)
inventory 재고
warehouse 물류 창고
give quantity[volume] discounts 대량 구매 할인을 제공하다
you've reached ~ ~에 연락하셨습니다
supplier 공급업체, 공급업자
manufacturer 제조업체, 제조업자

지불/배송

pay for ~값을 지불하다
payment methods 지불 수단
make a payment 지불하다
cash register 계산대(= checkout counter)
request a refund 환불을 요청하다
provide a refund 환불해주다
get[obtain] a refund 환불 받다
billing error 청구서 오류(= billing mistake)
be overcharged 바가지 쓰다, 너무 많이 청구되다
make a delivery 배달하다
waive a delivery fee 배송비를 면제해주다
shipment 선적, 배송
expedite 신속히 처리하다
return policy 환불 정책
shipping order 선적 지시
reimbursement process 상환 처리
pay in cash 현금으로 지불하다
in three working[business] days (공휴일을 제외한) 3영업일 안에

ETS 문제로 훈련하기

P3_47

STEP 01

문장 핵심 파악하기

먼저 질문의 키워드에 동그라미로 표시하며 질문 내용을 파악하세요. 대화를 듣고 주어진 질문에 답한 후 빈칸을 채워 보세요.

1 Where does this conversation probably take place?

(A) At a bookstore (B) At a travel agency

M1 Can I help you?
M2 Yes, I can't seem to ____________ the new ____________ of Indira Kumar.
M1 It's been very popular. I'm afraid that all of our ____________ of the ____________ have been sold.

2 What does the man ask for?

(A) Some product codes (B) Credit card information

W Hello. I recently _________ _________ _________ with your company for a large shipment of _________ _________. It arrived today, but the order isn't quite _________.
M Let me look up your order on the computer. Could you give me the last four digits of the _________ _________ _________ you used for this order?
W Sure. Let's see, the _________ is thirty-eight eighty-nine.

STEP 02

실전에 가깝게 훈련하기

질문의 키워드에 동그라미로 표시한 후, 대화를 듣고 주어진 질문에 답하세요.

3 Why does the man apologize?

(A) A product has sold out.
(B) A reservation was incorrect.
(C) An order was misplaced.
(D) A bill was not accurate.

4 What does the man suggest?

(A) Contacting another store
(B) Requesting a refund
(C) Placing an order
(D) Rescheduling an event

PART 3 | UNIT 07

ETS 실전 테스트

1. What supplies do the speakers need?
   (A) Paper clips
   (B) Business cards
   (C) Printing paper
   (D) Shipping boxes

2. What is the problem?
   (A) A delivery is late.
   (B) An item is defective.
   (C) An incomplete order arrived.
   (D) A wrong item was delivered.

3. What will the company receive?
   (A) A discount
   (B) Free merchandise
   (C) A letter of apology
   (D) Free shipping

---

4. Where most likely does the man work?
   (A) At a post office
   (B) At a restaurant
   (C) At a print shop
   (D) At a travel agency

5. What has changed about an event?
   (A) Its starting time
   (B) Its location
   (C) The number of guests
   (D) The room size

6. What does the man ask the woman to do?
   (A) Revise her order online
   (B) Confirm her telephone number
   (C) Call another vendor
   (D) Submit a credit card payment

7. Where does the conversation most likely take place?
   (A) At an event-planning company
   (B) At a supermarket
   (C) At a farm
   (D) At a café

8. Why does the man say, "the party's tonight"?
   (A) To express excitement
   (B) To extend an invitation
   (C) To indicate an immediate need
   (D) To correct a scheduling error

9. What does the woman suggest doing?
   (A) Buying a different product
   (B) Calling a friend
   (C) Parking in another location
   (D) Paying with cash

---

10. Who most likely is the woman?
    (A) A delivery truck driver
    (B) A customer service agent
    (C) A hotel clerk
    (D) A bank teller

11. Why is the man using the Web site?
    (A) To enter a complaint
    (B) To compare some prices
    (C) To place an order
    (D) To apply for a job

12. What does the woman explain?
    (A) How to ship to multiple locations
    (B) How to request a refund
    (C) How to change a reservation
    (D) How to upload a document

13. What does the woman want to purchase?
(A) A camera
(B) A computer
(C) Some software
(D) Some art supplies

14. What would the woman like to improve?
(A) The speed of her Internet
(B) The quality of some photos
(C) The price of a service
(D) The design of a product

15. According to the man, what will the woman have to do?
(A) Visit a different store
(B) Spend more than expected
(C) Speak with a technician
(D) Keep a receipt

---

16. What product are the speakers discussing?
(A) A digital camera
(B) A laptop computer
(C) A mobile phone
(D) A television set

17. According to the customer, what is the problem with the product?
(A) Its warranty has expired.
(B) Its assembly instructions are incorrect.
(C) It will not turn on.
(D) It is missing an accessory.

18. What does the man offer the customer?
(A) Free shipping
(B) Repair services
(C) A gift card
(D) A payment plan

STORE DIRECTORY

Products	Aisle
Fresh Produce	1
Meat and Fish	2
Paper Products	3
Dairy	4
Beverages	5

19. Look at the graphic. Where are the items the man wants to buy?
(A) In Aisle 1
(B) In Aisle 3
(C) In Aisle 4
(D) In Aisle 5

20. What event is the man shopping for?
(A) A training seminar
(B) An awards banquet
(C) A company picnic
(D) A retirement party

21. What will the woman most likely do next?
(A) Call her manager
(B) Get a shopping cart
(C) Copy some documents
(D) Start preparing a meal

정답 및 해설 p. 178

UNIT 08 식당/호텔

식당·호텔의 예약, 예약 변경이나 취소, 불평·불만 사항, 음식 주문, 기타 문의 등에 관련된 대화가 주로 출제됩니다.

기출 문제풀이 전략

P3_49

STEP 01 질문 파악 질문을 먼저 읽으면서 키워드를 파악하세요.

1 When is the conversation taking place? (A) In the morning (B) At noon (C) In the afternoon (D) In the evening	2 What does the man suggest? (A) Placing an order quickly (B) Going to another restaurant (C) Coming back another time (D) Ordering a light snack	3 What does the man say about his restaurant? (A) It is usually quiet on weeknights. (B) It is especially popular on weekends. (C) It has lunch specials every day. (D) It closes at nine every day.

STEP 02 정답 고르기 대화를 들으며 키워드의 단서를 찾아 정답을 고르세요.

W **1** Good evening. I'd like a table for one. Are you still serving dinner?

M I'm sorry, but we're closing in a few minutes; we close at nine. **2** You could try the restaurant across the street. It's open until eleven.

W Well, it looks like they have quite a crowd over there, but I might do that. Do you close at nine every day? What are your weekend hours like?

M We have the same hours on the weekends; **3** we're open from nine to nine every day.

1. 키워드: 대화가 일어난 때

Good evening, dinner 등의 어휘에 유의 → 정답은 (D)

2. 키워드: 남자가 제안하는 것

길 건너 식당에 가보라는 말에 유의 → 정답은 (B)

Paraphrasing try the restaurant across the street → Going to another restaurant

3. 키워드: 남자가 식당에 대해 하는 말

매일 9시부터 9시까지 영업한다는 말에 유의 → 정답은 (D)

—

여 안녕하세요. 한 사람 앉을 자리 부탁해요. 아직 저녁 식사가 되는 거죠?
남 죄송합니다만 저희는 몇 분 후에 문을 닫습니다. 9시에 닫거든요. 길 건너편에 있는 식당에 가 보세요. 그곳은 11시까지 영업을 합니다.
여 음, 저기 사람들이 꽤 많은 것처럼 보이지만 저 식당으로 가 봐야겠네요. 매일 9시에 문을 닫나요? 주말 영업시간은 어떤가요?
남 주말에도 영업시간은 같아요. 저희는 매일 9시부터 9시까지 영업합니다.

정답 및 해설 p. 185

CHECK UP

Step 1 다음 3개의 질문을 읽으며 키워드에 표시하세요.

Step 2 대화를 들으며 정답의 단서를 찾아 정답을 고르세요.

P3_50

1 Why is the woman calling the man?

(A) To report a problem

(B) To place an order

2 Who most likely is the man?

(A) A computer technician

(B) A hotel receptionist

3 What does the man say he will do?

(A) Adjust a bill

(B) Send some information by e-mail

정답 및 해설 p. 185

기출로 익히는 패러프레이징

기출 문제에 등장했던 상황과 문장을 보고 정답이 어떤 식으로 패러프레이즈 되는지 확인해보세요.

대화 내 단서 포착	패러프레이징 된 정답 찾기
I wanted to book a room online last week, but I didn't have the time. 지난주에 온라인으로 방을 예약하고 싶었는데, 시간이 없었어요.	**Q. 대화의 주제?** **A.** Reserving a hotel room 호텔 방 예약하기
I'm sorry, our restaurant is closed on Mondays. 죄송합니다만, 저희 식당은 월요일에 문을 닫습니다.	**Q. 여자가 언급한 문제는?** **A.** A business will not be open. 사업체가 문을 열지 않는다.
Would you like to go to lunch with the accounting team today? 오늘 경리팀과 점심 같이 하러 갈까요?	**Q. 대화의 주제?** **A.** Lunch arrangements 점심 약속
Could you add some fruit to the breakfast items? 조식 메뉴에 과일 몇 가지를 추가할 수 있나요?	**Q. 여자가 요청하는 변경 사항?** **A.** Additional food items 추가 식품 메뉴

주제별 기출 어휘

P3_51

식당

meal 식사
bill 계산서(= check)
entrée 주요리
today's special 오늘의 요리
server 서빙하는 사람
diner 식사하는 사람
dine out 외식하다(= eat out)
reserve[book] a table 자리를 예약하다
make a reservation for ~을 위해 예약하다
a party of four 4명 일행
cater (행사 등에) 음식을 공급하다
patio 옥외 테라스
serve the food 음식을 제공하다
private room (식당 등의) 별실, 개별 룸
allergic 알레르기 체질의
beverage 음료
cuisine 요리법, (고급 식당의) 요리
culinary 요리의
flavor 맛, 풍미
gourmet 미식가; (음식이) 고급인
low in fat 지방 함량이 낮은
light snack 가벼운 식사
leave a tip 팁을 남기다
ingredient (요리) 재료
nutritious 영양가 높은
recipe 요리법
online booking system 온라인 예약 시스템
pay for one's meal ~의 식대를 지불하다
grab a bite (to eat) 요기하다, 끼니를 간단히 때우다
specialize in ~을 전문으로 하다
recommend a dish 요리를 추천하다
All tables are booked. 모든 테이블은 예약되었습니다.
No tables are available. 자리가 없습니다.
Thanks for calling ~. ~에 전화 주셔서 감사합니다.
Everything is in order.
모든 것이 순조롭게 진행되고 있습니다.

호텔

accommodations 숙박 시설
room reservation 객실 예약
suite (호텔의) 스위트룸, 특별실
vacancy 빈 방
wake-up call 모닝콜
hotel guest 호텔 투숙객
confirm 확인하다(= double check)
confirmation number[code] 예약 확인 번호
available 이용할 수 있는, 비어 있는
banquet hall 연회장
spacious 넓은
stay 체류; 머물다
concierge service 접객 서비스
housekeeping (호텔의) 시설 관리
at the same rate 같은 요금으로
check in (호텔에) 투숙 절차를 밟다, 체크인하다
check out (호텔에서) 나가다, 체크아웃하다
reservation under the name (of)+이름
~의 이름으로 한 예약

ETS 문제로 훈련하기

P3_52

STEP 01

문장 핵심 파악하기

먼저 질문의 키워드에 동그라미로 표시하며 질문 내용을 파악하세요. 대화를 듣고 주어진 질문에 답한 후 빈칸을 채워 보세요.

1 What are the speakers doing?

(A) Waiting for a table (B) Placing an order for delivery

W The host just told me that it'll be a half hour before we can ________ ________ ________.
M Do you want to leave and ________ at a different ________?
W No, let's stay. Everyone at work says the ________ ________ is delicious.

2 Who is the woman most likely talking to?

(A) A hotel employee (B) A restaurant employee

W Hi, this is Julia Thomas. I'm calling to confirm my ________ ________ for October 20th.
M Yes, we have your reservation — you're ________ at the special convention rate for two ________.
W That's right, but I probably won't arrive until about 8 P.M., so please tell the ________ desk I'll be late.

STEP 02

실전에 가깝게 훈련하기

질문의 키워드에 동그라미로 표시한 후, 대화를 듣고 주어진 질문에 답하세요.

3 According to the woman, why will the daily special be changed?

(A) Some customers have complained.
(B) A meal is sold out.
(C) A shipment did not arrive.
(D) A chef cooked the wrong dish.

4 Look at the graphic. How much will the new special cost?

(A) $7.25
(B) $9.99
(C) $10.50
(D) $12.99

Today's Specials	
Vegetable stir fry with rice	$7.25
Fish sandwich	$9.99
Roasted chicken pasta	$10.50
Beef curry	$12.99

정답 및 해설 p. 186

ETS 실전 테스트

1. Why is the man calling?
   (A) To respond to an invitation
   (B) To reserve a hotel room
   (C) To get directions
   (D) To arrange a shuttle service

2. What does the man ask about?
   (A) A discount rate
   (B) A payment method
   (C) Public transportation
   (D) Local attractions

3. What does the woman say the man will need to show?
   (A) A registration form
   (B) A coupon
   (C) Proof of employment
   (D) A credit card

---

4. What is the conversation mainly about?
   (A) Making a reservation
   (B) Picking up a forgotten item
   (C) Scheduling a meeting
   (D) Applying for a job

5. Why is Mr. Wu unavailable this afternoon?
   (A) He is making a client presentation.
   (B) He is training a new employee.
   (C) He is participating in a job fair.
   (D) He is attending a fund-raising event.

6. What does the woman offer to do?
   (A) Update her résumé
   (B) Speak to her manager
   (C) Add more chairs at a table
   (D) Work an extra shift

7. Where most likely are the speakers?
   (A) In a convention center
   (B) In an apartment building
   (C) In a hotel
   (D) In an airport

8. What does the man say he forgot?
   (A) A shirt
   (B) A room number
   (C) Some paperwork
   (D) Some driving directions

9. What will the woman most likely do next?
   (A) Call a taxi service
   (B) Look for some luggage
   (C) Cancel an order
   (D) Draw a map

---

10. Where most likely are the speakers?
    (A) In a grocery store
    (B) In an electronics store
    (C) In a restaurant
    (D) In a garden center

11. Why does the woman say, "I think it's supposed to rain"?
    (A) To decline an offer
    (B) To correct some information
    (C) To suggest a schedule change
    (D) To explain a delay

12. What does the man offer to do?
    (A) Arrange a display
    (B) Check some inventory
    (C) Return some products
    (D) Discount a purchase

P3_53

13. What do the women like about the restaurant?
(A) The food
(B) The atmosphere
(C) The service
(D) The prices

14. What event do the women want to have at the restaurant?
(A) A client meeting
(B) A department luncheon
(C) A birthday party
(D) A retirement celebration

15. What convenience does the man mention?
(A) Wireless Internet access
(B) Free delivery
(C) Advance ordering
(D) Party-planning consultations

---

16. Why is the woman calling?
(A) To complain about noise levels
(B) To report a broken television set
(C) To request a different room
(D) To inquire about nearby attractions

17. What does the man say about the other hotel guests?
(A) They are in the fitness center.
(B) They are waiting in the lobby.
(C) They are going to have a meal.
(D) They are attending a conference.

18. What does the woman ask the man to do?
(A) Contact a supervisor
(B) Send an employee to a room
(C) Book a reservation at a restaurant
(D) Provide a list of movies

Basic Bread Recipe
- 6 cups all-purpose flour
- 3 cups warm water
- 1/8 cup vegetable oil
- 2 tablespoons honey
- 1 tablespoon salt
- 1 package yeast

19. What will happen in September?
(A) A seasonal menu will change.
(B) A cooking competition will take place.
(C) A restaurant will participate in a food festival.
(D) A shop will move to a new location.

20. Look at the graphic. Which amount did the man change?
(A) 6 cups
(B) 3 cups
(C) 2 tablespoons
(D) 1 tablespoon

21. What does the woman say she will do?
(A) Talk to a chef
(B) Update a food order
(C) Check some prices
(D) Create a flyer

정답 및 해설 p. 188

UNIT 09

각종 편의시설

은행이나 우체국, 병원, 도서관, 서점, 약국, 수리센터 등 각종 관공서나 공공장소, 일상생활의 편의를 위한 장소에서 나눌 수 있는 대화가 출제됩니다.

기출 문제풀이 전략

P3_54

STEP 01 **질문 파악** 질문을 먼저 읽으면서 키워드를 파악하세요.

1 Where is the conversation probably taking place? (A) In a parking garage (B) At a car repair shop (C) At a doctor's office (D) In an art studio	2 What does the woman ask the man about? (A) Replacing a sign (B) Treating a cut (C) Painting a car (D) Paying a bill	3 What does the woman say she will do? (A) Return later (B) Wait in the office (C) Get a second opinion (D) Do the work herself

STEP 02 **정답 고르기** 대화를 들으며 키워드의 단서를 찾아 정답을 고르세요.

M Hi. How can I help you?

W **1** I hit my car door on a concrete post in a parking garage last night and a little bit of paint came off. **2** How long would it take to touch up the paint?

M It looks like a small job, but I won't be able to get to it for about an hour.

W An hour? I guess I don't have time to wait right now. **3** I'll have to come back after work.

1. 키워드: 대화 장소
차가 부딪혀서 칠이 벗겨졌다고 설명하는 부분에 유의 → 정답은 (B)

2. 키워드: 여자가 묻는 것
페인트 작업 소요 시간을 묻는 점에 유의 → 정답은 (C)
Paraphrasing touch up the paint → Painting a car

3. 키워드: 여자가 할 일
퇴근 후 다시 온다는 말에 유의 → 정답은 (A)
Paraphrasing come back after work → Return later

—

남 안녕하세요. 무엇을 도와 드릴까요?
여 어젯밤 주차장 콘크리트 기둥에 차 문을 부딪혀서 칠이 살짝 벗겨졌어요. 페인트 칠을 손보는 데 얼마나 걸릴까요?
남 간단한 일처럼 보이긴 하는데, 약 한 시간 후에야 일을 시작할 수 있을 거예요.
여 한 시간이요? 지금 기다릴 시간은 없을 것 같아요. 퇴근 후에 다시 와야겠네요.

정답 및 해설 p. 195

CHECK UP

Step 1 다음 3개의 질문을 읽으며 키워드에 표시하세요.

Step 2 대화를 들으며 정답의 단서를 찾아 정답을 고르세요.

P3_55

1 Where is this conversation most likely taking place?

(A) At a post office

(B) At a bank

2 What does the woman give the man?

(A) An application form

(B) An e-mail address

3 What does the woman suggest that the man do?

(A) Mail in a document

(B) Send an e-mail

정답 및 해설 p. 196

기출로 익히는 패러프레이징

기출 문제에 등장했던 상황과 문장을 보고 정답이 어떤 식으로 패러프레이즈 되는지 확인해보세요.

대화 내 단서 포착	패러프레이징 된 정답 찾기
It won't shut down when I try to turn it off. 끄려고 할 때 꺼지질 않아요.	**Q. 문제점?** **A.** The computer is not working properly. 컴퓨터가 제대로 작동하지 않는다.
I'm calling to find out if your bank is open on weekends. 은행이 주말에 문을 여는지 알고 싶어 전화 드립니다.	**Q. 남자가 은행에 전화한 이유?** **A.** To inquire about operating hours 영업시간에 대해 문의하려고
We do offer an expedited overseas service. 저희는 신속한 해외 배송 서비스를 제공합니다.	**Q. 남자가 제안하는 것?** **A.** A faster service 더 빠른 배송 서비스
If you wish to reschedule or cancel, please contact me at this number twenty-four hours before the appointment. 약속을 다시 잡거나 취소하고 싶으시면, 약속 24시간 전에 이 번호로 저에게 연락 주십시오.	**Q. 약속을 바꾸기 위해 남자가 해야 할 일?** **A.** Inform the woman in advance 여자에게 미리 알려주기

주제별 기출 어휘

은행

deposit 예금(액); 예금하다
bank teller 은행 창구 직원
(bank) account 계좌
savings account 보통 예금 계좌
interest 이자
transfer 송금; 송금하다
transaction 거래
(photo) identification (사진이 부착된) 신분증
balance 잔고
open an account 계좌를 개설하다
make a withdrawal 인출하다(= withdraw)
make a deposit 예금하다
make a transfer 송금하다(= wire)
get a loan 대출을 받다
pay for a loan 대출을 갚다
approve a loan 대출 승인을 하다

병원/약국

patient 환자
clinic 개인 병원, 진료소(= doctor's office)
medicine 약
medical 의학의, 의료의
medical appointment 병원 예약
pharmacy 약국(= drugstore)
pharmacist 약사
prescription 처방전, 처방약
(physical/annual) checkup (신체/연례) 건강 검진
dentist 치과의사
physician (내과)의사
be not feeling well 몸이 안 좋다
be in good shape 건강 상태가 좋다
see a doctor 진료를 받다
fill a prescription 처방전에 따라 약을 조제하다
take medicine 약을 복용하다
examine a patient 환자를 진찰하다
have a routine test done 정기 검진을 받다
have a dental appointment 치과 진료 예약이 있다
get vaccinations 예방 접종하다

우체국/도서관/기타

parcel 소포(= package)
fragile 손상되기 쉬운
postage 우편요금
postal code 우편번호(= zip code)
express mail 속달
postal carrier 우편배달부
track packages 택배 위치를 추적하다
weigh a package 소포의 무게를 달다
librarian 사서
overdue (지불·반납 등의) 기한이 지난
late fee 연체료(= fine)
borrow[check out] a book 책을 빌리다[대출하다]
return a book 책을 반납하다
issue a library card 도서 대출 카드를 발급하다
have one's hair trimmed[cut] 머리를 다듬다[자르다]
drop off[pick up] dry cleaner's 세탁소에 옷을 맡기다[가지러 가다]
press the clothes 다림질하다
take the stain out 얼룩을 제거하다

ETS 문제로 훈련하기

P3_57

STEP 01

문장 핵심 파악하기

먼저 질문의 키워드에 동그라미로 표시하며 질문 내용을 파악하세요. 대화를 듣고 주어진 질문에 답한 후 빈칸을 채워 보세요.

1 Why is the man calling?

(A) To volunteer for a task (B) To reschedule an appointment

W Newton National ________. This is Ranger Kim speaking.

M Yes—hi. I read in your newsletter that you're organizing a forest ________ day for next Saturday and need ________. I'd like to ________.

W Great! We need people to ________ the branches that have fallen on our trails.

2 What does the man want to do?

(A) Change an order (B) Fill a prescription

M Good morning, I just got a new eyeglasses ________ from my ________ ________. She suggested coming to your store to ________ ________ ________.

W Certainly. We have a great selection of frames—we just got a ________ yesterday.

M Great. I did want to get some new ________.

STEP 02

실전에 가깝게 훈련하기

질문의 키워드에 동그라미로 표시한 후, 대화를 듣고 주어진 질문에 답하세요.

3 What is the woman trying to do?

(A) Find a dressing room
(B) Use an appliance
(C) Play a game
(D) Purchase a machine

4 What problem does the man mention?

(A) A price tag is incorrect.
(B) A staff member is unavailable.
(C) A dress is torn.
(D) A door does not close.

정답 및 해설 p. 196

ETS 실전 테스트

1. Who most likely is the woman?
   (A) A florist
   (B) A bus driver
   (C) A travel agent
   (D) A postal worker

2. What does the man say he cannot find?
   (A) A credit card
   (B) A delivery notice
   (C) A trip itinerary
   (D) A revised invoice

3. What does the woman ask the man to bring with him?
   (A) Proof of payment
   (B) An account number
   (C) Photo identification
   (D) Some packaging supplies

---

4. Where does the woman work?
   (A) At an electronics store
   (B) At a grocery store
   (C) At a restaurant
   (D) At a pharmacy

5. Why does the man apologize?
   (A) He called the wrong store.
   (B) He provided an incorrect date.
   (C) He lost a sales receipt.
   (D) He forgot his discount card.

6. What does the woman offer to do?
   (A) Call the man back
   (B) Authorize a refund
   (C) Change a reservation
   (D) Place an order

7. What does the woman want to do?
   (A) Volunteer at the library
   (B) Join a committee
   (C) Get a library card
   (D) Renew a book

8. What does the man say the woman has to do?
   (A) Provide proof of her address
   (B) Make a payment
   (C) Attend an orientation
   (D) Sign up at the front desk

9. What does the man give the woman?
   (A) A registration form
   (B) A policy document
   (C) A schedule
   (D) A reading list

---

10. Where most likely are the speakers?
    (A) At a train station
    (B) At a construction site
    (C) At a travel agency
    (D) At an automobile dealership

11. Which feature does the woman say is important?
    (A) Price
    (B) Safety
    (C) Efficiency
    (D) Size

12. What is the woman asked to provide?
    (A) A driver's license
    (B) A credit card
    (C) An itinerary
    (D) A receipt

13. Where does the woman work?
(A) At a law firm
(B) At a travel agency
(C) At a health clinic
(D) At a hair salon

14. What does the man say he will be doing next month?
(A) Leading a workshop
(B) Starting a job at a different company
(C) Taking a holiday overseas
(D) Writing a travel guide

15. What does the man imply when he says, "I work until 3 o'clock on Tuesdays"?
(A) He wishes that he worked full-time.
(B) He needs a later appointment.
(C) He would prefer to come in on the weekend.
(D) He will be departing early for an event.

---

16. Where does this conversation most likely take place?
(A) At a software company
(B) At a plastics factory
(C) At an electronics store
(D) At an auto repair shop

17. What problem does the man mention?
(A) A part needs to be replaced.
(B) No technicians are available.
(C) Some supplies are out of stock.
(D) A workplace is noisy.

18. What does the woman want to know?
(A) When a task will be completed
(B) How much an item will cost
(C) Where a branch is located
(D) How long a warranty lasts

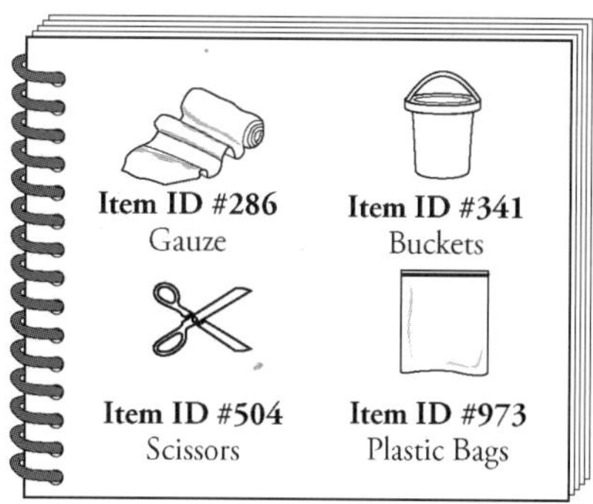

19. Who most likely is the woman?
(A) A salesperson
(B) A maintenance supervisor
(C) A safety inspector
(D) A veterinarian

20. According to the man, what has Ms. Jones requested?
(A) A signed form
(B) A phone call
(C) A rescheduled appointment
(D) A printed invoice

21. Look at the graphic. What item ID number will the man use in the order?
(A) 286
(B) 341
(C) 504
(D) 973

정답 및 해설 p. 198

PART 3

Directions: You will hear some conversations between two or more people. You will be asked to answer three questions about what the speakers say in each conversation. Select the best response to each question and mark the letter (A), (B), (C), or (D) on your answer sheet. The conversations will not be printed in your test book and will be spoken only one time.

32. Who most likely is the man?
(A) A dietitian
(B) A repair person
(C) A sales associate
(D) A safety inspector

33. Why does the man need a week to complete some work?
(A) He has to order a new part.
(B) He wants to consult with an expert.
(C) He must wait until an office is closed.
(D) He needs assistance from some coworkers.

34. What does the woman say she will do?
(A) Post a notice
(B) Check a manual
(C) Reschedule an event
(D) Make a lunch reservation

35. According to the man, why is an interview well-timed?
(A) He just hired a new executive director.
(B) His company is about to launch a new product.
(C) It is the only time he is available this week.
(D) It is his company's anniversary.

36. What did the woman research?
(A) A popular trend
(B) A family background
(C) Product sales
(D) Workplace culture

37. According to the man, what is responsible for the success of his business?
(A) His willingness to work hard
(B) His father's business contacts
(C) The uniqueness of the products
(D) The creativity of the marketing

38. What are the speakers discussing?
(A) A client visit
(B) A training session
(C) A company luncheon
(D) An expense report

39. Why is the woman concerned?
(A) A budget has not been increased.
(B) A schedule has not been set up.
(C) A location is too far away.
(D) Some employees are not available.

40. What does the woman suggest doing?
(A) Talking to other employees
(B) Getting approval from a supervisor
(C) Checking some sales figures
(D) Reserving an event venue

41. What service does the man's business provide?
(A) Travel planning
(B) Interior decorating
(C) Property management
(D) Industrial shipping

42. What does the woman ask the man about?
(A) A business referral
(B) An insurance policy
(C) Some pricing information
(D) Some customer feedback

43. What does the man suggest the woman do?
(A) Review an invoice
(B) Read about some regulations
(C) Look at some photographs
(D) Create an account

44. What are the speakers mainly discussing?
(A) A maintenance request
(B) A job promotion
(C) An office relocation
(D) An online payment system

45. What will the woman do next week?
(A) Go on a vacation
(B) Schedule an interview
(C) Clean out a file cabinet
(D) Lead a training workshop

46. Which department does the man say he contacted?
(A) Maintenance
(B) Marketing
(C) Purchasing
(D) Accounting

47. Where do the speakers most likely work?
(A) At a factory
(B) At a restaurant
(C) At a kitchen supply store
(D) At a gardening center

48. What is the man concerned about?
(A) Covering a work shift
(B) Needing additional supplies
(C) Receiving negative feedback
(D) Damaging some equipment

49. What information does the man ask Paloma to repeat?
(A) The duration of a task
(B) The location of an item
(C) A temperature setting
(D) A closing time

50. Why does the woman say, "Do you know what time it is"?
(A) To express enthusiasm
(B) To request more preparation time
(C) To note that the man is late
(D) To determine the length of a meeting

51. What problem does the man mention?
(A) His flight has been delayed.
(B) There are no taxis nearby.
(C) An e-mail was deleted.
(D) There is a lot of traffic.

52. What does the man say he just did?
(A) He revised a sales report.
(B) He contacted a colleague.
(C) He boarded a train.
(D) He met with a client.

53. What are the speakers mainly discussing?
(A) A product launch
(B) A company merger
(C) A construction project
(D) A hiring initiative

54. What concern does the woman mention?
(A) An opening was delayed.
(B) Some staff members were late.
(C) A flight has been canceled.
(D) A budget has been exceeded.

55. What does the man offer to do?
(A) Resend a document
(B) Set up a conference call
(C) Open an investigation
(D) Reduce the staffing level

GO ON TO THE NEXT PAGE

56. Who most likely is the man?

(A) A software engineer
(B) A financial analyst
(C) A marketing specialist
(D) A security guard

57. What kind of business do the women run?

(A) A magazine publishing company
(B) A travel-booking Web site
(C) A video-streaming service
(D) A nutritional consulting practice

58. What information will the women most likely provide next?

(A) A budget estimate
(B) A project deadline
(C) An account number
(D) A business closing time

---

59. Why did the man miss a meeting yesterday?

(A) His car broke down.
(B) He was conducting an interview.
(C) He needed to make some home repairs.
(D) He was visiting a storage facility.

60. Why does the woman say, "The board usually takes a long time to make decisions"?

(A) To express doubt
(B) To ask for more time
(C) To recommend a new process
(D) To complain about a policy

61. What does the man say he is concerned about?

(A) Some requests from a client
(B) The qualifications of a worker
(C) An interruption in a work assignment
(D) Some policy guidelines

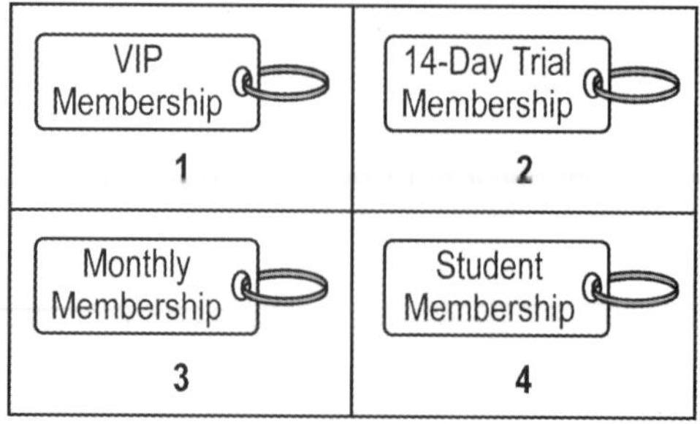

62. Where most likely are the speakers?

(A) At a museum
(B) At a university
(C) At a fitness center
(D) At a community garden

63. What does the woman provide assistance with?

(A) Finding a lost object
(B) Renewing a membership
(C) Joining a tour
(D) Making a payment

64. Look at the graphic. Which card belongs to the man?

(A) Card 1
(B) Card 2
(C) Card 3
(D) Card 4

Wednesday, April 12	Perton Foundation
Thursday, April 13	Aplicon LLC
Friday, April 14	Partel Agency
Saturday, April 15	Dreamvilla Productions

65. What type of service does the speakers' business provide?
(A) Tax form preparation
(B) Legal counseling
(C) Banquet hall rental
(D) Photography

66. Look at the graphic. Which company will the man contact?
(A) Perton Foundation
(B) Aplicon LLC
(C) Partel Agency
(D) Dreamvilla Productions

67. Why will the speakers talk to Maria?
(A) To ask her to update some Web site photos
(B) To obtain her input about pricing
(C) To confirm a business address
(D) To request that a schedule be adjusted

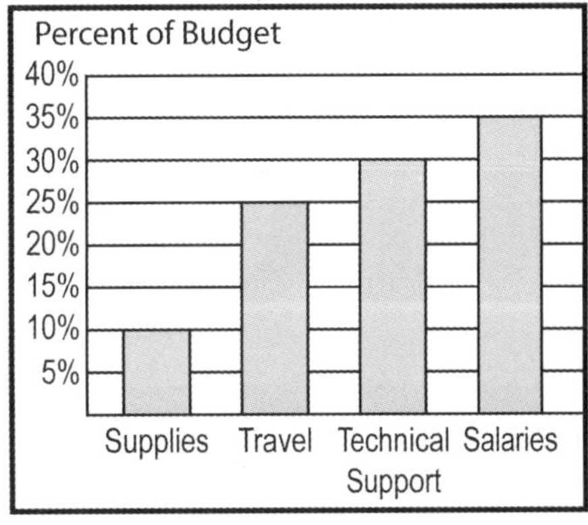

68. What department do the speakers work in?
(A) Customer Service
(B) Human Resources
(C) Manufacturing
(D) Marketing

69. Look at the graphic. What percentage do the speakers want to reduce?
(A) 10%
(B) 25%
(C) 30%
(D) 35%

70. What does the man say he will do this afternoon?
(A) Discuss a topic at a meeting
(B) Plan a workshop agenda
(C) Make a hotel reservation for a client
(D) Post a job advertisement

LC

PART 04

짧은 담화

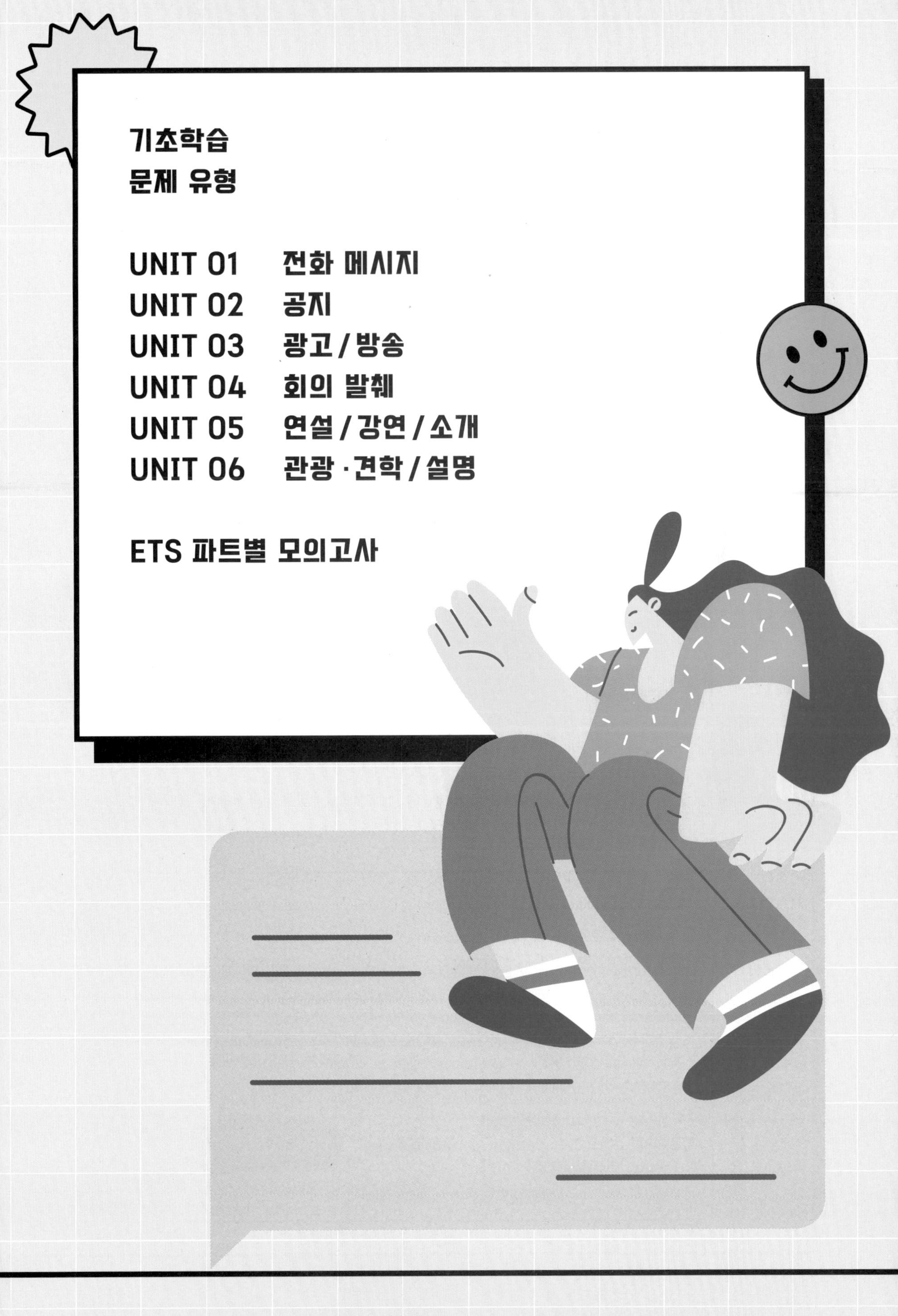

기초학습
문제 유형

UNIT 01 전화 메시지
UNIT 02 공지
UNIT 03 광고/방송
UNIT 04 회의 발췌
UNIT 05 연설/강연/소개
UNIT 06 관광·견학/설명

ETS 파트별 모의고사

PART 4 | 짧은 담화

30문항

Part 4 시험은 이렇게 나와요

짧은 담화문을 듣고, 이에 딸린 문제 3개를 풀게 됩니다. 담화당 3문제씩 푸는 패턴이 10번 반복되어 총 30문제(71번~100번)로 구성됩니다.

문제지

71. What is being advertised?
    (A) A recipe book
    (B) A fitness drink
    (C) Some exercise clothing
    (D) Some athletic equipment

72. What does the speaker say is surprising about the product?
    (A) Its money-back guarantee
    (B) Its simple instructions
    (C) Its affordable price
    (D) Its wide availability

73. What can the listeners do on a Web site?
    (A) Subscribe to a podcast
    (B) Receive discount coupons
    (C) Chat with personal trainers
    (D) Access some videos

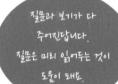

질문과 보기가 다
주어진답니다.
질문은 미리 읽어두는 것이
도움이 돼요.

음원

Questions 71-73 refer to the following advertisement.

W-Am Do you like to exercise and need a quick, healthy way to get energy? [71] If you want more power for your fitness routine, try drinking Rita's Shakes. Our delicious beverages provide all the nutrients you need. And if you're used to paying a lot for fitness drinks, [72] you'll be pleasantly surprised at our affordable price. Rita's is the economical choice. Plus, [73] if you go to our Web site, you can sign up for exclusive access to exercise videos led by famous fitness instructors.

71. What is being advertised?
72. What does the speaker say is surprising about the product?
73. What can the listeners do on a Web site?

이런 음원이 들려요.

ETS가 제안하는 꿀팁!

Part 4는 담화를 들으면서 질문과 보기를 읽기도 해야 하는 고난도의 파트입니다. 다음과 같은 사항에 주의하세요.

① 담화문을 듣기 전에 미리 질문을 읽으며 키워드를 파악하세요.

담화를 듣기 전에 문제의 의도를 잘 파악해야 정답을 찾기가 쉽습니다.

71. What is being advertised?	광고되고 있는 것은?
72. What does the speaker say is surprising about the product?	화자가 제품에 대해 놀랍다고 하는 것은?
73. What can the listeners do on a Web site?	청자들이 웹사이트에서 할 수 있는 것은?

② 화자와 청자를 구분하세요.

Part 4는 화자가 한 명이므로 남녀를 구분할 필요는 없지만, 질문에 speaker(화자)와 listener(청자)를 제시하는 경우가 있으니 질문의 주어를 꼭 확인하세요.

What will the speaker probably do next? → **화자가 할 일**	화자가 다음에 할 일은?
What can the listeners do on a Web site? → **청자가 할 일**	청자들이 웹사이트에서 할 수 있는 것은?

③ 문제 순서대로 답이 들립니다!

담화가 전개되는 순서에 따라 대부분 답이 나와요.

전반부	Do you like to exercise and need a quick, healthy way to get energy? [71] If you want more power for your fitness routine, try drinking Rita's Shakes.	**71.** What is being advertised? → **A fitness drink**
중반부	Our delicious beverages provide all the nutrients you need. And if you're used to paying a lot for fitness drinks, [72] you'll be pleasantly surprised at our affordable price. Rita's is the economical choice.	**72.** What does the speaker say is surprising about the product? → **Its affordable price**
후반부	Plus, [73] if you go to our Web site, you can sign up for exclusive access to exercise videos led by famous fitness instructors.	**73.** What can the listeners do on a Web site? → **Access some videos**

기초학습

Paraphrasing(바꿔 표현하기) 익히기

Part 4에서도 Part 3과 마찬가지로 담화에 나온 단어나 구를 정답에 그대로 제시하는 경우보다 같은 의미를 가진 다른 말로 바꿔 표현하는 경우가 많습니다. Part 4에서 자주 출제되는 paraphrasing 유형을 배워봅시다.

① 동의어/유사 표현 의미가 같지만 다른 표현을 사용하는 경우입니다.

담화 내 단서	질문 및 정답
Our office building will be undergoing some repairs Saturday morning and the electricity will be off for about three hours. 우리 사무실 건물이 토요일 아침에 보수공사를 할 예정이라, 대략 3시간 동안 전기가 차단될 것입니다.	**Q. 문제점?** **A.** A building will be without power. 건물에 전기가 들어오지 않을 것이다.
Remember all our members receive a ten percent discount on all purchases, not just books, so sign up for the program today. 저희의 모든 회원은 책뿐만 아니라, 모든 구매품에 10퍼센트 할인을 받는다는 것을 기억하십시오, 그러니 오늘 프로그램을 신청하세요.	**Q. 청자에게 권하는 것?** **A.** Enroll in a program 프로그램 등록

② 포괄적 상위어 표현 상위 개념의 어휘를 사용하는 경우입니다.

담화 내 단서	질문 및 정답
Please make some changes and bring the revised proposal to my office, by the end of the day if possible. 변경을 해서 수정된 제안서를 제 사무실로 가지고 오세요.	**Q. 청자에게 가져오라고 요청한 것?** **A.** A document 서류
We'll offer complimentary coffee, tea and soft drinks. 무료 커피, 차, 그리고 탄산음료를 제공할 겁니다.	**Q. 다음에 일어날 일?** **A.** provide free beverages 무료 음료를 제공

③ 축약 표현 길게 풀어 쓴 표현을 간단히 요약하여 말하는 경우입니다.

담화 내 단서	질문 및 정답
Please contact my colleague in software development, Jason Lee, at extension 331. 소프트웨어 개발팀의 제 동료인 제이슨 리에게 연락하십시오.	**Q. 제이슨 리는 누구인가?** **A.** A software specialist 소프트웨어 전문가
And now, for the top stories from today's financial news. 이제, 오늘 경제 뉴스의 주요 기사들입니다.	**Q. 청자들이 다음에 들을 것?** **A.** Some news stories 몇 가지 뉴스

CHECK UP

1-5. 다음 밑줄 친 부분을 가장 잘 바꾸어 표현한 것을 고르세요.

1. The price of your tour ticket includes free entry to the museum.

   (A) parking (B) admission

2. Because of the long wait times tonight, we're offering every customer a free dessert.

   (A) discount voucher (B) a complimentary menu item

3. National Airlines flight 415 will be leaving from gate 14 instead of gate 3.

   (A) a change in departure gate (B) a delay in departure time

4. Please go to my Web site to see testimonials from customers I've worked with before.

   (A) read customer feedback (B) find a list of consultants

5. Visit the Mishu Web site to read for yourself what our customers are saying about their devices.

   (A) purchase a product (B) read customer reviews

6-10. 다음 음원을 듣고 질문에 알맞은 말을 고르세요. P4_01

6. What does the speaker offer the listener?

   (A) A replacement product (B) A future discount

7. What change will be implemented?

   (A) Buses will be added. (B) Travelers will be reimbursed.

8. What will the audience do?

   (A) Learn to create a secure Web site (B) Take a tour of a business

9. What is the problem?

   (A) Some receipts are missing. (B) A form has not been received.

10. Why does the speaker say she is concerned?

    (A) A supplier has raised its prices. (B) A competitor opened a store nearby.

정답 및 해설 p. 220

문제 유형

기본 문제 유형 알아보기

① 전체 내용을 묻는 문제

담화의 주제나 장소, 화자의 신분 등을 묻는 일반적인 질문은 주로 담화의 시작 부분에서 답을 알 수 있습니다. 질문의 주요 키워드를 먼저 파악한 후, 담화의 앞 부분을 잘 들으며 단서를 잡으세요..

1. 주제/목적 문제

• What is the purpose of the talk[call]?	담화[전화]의 목적은?
• What is the main topic of the talk?	담화의 주요 주제는?
• What type of event is being held?	어떤 행사가 열리고 있는가?
• What position is being advertised?	어떤 자리가 광고되고 있는가?

정답이 들리는 단서 표현

전화 메시지	**I'm calling to** confirm the delivery of your new air conditioner tomorrow morning. 내일 오전에 있을 고객님의 새 에어컨 배송 확인차 전화 드립니다.
회의 발췌	In today's meeting, **I want to discuss** how the needs of each of you might be better addressed. 오늘 회의에서는 여러분 개개인의 요구사항을 어떻게 하면 더 잘 해결할지 논의하고 싶습니다.
공지	**A reminder that** the city's annual bicycle race is taking place tomorrow. 시에서 개최하는 연례 자전거 경주가 내일 있을 예정이니 기억하시기 바랍니다.

2. 신분/장소 문제

신분/직업	• Who is the announcement for?	누구를 위한 공지인가?
	• What industry does the speaker work in?	화자는 어떤 업계에 종사하는가?
	• Who is the audience for the talk?	담화의 청중은 누구인가?
장소/근무지	• Where is the speaker?	화자가 있는 곳은?
	• Where does the talk take place?	담화가 일어나고 있는 곳은?
	• Where does the woman work?	여자가 일하는 곳은?

정답이 들리는 단서 표현

전화 메시지	This is Steve **from Dr. Chang's office.** 저는 장 박사님 진료실의 스티브입니다.
방송	The club is especially happy to have Ms. Charlotte Blake, **the film's screenwriter,** here with us today. 저희 클럽은 특히 오늘 이곳에 이 영화의 시나리오 작가인 샬롯 블레이크 씨를 모시게 되어 기쁩니다.
관광/견학	**Welcome to the factory** tour of Indigolab Fragrances. 인디고랩 향수 공장 견학에 오신 것을 환영합니다.

P4_02

문제 유형 맛보기

Are you looking for an exciting new career in the banking industry? Premier National Bank is opening seven new locations in the area over the next twelve months, and we are looking for dynamic people with good communication and management skills. If you are interested in a job with great advancement potential, visit our Web site for more information today.

What is the main purpose of the advertisement?
(A) To announce new prices
(B) To recruit new workers
(C) To promote a new product
(D) To describe an office location

STEP 01 키워드 보고 문제 유형 파악하기

목적 문제

STEP 02 보기 보면서 담화 앞부분 집중해서 듣기

새 일자리를 찾고 있냐는 질문과 사람을 구하고 있다는 말에 유의

STEP 03 Paraphrasing 표현에 유의하기

looking for an exciting new career → recruit new workers

정답 (B)

–

은행업에서 흥미로운 새 직업을 찾고 계십니까? 프리미어 내셔널 은행은 앞으로 12개월 동안 우리 지역에 7개의 새 지점을 열며, 의사소통 능력과 관리 기술이 뛰어난 활동적인 사람을 찾고 있습니다. 발전 가능성이 큰 일자리에 관심이 있으시다면, 오늘 추가 정보를 얻기 위해서 저희 웹사이트를 방문해주세요.

광고의 주요 목적은 무엇인가?
(A) 새로운 가격 공지
(B) 신입 사원 채용
(C) 신제품 홍보
(D) 사무실 위치 설명

CHECK UP 질문의 키워드를 먼저 파악한 후 담화를 들으면서 정답을 고르세요.

1. Who most likely is the speaker?
   (A) A bus driver
   (B) A transportation official
   (C) A train passenger
   (D) A news reporter

2. Where does the speaker most likely work?
   (A) At a department store
   (B) At a fitness center
   (C) At a newspaper
   (D) At a bank

정답 및 해설 p. 222

② 세부 사항을 묻는 문제

주로 담화의 중반부에서 나오는 질문으로, 최근에는 전체 내용을 묻는 질문이 나오지 않으면 세부 사항 묻는 문제가 두 개 나오기도 합니다. 주요 키워드 파악이 매우 중요하니, 키워드를 재빨리 파악한 후 단서를 기다리며 집중하여 들으세요.

1. 문제점/걱정거리 문제

• What is the problem?	문제가 무엇인가?
• What problem does the speaker mention?	화자가 언급한 문제는?
• Why is the caller concerned?	전화한 사람은 왜 걱정하는가?
• What is wrong with the order?	주문에 무슨 문제가 있는가?

정답이 들리는 단서 표현

취소/중단/만료	canceled / no longer / expire	취소된 / 더 이상 ~ 않다 / 만료되다
폐쇄/차단	closed / blocked (off) / under construction	닫힌 / 폐쇄된 / 공사 중
변경/고장	reschedule / policy changes / broken down	일정을 다시 잡다 / 정책 변경 / 고장 나다
부재	out of office / absent	부재 중 / 결근한
교통 문제	backup / heavy traffic / long commute	차량 지체 / 교통 체증 / 긴 출퇴근 시간

2. 이유/원인 문제

• Why was the event canceled?	행사가 취소된 이유는?
• Why does the speaker recommend the Web site?	화자가 웹사이트를 추천한 이유는?
• Why is Ann Douglas asked to arrive early?	앤 더글라스가 일찍 오라고 요청 받은 이유는?

정답이 들리는 단서 표현

연락 이유	**I'm calling because** we need to reschedule your appointment. 귀하의 예약 시간을 변경해야 해서 전화 드립니다.
사과 이유	**I want to apologize for** missing our meeting this morning. 오늘 아침 회의에 빠진 것에 대해 사과하고 싶습니다.
인기 이유	Alton computers have been very **popular with consumers because of** their light weight. 알톤 컴퓨터는 가벼운 무게 때문에 소비자들에게 매우 인기가 있어 왔다.

3. 기타 세부 사항 문제

• What is the flight's destination?	이 비행편의 목적지는?
• What time does the woman say she is leaving today?	여자가 오늘 퇴근할 시간은?
• According to the report, how will the weather be tomorrow?	보도에 따르면, 내일 날씨는 어떠할 것인가?

정답이 들리는 단서 표현

기타 세부 사항 문제는 다양한 정보를 묻기에, 의문사, 명사, 동사 위주의 **키워드**를 잘 파악해야 합니다.

문제 유형 맛보기

P4_04

Hello, this is Sandy Johnson. I placed a print order with your company last week. I just received my order, and there's a problem. I ordered two hundred flyers printed on orange paper, but instead, the flyers came printed on blue paper. I had planned to send the orange flyers out to my customers this week to advertise a special sale. I need you to correct this error as soon as possible. Thank you.

What is wrong with the order?
(A) It has arrived late.
(B) The prices are wrong.
(C) There are not enough flyers.
(D) The flyers are the wrong color.

STEP 01 키워드 보고 문제 유형 파악하기

문제점 문제

STEP 02 보기 보면서 담화 중반부 집중해서 듣기

오렌지색으로 주문했는데 파란색으로 왔다는 말에 유의

STEP 03 Paraphrasing 표현에 유의하기

the flyers came printed on blue paper → The flyers are the wrong color.

정답 (D)

–

안녕하세요, 저는 샌디 존슨입니다. 지난주에 귀사에 인쇄 발주를 했습니다. 막 주문품을 받았는데, 문제가 있네요. 오렌지색 용지로 전단 200부를 주문했는데, 대신, 전단이 파란색 용지에 인쇄되어 왔습니다. 특별 할인 행사를 광고하기 위해 이번 주에 고객들에게 오렌지색 전단을 보낼 계획이었습니다. 가능한 한 빨리 이 오류를 바로 잡아 주세요. 감사합니다.

주문에 무슨 문제가 있는가?
(A) 늦게 도착했다.
(B) 가격이 틀리다.
(C) 전단이 충분하지 않다.
(D) 전단 색이 잘못됐다.

CHECK UP 질문의 키워드를 먼저 파악한 후 담화를 들으면서 정답을 고르세요.

04_05

1. Why are visitors invited to the Ashton Ball Room?
   (A) To meet people
   (B) To attend a presentation
   (C) To register for an event
   (D) To eat breakfast

2. What anniversary is the conference celebrating?
   (A) 2 years
   (B) 5 years
   (C) 10 years
   (D) 20 years

정답 및 해설 p. 223

③ 요청·제안/앞으로 일어날 일 문제

담화의 후반부에는 주로 청자에게 요청하거나 제안하는 내용, 또는 앞으로 일어날 일에 대한 암시나 제시가 나오는 경우가 많습니다. 보기의 내용이 긴 경우가 많으므로 시간이 된다면 미리 읽어두는 편이 유리합니다.

1. 요청·제안 문제

• What are callers asked to do?	전화한 사람들이 요청 받는 것은?
• What does the speaker say the listeners should do?	청자들이 해야 할 일은?
• What are listeners advised to do?	청자들이 해야 할 일은?
• What does the speaker recommend?	화자가 제안하는 것은?
• What does the speaker suggest about the project?	화자가 프로젝트에 대해 제안하는 것은?

2. 앞으로 일어날 일 문제

• What will the speaker probably do next?	화자가 다음에 할 일은?
• What will listeners probably hear next?	청자들이 다음에 듣게 될 것은?
• What most likely will happen next?	다음에 일어날 일은?
• What does the speaker say he will do?	화자가 곧 할 일은?
• What is Mayumi Toshida planning to do?	마유미 토시다가 하려는 것은?

정답이 들리는 단서 표현

요청/앞으로 일어날 일	**Would you please** step forward to accept your prize? 상을 받기 위해 앞으로 나와 주시겠어요? **We ask that you** bring your final selections to the cashier counters at this time. 지금 계산대로 여러분이 마지막으로 선택한 물건들을 가지고 오실 것을 부탁드립니다. And **don't forget to** come back in November, when our featured exhibit will change to prints from our permanent collection. 그리고 특별 전시회가 저희 영구 소장품의 판화로 교체되는 11월에 꼭 다시 찾아 주시기 바랍니다. So next time you're traveling on business, **make sure you** book a room at a Vella hotel. 이제 다음 출장에는, 벨라 호텔을 예약하십시오.
제안/앞으로 일어날 일	**We hope you'll** stop by to meet Chef Ramos, and consider purchasing a copy of the book. 주방장 라모스를 만나러 들러 주시기 바라며, 책 구입도 고려해 보시기 바랍니다. Just **remember to** use some of the money you'll save to buy Weebli's fast-paced racing game, Future Sprint, when it comes out this fall. 절약한 금액은 이번 가을에 출시될 위블리의 속도감 높은 경주 게임인 퓨처 스프린트를 구입하는 데 써 주세요. **I encourage you to** walk around and see all the offerings before making your choices. 선택하시기 전에 돌아다니면서 모든 물품들을 구경하실 것을 권해 드립니다.

문제 유형 맛보기

P4_06

And now for a look at Brooktown's roads. There's actually very little to report this morning. Most roads are clear; however, there is one trouble spot on Carter Highway. This is the fifth day of construction on the Carter Highway Bridge. Due to the work, officials have closed one of the two southbound lanes. If you plan on traveling south, I recommend taking Dairy Road or Valley Drive instead. Now over to Ann for the weather report.

What does the speaker suggest?
(A) Taking a different route
(B) Using public transportation
(C) Canceling a trip
(D) Leaving early

STEP 01 키워드 보고 문제 유형 파악하기

제안 문제

STEP 02 보기 보면서 담화 후반부 집중해서 듣기

데어리 로나 밸리 도로를 택하라고 권한다는 말에 유의

STEP 03 Paraphrasing 표현에 유의하기

Dairy Road or Valley Drive instead → a different route

정답 (A)

—

이제 브룩타운 도로들을 보겠습니다. 오늘 오전에는 알려드릴 것이 거의 없습니다. 대부분의 도로는 훤히 뚫려 있지만, 카터 고속도로에 문제 지점이 한 군데 있습니다. 오늘은 카터 고속도로 다리 공사가 5일째인데요. 이 공사 때문에, 관계자들은 남행 두 차선 중 한 개를 폐쇄했습니다. 남쪽으로 이동하실 계획이면, 데어리 로나 밸리 도로를 대신 이용하실 것을 추천 드립니다. 이제 일기예보를 듣기 위해 앤에게 넘기겠습니다.

화자가 제안하는 것은 무엇인가?
(A) 다른 도로 이용
(B) 대중 교통 이용
(C) 여행 취소
(D) 이른 출발

CHECK UP 질문의 키워드를 먼저 파악한 후 담화를 들으면서 정답을 고르세요.

04_07

1. What does the speaker suggest?
   (A) Taking photographs
   (B) Eating at the café
   (C) Visiting the gift shop
   (D) Going to the library

2. What will the speaker probably do next?
   (A) Give someone an award
   (B) Read a poem
   (C) Take a picture of a guest
   (D) Show a documentary film

정답 및 해설 p. 224

고난도 유형 알아보기

① 의도 파악 문제

화자의 의도 파악 문제는 제시된 문장을 말한 이유나 의미, 암시하는 바를 파악하는 문제입니다. 같은 표현이라도 문맥에 따라, 화자의 어조에 따라 의미가 달라질 수 있으므로, 제시된 문장의 앞뒤 맥락을 잘 파악해야 합니다.

1 질문에 제시된 인용 문장을 미리 읽어 두세요.

2 그 인용 문장이 언제 나올지 기다리며 앞뒤 문맥을 집중해서 잘 들어보세요.

• **Why** does the speaker **say**, **"Did everyone bring a camera"**?	화자는 왜 "여러분 모두 사진기 가져오셨나요"라고 말하는가?
• **What** does the speaker **imply** when she says, **"That's one way of doing it"**?	여자가 "그것도 하나의 방법입니다"라고 말할 때 암시하는 바는 무엇인가?

맥락에 따른 화자의 의도 파악하기

화자의 의도 파악 질문은 담화의 맥락과 화자들의 상황을 이해하는 것이 무엇보다 중요합니다. 다음 담화문을 통해 문장이 의미하는 바가 문맥에 따라 어떻게 달라지는지 알아보세요.

What does the speaker mean when she says, "I hear what you're saying?" (A) She understands the listener's concerns. (B) She wants to express her opinion.	여자가 "무슨 말을 하는지 알겠어요"라고 말할 때 의미하는 바는 무엇인가? (A) 그녀는 청자의 걱정을 이해한다. (B) 그녀는 자신의 주장을 표현하고 싶어한다.

Hi, Faith. I thought about our conversation, and I hear what you're saying. I see how my presentation might be a little confusing. I've made some changes, and I'd be appreciate it if you could look at them. I'll send you a revision soon.	안녕하세요, 페이쓰. 우리의 대화에 대해 생각해봤는데, **무슨 말을 하는지 알겠어요.** 제 발표가 좀 혼란스러울지도 모른다는 것에 대해 이해합니다. 변경을 좀 했으니 한번 봐 주시면 고맙겠습니다. 수정 사항을 곧 보내 드리겠습니다. → '청자의 걱정을 이해한다'는 의미
I guess we'd better discuss it later. I hear what you're saying but first of all, we need to meet the release date. I'll set up a meeting to talk about the promotion campaign right after the release date.	그건 나중에 얘기하는 게 좋겠어요. **무슨 말을 하는지 알겠어요,** 하지만 우 리는 먼저 출시일을 맞춰야 하잖아요. 출시일 직후에 바로 홍보 캠페인에 대해 얘기할 회의를 잡을게요. → '자신의 주장을 표현하고 싶어한다'는 의미

P4_08

문제 유형 맛보기

Thank you for participating in today's research study. Before we get started, I need everyone to fill out these forms. They just ask some basic questions about your medical history. It should not take more than a minute or two. I'll wait for everyone to finish, and then collect all the forms at once.

Why does the speaker say, "It should not take more than a minute or two"?
(A) To explain a schedule change
(B) To indicate that a task is easy
(C) To apologize for being late
(D) To criticize the speed of a project

STEP 01
키워드 보고 문제 유형 파악하기
의도 파악 문제

STEP 02
제시 문장 기다리며 듣고, 전후 맥락 파악하기
몇 가지 기본적인 질문만을 한다는 말에 유의

STEP 03
Paraphrasing 표현에 유의하기
just ask some basic questions
→ a task is easy

정답 (B)

오늘 조사 연구에 참가해 주셔서 감사합니다. 시작하기 전에 모든 분이 이 양식을 작성해 주시기 바랍니다. 양식에서는 여러분의 병력에 관한 몇 가지 기본적인 질문을 묻고 있습니다. **1~2분 이상 걸리지 않을 것입니다.** 모든 분이 완료하실 때까지 기다려서 한꺼번에 걷겠습니다.

화자는 왜 "1~2분 이상 걸리지 않을 것입니다"라고 말하는가?
(A) 일정 변경을 설명하기 위해
(B) 과제가 쉽다는 것을 나타내기 위해
(C) 늦은 것에 대해 사과하기 위해
(D) 프로젝트의 속도를 비난하기 위해

CHECK UP 질문의 키워드를 먼저 파악한 후 담화를 들으면서 정답을 고르세요.

04_09

1. Why does the speaker say, "Did everyone bring a camera"?
(A) He is worried a camera has been lost.
(B) He would like to borrow a camera.
(C) Photography is not allowed on the tour.
(D) The listeners are encouraged to take photographs.

2. What does the speaker imply when he says, "Ms. Chung, however, has worked in finance for thirty years"?
(A) Changing careers is difficult.
(B) Ms. Chung should retire soon.
(C) The financial industry is stable.
(D) Listeners should trust Ms. Chung.

정답 및 해설 p. 225

② 시각정보 연계 문제

시각정보 연계 문제는 일상 생활이나 업무에서 흔히 볼 수 있는 리스트, 쿠폰, 표지판, 평면도 등 다양한 시각정보가 함께 제시되는 문제입니다.

1 시각정보는 질문 윗부분에 제시되므로 담화를 듣기 전에 미리 파악해 두세요.

2 시각정보 연계 문제는 시각정보만으로는 답을 알 수 없고, 담화 내용과 연결시켜야만 정답을 찾을 수 있다는 점에 주의하세요.

• Look at the **graphic. On what day** is the talk **taking place**? 시각정보에 따르면, 강연은 어느 요일에 열리게 되는가?

시각정보 종류 알아보기

표/그래프/차트

표는 전화 메시지에서 주문 내용을 확인하거나 변동이 생겼을 때 등장할 가능성이 높고, 그래프나 차트도 공지, 회의 자료 등으로 등장할 수 있다.

Order Form 10-Sep-09

10-Sep-09
June Summers
123 Main St
Toronto, ON M5M 5M5

Product	Price	Qty	Total
Sweater	$ 15.00	5	$ 75.00
Shirt	$ 12.00	3	$ 36.00

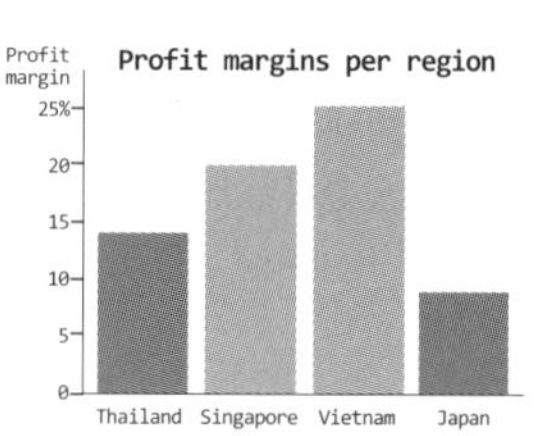

라벨/영수증

광고에서 상품 설명을 하면서 라벨이나 할인 쿠폰이 등장할 수 있고, 개업 행사를 알리는 전단 또는 구매 영수증이 등장할 수 있다.

Nutrition Facts
Serving Size 30 g (1.1 oz)
Servings Per Container 3.6

Amount Per Serving	
Calories 140 Calories from Fat 70	
	% Daily Value*
Total Fat 8g	13%
Saturated Fat 0g	0%
Trans Fat 0g	
Cholesterol 0mg	0%
Sodium 360mg	15%
Total Carbohydrate 15g	5%

A-Plus Transport
129 Goldfinch Way

March 3

Adult ticket	$29.00
Bag handling fee	$ 5.00
TOTAL:	$34.00

지도/평면도

관광 및 견학 안내에서 관광 지도, 추천 일정 등이 등장하거나, 교통 관련 뉴스에서 도로가 등장할 수 있다.

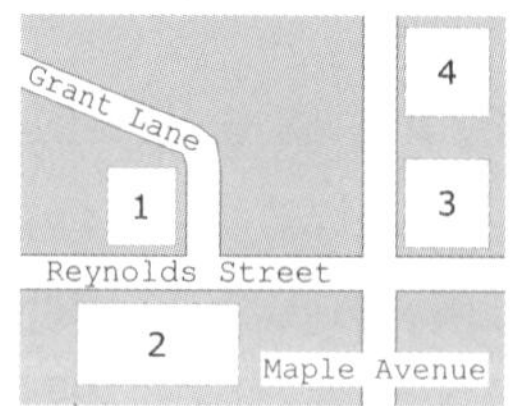

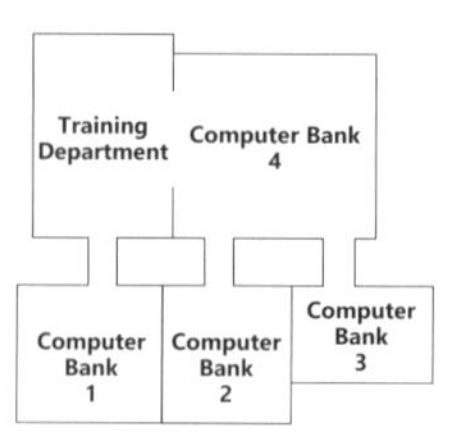

P4_10

문제 유형 맛보기

Hello. I'm Deanna Graves, and today is my first day on the job. I'm looking forward to working with all of you. I saw in some orientation materials that we're the largest department in Valorie Manufacturing, so it might take a while to meet all of you. If you have time, though, my desk is there in the corner, so please stop by and say hello.

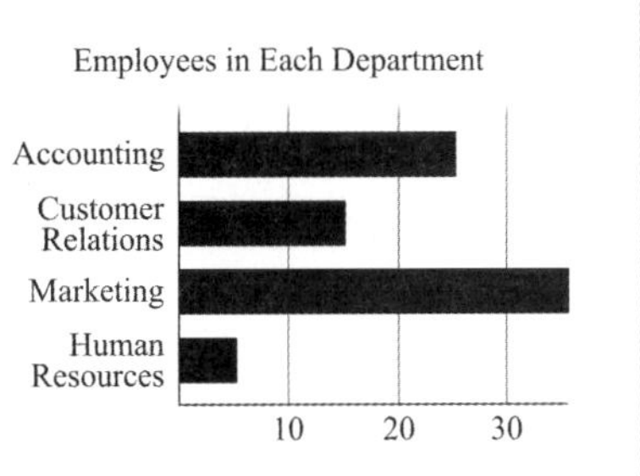

Look at the graphic. Which department does the speaker work in?

(A) Accounting

(B) Customer Relations

(C) Marketing

(D) Human Resources

STEP 01 **키워드 보고 문제 유형 파악하기**

시각정보 연계 문제

STEP 02 **시각정보와 관련된 내용에 집중하기**

우리가 가장 큰 부서라는 말에 유의

STEP 03 **담화 내용과 시각정보를 연관 지어 정답 찾기**

그래프에서 가장 직원수가 많은 부서는 Marketing인 것을 알 수 있음

정답 (C)

안녕하세요. 저는 디아나 그레이브스인데, 오늘이 출근 첫날입니다. 여러분과 함께 근무하는 것을 고대하고 있습니다. 오리엔테이션 자료에서 우리가 발로리 제조사에서 가장 큰 부서라고 보았습니다. 그러니 여러분 모두를 만나보는 데 시간이 좀 걸릴지도 모릅니다. 하지만 여러분 시간이 된다면 제 자리는 저기 모퉁이에 있으니 잠깐 들러서 인사해 주세요.

화자는 어느 부서에 근무하는가?

(A) 회계부

(B) 고객관리부

(C) 마케팅부

(D) 인사부

CHECK UP 질문의 키워드를 먼저 파악한 후 담화를 들으면서 정답을 고르세요.

04_11

1. Look at the graphic. On what day is the talk taking place?

(A) Monday

(B) Tuesday

(C) Wednesday

(D) Thursday

Class	Day
Intro to finance	Monday
Computer basics	Tuesday
Budgeting software	Wednesday
Tools for the future	Thursday

2. Look at the graphic. Which power station is being repaired?

(A) Slatterly

(B) Coleman

(C) Riverside

(D) Silver Quarry

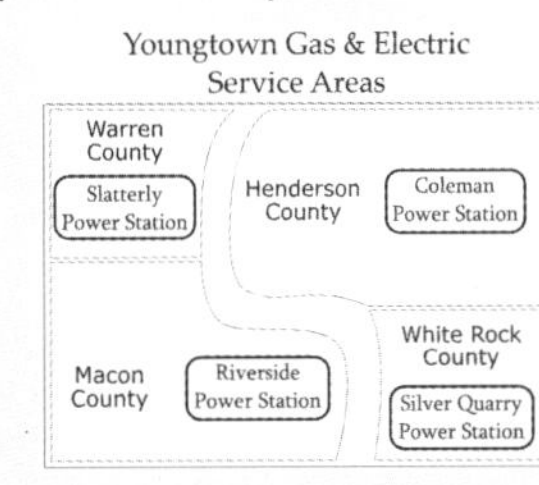

정답 및 해설 p. 225

UNIT 01 전화 메시지

전화 메시지는 전화를 건 사람이 남기는 음성 메시지와 회사나 상점에서 안내하는 자동 안내 메시지 등이 출제됩니다.

기출 문제풀이 전략

P4_12

STEP 01 **질문 파악** 질문을 먼저 읽으면서 키워드를 파악하세요.

1 What is the purpose of the message?	2 What does the speaker say he has to do on Wednesday?	3 What does the speaker say the listener will enjoy?
(A) To recommend a service	(A) Arrange a business trip	(A) A museum
(B) To extend a compliment	(B) Meet with a client	(B) A restaurant
(C) To postpone a lunch	(C) Wait for a delivery	(C) A community park
(D) To plan a dinner menu	(D) Go to a dentist	(D) A shopping center

STEP 02 **정답 고르기** 담화를 들으며 키워드의 단서를 찾아 정답을 고르세요.

화자 소개 Hi Marge, this is Yaniv.

세부 사항 1 I'm going to have to change our lunch meeting this week. 2 We were originally going to meet on Wednesday at noon, but I forgot I'm supposed to be at the dental clinic then, and my dentist is only available on Wednesday.

요청/추가 사항 Could we meet Thursday at noon, instead? 3 You'll love Miguel's Bistro. I think they even have a lunch special on Thursdays. Let me know if that works for you. I'll talk to you soon.

1. 키워드: 메시지의 목적

점심 모임을 바꿔야 할 것 같다는 말에 유의 → 정답은 (C)

Paraphrasing change our lunch meeting → postpone a lunch

2. 키워드: 수요일에 화자가 할 일

수요일 치과 약속을 깜박했다는 말에 유의 → 정답은 (D)

3. 키워드: 청자가 좋아할 것

미겔스 비스트로가 마음에 들 거라는 말에 유의 → 정답은 (B)

Paraphrasing Bistro → restaurant

안녕하세요 마지, 야니브예요. 이번 주 점심 모임을 바꿔야 할 것 같아요. 원래 수요일 정오에 만나기로 했잖아요. 그런데 내가 그때 치과에 가야 한다는 걸 깜빡했어요. 치과의사가 수요일에만 시간이 되어서요. 대신 목요일 정오에 만날 수 있을까요? 미겔스 비스트로가 아주 마음에 들 거예요. 목요일에는 점심 특선 메뉴도 있는 것 같아요. 괜찮은지 알려주세요. 곧 전화할게요.

정답 및 해설 p. 227

CHECK UP

Step 1 다음 3개의 질문을 읽으며 키워드에 표시하세요.

Step 2 담화를 들으며 정답의 단서를 찾아 정답을 고르세요

P4_13

1 Where most likely does the speaker work?

(A) At a jewelry shop

(B) At a clothing store

2 What does the speaker say about a product?

(A) It comes in different sizes.

(B) Its design has changed.

3 What does the speaker ask the listener to do?

(A) Pay by credit card

(B) Confirm an order

정답 및 해설 p. 227

기출로 익히는 패러프레이징

기출 문제에 등장했던 상황과 문장을 보고 정답이 어떤 식으로 패러프레이즈 되는지 확인해보세요.

담화 내 단서 포착	패러프레이징 된 정답 찾기
I'm a recruiter in the human resources department at Dellvue Electronics. 저는 델뷰 전자회사 인사부의 채용 담당자입니다.	**Q. 남자는 누구?** **A.** A human resources employee 인사부 직원
If you're available, we'd like you to come in for an interview on Wednesday, May 9th, at ten o'clock. 괜찮으시다면, 5월 9일 수요일 10시 면접에 오시면 좋겠습니다.	**Q. 전화 메시지의 목적?** **A.** To set up an appointment 약속을 잡기 위해
Please give me a call and I'd be happy to schedule a meeting with you. 저에게 전화 주시면 기꺼이 회의 약속을 잡겠습니다.	**Q. 전화 건 사람의 제안?** **A.** Meet with an employee 직원과 회의하기
Could you please call me back today before five o'clock, or tomorrow between ten and six? 오늘 5시 전이나 내일 10시와 6시 사이에 저에게 다시 전화 주시겠어요?	**Q. 전화 건 사람이 요청하는 것?** **A.** Return a telephone call 다시 전화하기

주제별 기출 어휘

P4_14

전화 녹음 메시지

urgent 긴급한

confirm (사실임을) 확인해주다, 확정하다

appointment 예약, 약속

postpone 연기하다

contact 연락하다

inquire 문의하다

regarding ~에 관해서(= about)

response 응답

currently 현재

repeat 반복; 반복하다

return a call to ~ ~에게 응답 전화를 하다

let ~ know ~에게 알려주다

This is ~ from... 저는 …의 ~입니다

This is a message for ~
~에게 전하는 메시지입니다(= I'm calling for ~)

This is a reminder of ~ ~을 알려드립니다

You can reach me at ~
~ 번호로 제게 연락하세요

I'm calling about[regarding] ~
~에 관해서 전화 드립니다

We're having[experiencing] problems with ~ ~에 문제가 생겼습니다

Please call me on my cell phone.
제 휴대전화로 전화 주십시오.

For inquiries about ~ ~에 대해 문의가 있으시면

자동 응답 메시지 (ARS)

hold 기다리다

reach (전화로) 연락하다

automated message 자동 메시지

busy 통화 중인

customer service representative
고객 서비스 직원

agent 상담원

extension number 내선 번호

business hours 영업시간, 운영 시간

transfer (전화를) 돌리다

connect (전화로) 연결시키다

pound key 우물 정(#)자 버튼

power failure 정전(= electric interruption, electric service outage, blackout)

repairs 보수

renovation 개조

dial 다이얼을 돌리다, 전화를 걸다

voice mail 음성 메일

operator 전화 교환원

at the moment 지금은

after the tone 신호음이 나온 후에

during the hours of operation 영업시간 동안

be advised that ~ ~을 숙지하다(= note that ~)

leave a message 메시지를 남기다

put A through B A를 B에게 연결하다

stay on the line 전화를 끊지 않고 기다리다
(= remain on the line)

Thank you for calling ~
~에 전화 주셔서 감사합니다

You've reached ~ ~에 연락하셨습니다

To do ~, (please) press + 번호
~하려면 …번을 누르세요

To hear this message again, please press ~ 이 메시지를 다시 듣고 싶으시면, ~번을 누르세요

The office will be closed on ~
사무실은 ~에 문을 닫습니다

ETS 문제로 훈련하기

P4_15

STEP 01 문장 핵심 파악하기

먼저 질문의 키워드에 동그라미로 표시하며 질문 내용을 파악하세요. 담화를 듣고 주어진 질문에 답한 후 빈칸을 채워 보세요.

1 Why is the speaker calling Ms. Newberry?

(A) To sell her an item (B) To give her an update

> Hello, this is Daniel Green from the Town ________. This message is for Estelle Newberry. Ms. Newberry, you recently came to the library and ________ ________ a book titled *Cool River*, by Karl McDonald. That book has just been ________, and I've ________ it in your name. Please come by the library at your convenience to ________ ________ ________ at the front desk.

2 What change does the speaker mention about the cafe?

(A) It has hired a new baker. (B) It has moved to a new location.

> Thank you for calling Lindenbrook Bakery and Café. We are currently ________, but please stay on the line for an important ________. We are now open at our ________ ________ at 24 Owensview Road. Business hours are ________ ________, and we are still offering ________ pastry-making ________ every Thursday at two P.M. For inquiries about scheduling an event with us, please ________ ________ ________ and we'll return your call as soon as we can.

STEP 02 실전에 가깝게 훈련하기

질문의 키워드에 동그라미로 표시한 후, 담화를 듣고 주어진 질문에 답하세요.

3 Who most likely is the speaker?

(A) A hotel employee
(B) A property manager
(C) A travel agent
(D) A job recruiter

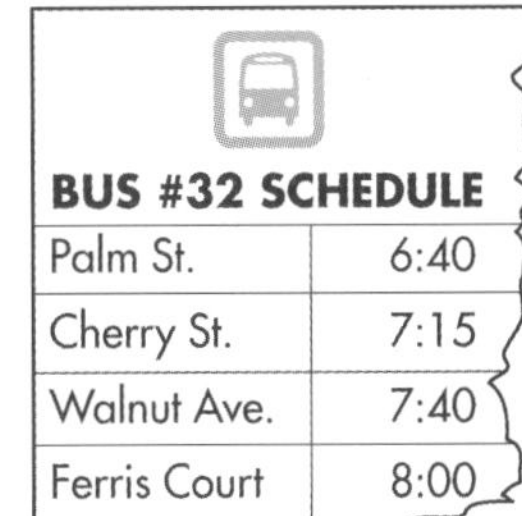

BUS #32 SCHEDULE

Palm St.	6:40
Cherry St.	7:15
Walnut Ave.	7:40
Ferris Court	8:00

4 Look at the graphic. When should the listener board the bus?

(A) 6:40
(B) 7:15
(C) 7:40
(D) 8:00

PART 4 | UNIT 01

정답 및 해설 p. 228

ETS 실전 테스트

1. Why is the speaker calling?
   (A) To order a prescription
   (B) To recommend a specialist
   (C) To confirm an appointment
   (D) To provide driving directions

2. What is being updated?
   (A) An office building
   (B) A company policy
   (C) A security system
   (D) A computer database

3. What is the listener instructed to bring?
   (A) A copy of her résumé
   (B) A list of medications
   (C) A confirmation number
   (D) A recent invoice

---

4. What type of business does the message refer to?
   (A) A hotel
   (B) A travel agency
   (C) A real estate office
   (D) A fitness club

5. According to the speaker, why should listeners visit a Web site?
   (A) To update contact information
   (B) To make a reservation
   (C) To view photos
   (D) To sign up for discounts

6. What does the speaker say will take place on Saturday?
   (A) An open house
   (B) A special sale
   (C) A free workshop
   (D) A holiday event

7. What is the speaker planning for next week?
   (A) An awards ceremony
   (B) A poetry reading
   (C) A gardening lecture
   (D) A glassmaking workshop

8. What does the speaker say she sent to the listener?
   (A) An outline
   (B) A credit card number
   (C) A pamphlet
   (D) A coupon

9. Why does the speaker say, "but we're also available on Tuesday"?
   (A) To ask for a budget increase
   (B) To confirm attendance
   (C) To complain about a scheduling conflict
   (D) To suggest holding an additional class

---

10. What department does the speaker work in?
    (A) Marketing
    (B) Personnel
    (C) Finance
    (D) Travel

11. Why is the speaker calling?
    (A) To make a job offer
    (B) To describe a training session
    (C) To explain an enrollment procedure
    (D) To request a document

12. What is the listener asked to do?
    (A) Go to the post office
    (B) Attend a department meeting
    (C) Call the registration office
    (D) Contact an employment agency

13. What type of business is the speaker calling from?
(A) A bank
(B) A manufacturing company
(C) A medical clinic
(D) A fitness center

14. Why does the speaker say, "there was a problem with some of our equipment"?
(A) To explain a delay
(B) To justify an expense
(C) To question a decision
(D) To express surprise

15. What does the speaker say he will do?
(A) Send an order code
(B) Change an appointment
(C) Give a discount
(D) Provide a recommendation

---

16. Why is the speaker calling?
(A) To recommend a job candidate
(B) To decline an invitation
(C) To schedule a photo shoot
(D) To order a product

17. What does the speaker plan to do next Wednesday?
(A) Meet with clients
(B) Take some time off
(C) Attend a business convention
(D) Conduct some interviews

18. What does the speaker ask the listener to provide?
(A) Feedback about some training
(B) Details of an itinerary
(C) A list of participants
(D) Photos from a job applicant

Schedule	
Wednesday	10 A.M.–4 P.M.
Thursday	OFF
Friday	10 A.M.–4 P.M.
Saturday	5 P.M.–11 P.M.
Sunday	7 A.M.–1 P.M.

19. Why does the speaker congratulate the listener?
(A) For winning an award
(B) For getting a new job
(C) For completing a certification
(D) For receiving a good review

20. According to the speaker, where can the listener find a schedule?
(A) On a bulletin board
(B) In an e-mail
(C) In a folder
(D) On a Web site

21. Look at the graphic. Which day does the speaker want the listener to confirm?
(A) Thursday
(B) Friday
(C) Saturday
(D) Sunday

정답 및 해설 p. 230

UNIT 02 공지

직장에서 업무·회의 관련 사항을 직원들에게 공지하는 내용이나, 공항·비행기, 쇼핑몰, 공연장 등의 공공장소에서 공지 사항을 전달하는 내용이 출제됩니다.

기출 문제풀이 전략

P4_17

STEP 01 **질문 파악** 질문을 먼저 읽으면서 키워드를 파악하세요.

1 Where is the announcement being made?	2 What are the listeners asked to do?	3 Why should Mr. Tanaka come to the service desk?
(A) In an airport (B) In a train station (C) In a bus terminal (D) In a travel agency	(A) Have their passports ready (B) Listen for their names (C) Remain in their seats (D) Go to a different gate	(A) To pay for an upgrade (B) To recover a lost item (C) To meet a travel companion (D) To pick up a ticket

STEP 02 **정답 고르기** 담화를 들으며 키워드의 단서를 찾아 정답을 고르세요.

주의 환기/주제 **1** Attention, all passengers. Boarding will now begin for flight 257 to Boston.

세부 사항 **2** Be sure to have your passports ready to present to the gate attendant—this will make the boarding process faster. And please be aware that your carry-on luggage may be inspected as you board the plane.

추가 사항 **3** Passenger Satoru Tanaka, could you please make your way to the service desk? We have your standby ticket ready for you here.

1. 키워드: 공지 장소

승객, 탑승, 비행편 등의 어휘에 유의
→ 정답은 (A)

2. 키워드: 청자들이 할 일

여권을 보여줄 준비를 하라는 말에 유의 → 정답은 (A)

3. 키워드: 타나카 씨가 서비스 데스크로 가야 할 이유

대기표를 준비해 두었다는 말에 유의
→ 정답은 (D)

Paraphrasing make your way
→ come

—

승객 여러분, 주목해주십시오. 이제 보스턴행 257편 탑승이 시작됩니다. 여권을 게이트 직원에게 보여줄 준비를 하십시오. 이렇게 하면 탑승 절차가 더 빨라질 것입니다. 그리고 비행기에 탑승할 때 휴대 수하물 검사가 있을 수 있다는 점, 유념하십시오. 사토루 타나카 승객님, 서비스 데스크로 가 주시겠습니까? 대기표를 준비해 두었습니다.

정답 및 해설 p. 237

CHECK UP

Step 1 다음 3개의 질문을 읽으며 키워드에 표시하세요.
Step 2 담화를 들으며 정답의 단서를 찾아 정답을 고르세요

P4_18

1 Where is the announcement being made?
(A) At an electronics store (B) At a conference center

2 What is the announcement about?
(A) Purchasing some software (B) Reclaiming a lost item

3 Who most likely is Mr. Zaman?
(A) A security guard (B) A guest speaker

정답 및 해설 p. 237

기출로 익히는 패러프레이징

기출 문제에 등장했던 상황과 문장을 보고 정답이 어떤 식으로 패러프레이즈 되는지 확인해보세요.

담화 내 단서 포착	패러프레이징 된 정답 찾기
This is a reminder to all employees on the production line. 생산 라인의 모든 직원 여러분들께 알려 드립니다.	**Q. 공지의 대상?** **A.** Factory employees 공장 직원들
Our friend and colleague Marian Wilson announced she was retiring as the theater company's artistic director. 우리의 친구이자 동료인 메리앤 윌슨은 극단의 예술감독 직에서 은퇴한다고 발표했습니다.	**Q. 담화의 목적?** **A.** To announce a change in personnel 인사상의 변화 공지
The city's public works department has just informed us that Garden Road will be closed for maintenance work for two days. 도시공공사업부는 가든 로가 이틀 동안 유지보수로 인해 폐쇄된다고 막 알려 왔습니다.	**Q. 공지의 목적?** **A.** To inform employees about a road closure 직원들에게 도로 폐쇄에 대해 알리기
Unfortunately, her flight from London was delayed, so she just arrived in Denver fifteen minutes ago. 안타깝게도 런던에서 오는 비행기가 연착되어 그녀는 15분 전에 막 덴버에 도착했습니다.	**Q. 한 참가자가 늦은 이유?** **A.** Her plane arrived late. 비행기가 늦게 도착했다.

주제별 기출 어휘

P4_19

사내 공지

Attention. 주목해주십시오.
be sure to 반드시 ~하다
notice board 게시판
incentive 장려금, 성과급
reminder 공지, 알림
inspection 점검, 검사
company policy 회사 방침, 회사 규정
shift 교대 근무
security 보안
upcoming 다가올, 앞으로 있을
as you know 알다시피
first of all 우선, 무엇보다도, 먼저
on duty 당번인, 근무 중인
be required to ~해야 한다
make sure that ~을 확인하다
make a decision 결정하다
provide ~ with... ~에게 …을 제공하다
meet a goal 목표를 달성하다
shut down 폐쇄하다
I want to let you know ~을 알려 드리고자 합니다

교통 관련 공지

Please be aware~ 알고 계십시오
passenger 승객
a brief announcement 간단한 공지
flight 비행편, 항공기(= plane, airplane, aircraft)
flight attendant 비행 승무원(= cabin crew)
captain 기장(= pilot)
board 탑승하다
destination 목적지
leave 떠나다, 출발하다(= take off, depart)
fasten (안전벨트를) 매다
delay 지연; 지연하다
inconvenience 불편
be scheduled to ~할 예정이다
could you please make your way to ~ ~로 와주시겠습니까?
be subject to ~해야 한다, ~하기 쉽다
apologize for ~에 대해 사과하다
serve snacks and beverages 간식과 음료를 제공하다
Welcome aboard. 탑승하신 것을 환영합니다.
Thank you for your cooperation. 협조해 주셔서 감사합니다.

기타 공지

bargain (정상가보다) 싸게 사는 물건
volunteer 자원 봉사자; 자원하다
participant 참석자
audience 청중, 관중
performance 공연
appreciation 감사
refreshments 다과
gift certificate 상품권(= voucher)
a new line of ~의 신제품들
as scheduled 예정대로(= on schedule)
be proud to ~하게 되어 자랑스럽다
remind A of B A에게 B를 상기시키다
get started 시작하다
enroll in ~에 등록하다
stop by ~에 들르다
We will be closing in 30 minutes. 저희는 30분 후에 폐장합니다.

ETS 문제로 훈련하기

P4_20

STEP 01 문장 핵심 파악하기

먼저 질문의 키워드에 동그라미로 표시하며 질문 내용을 파악하세요. 담화를 듣고 주어진 질문에 답한 후 빈칸을 채워 보세요.

1 What will happen in three weeks?

(A) The company will receive new equipment.

(B) The company will move to another office.

> Well everyone, there are just three more weeks until we _________ to the _________ _________. We need to start _________. A good place to start is to organize your paper files. Go through _________ _________ and decide what can be thrown away and what must be moved to the _________ _________.

2 Why does the speaker say, "There's no time to wait"?

(A) To promote an athletic training program

(B) To encourage in-store purchases

> Attention, Arnold's Sporting Goods _________! Today is the last day of our big _________ _________. All the tennis equipment in our store is thirty percent off... We've extended our store hours to 11 P.M.—for today only—so everyone can pick up great goods at _________ _________. There's no time to wait!

STEP 02 실전에 가깝게 훈련하기

질문의 키워드에 동그라미로 표시한 후, 담화를 듣고 주어진 질문에 답하세요.

3 What is the main topic of the announcement?

(A) Company security

(B) Club membership

(C) Hotel keys

(D) Credit card purchases

4 According to the speaker, what are the cards needed for?

(A) Accessing databases

(B) Making purchases

(C) Opening doors

(D) Registering for classes

정답 및 해설 p. 238

ETS 실전 테스트

1. Who is the announcement probably for?
(A) Office supervisors
(B) Department store clerks
(C) Factory employees
(D) Hospital nurses

2. What are the instructions for?
(A) Starting a work shift
(B) Submitting a pay form
(C) Repairing a machine
(D) Changing a schedule

3. What are listeners asked to check for on the notice board?
(A) A list of supervisors
(B) A pay schedule
(C) Safety guidelines
(D) Daily announcements

---

4. Where is the announcement taking place?
(A) At a museum
(B) At a parking garage
(C) At a conference center
(D) At a restaurant

5. What is the problem?
(A) An event has been canceled.
(B) An exit is blocked.
(C) An employee is late.
(D) A receipt has been lost.

6. What type of assistance does the speaker mention?
(A) Setting up audio equipment
(B) Arranging an automatic payment
(C) Scheduling a group tour
(D) Finding alternate parking

7. Where does the speaker work?
(A) At a bakery
(B) At a restaurant supply company
(C) At a catering facility
(D) At a chocolate factory

8. What is the speaker mainly discussing?
(A) A change to a safety regulation
(B) An upcoming advertising campaign
(C) A partnership with another company
(D) A required training course

9. What event is scheduled for June?
(A) An awards ceremony
(B) A food festival
(C) A job fair
(D) A cooking class

---

10. Where is the announcement most likely being made?
(A) On a train
(B) On an airplane
(C) In a museum
(D) In a department store

11. Why does the speaker apologize?
(A) An area is closed.
(B) A price has changed.
(C) Tickets have been sold out.
(D) There was a delay.

12. What does the speaker mean when she says, "we accept credit cards and cash"?
(A) A Web site contained an error.
(B) A new procedure is more convenient.
(C) The listeners must pay for food.
(D) The listeners must present identification.

13. According to the speaker, which season is approaching?
(A) Winter
(B) Spring
(C) Summer
(D) Fall

14. What does the speaker encourage the listeners to buy?
(A) Food
(B) Books
(C) Electronics
(D) Clothing

15. How can the listeners receive a discount?
(A) By choosing a specific brand
(B) By purchasing a certain number of items
(C) By using a promotional code
(D) By completing a customer survey

---

16. What field does the speaker most likely work in?
(A) Catering
(B) Construction
(C) Manufacturing
(D) Real Estate

17. What does the speaker imply when she says, "I need to update the clients on this by the end of the day"?
(A) She is unable to attend an event.
(B) She needs more current data.
(C) She disagrees with a supervisor's suggestion.
(D) She wants employees to decide quickly.

18. What will the company do for some employees?
(A) Provide a meal
(B) Sign a certificate
(C) Arrange transportation
(D) Schedule extra days off

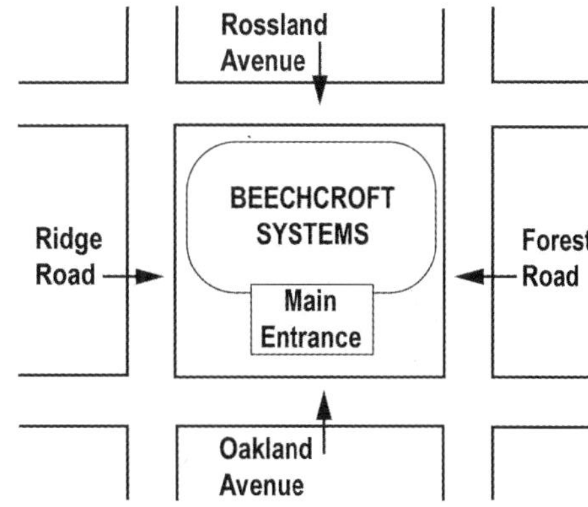

19. What will take place tomorrow morning?
(A) Some road construction
(B) A competition
(C) A street fair
(D) Employee training

20. Look at the graphic. Which street will be closed?
(A) Rossland Avenue
(B) Forest Road
(C) Oakland Avenue
(D) Ridge Road

21. What does the speaker suggest?
(A) Arriving at the office in the afternoon
(B) Participating in a company event
(C) Studying some materials
(D) Allowing extra time for travel

정답 및 해설 p. 239

UNIT 03 광고/방송

광고는 주로 업체나 행사 광고 또는 제품이나 서비스 광고 등이 출제되며, 방송은 비즈니스나 건강, 행사 등을 알리는 뉴스나 교통정보, 일기예보 등의 내용이 출제됩니다.

기출 문제풀이 전략

STEP 01 **질문 파악** 질문을 먼저 읽으면서 키워드를 파악하세요.

1 What business is being advertised?	2 What new service is now available?	3 How can listeners get a discount?
(A) A conference center (B) An office supply store (C) An electronics retailer (D) A delivery service	(A) Wireless Internet (B) 24-hour photocopying (C) Express shipping (D) An online reservation system	(A) By printing out a coupon (B) By becoming a member (C) By mentioning an advertisement (D) By booking four months in advance

STEP 02 **정답 고르기** 담화를 들으며 키워드의 단서를 찾아 정답을 고르세요.

업체 소개 **1** If you're looking for the best meeting facilities in town, then the Loma Vista Conference Center is for you.

세부 사항 We have a variety of large and small meeting rooms, and the most up-to-date electronic equipment. And **2** we've just made our copying services available twenty-four hours a day.

추가 정보 For more information and details on our rates, please call 555-1000. **3** Tell us you heard this advertisement and you'll get 10 percent off your next reservation.

1. 키워드: 광고 업체
회의 시설을 찾는다면 로마 비스타 컨퍼런스 센터가 있다고 한 말에 유의 → 정답은 (A)

2. 키워드: 이용 가능한 새로운 서비스
24시간 복사 서비스가 막 생겼다는 말에 유의 → 정답은 (B)

3. 키워드: 할인 받는 방법
이 광고를 들었다고 말하면 다음에 10퍼센트 할인해주겠다는 말에 유의 → 정답은 (C)

Paraphrasing Tell us you heard this advertisement → mentioning an advertisement

—
시내에서 가장 좋은 회의 시설을 찾고 있다면, 로마 비스타 컨퍼런스 센터가 있습니다. 저희는 크고 작은 다양한 회의실과 가장 최신의 전자 장비를 구비하고 있습니다. 또한 저희는 최근 저희 복사 서비스를 하루 24시간 제공하기 시작했습니다. 더 자세한 정보와 요금에 대한 상세한 내용을 알고 싶으시면 555-1000으로 전화하십시오. 이 광고를 들으셨다고 말씀해주시면 다음 예약에서 10퍼센트 할인해 드립니다.

정답 및 해설 p. 246

CHECK UP

Step 1 다음 3개의 질문을 읽으며 키워드에 표시하세요.

Step 2 담화를 들으며 정답의 단서를 찾아 정답을 고르세요

P4_23

1 What is the broadcast about?

(A) The opening of a new theater

(B) An upcoming performance

2 According to the speaker, what did Janice Leary do recently?

(A) She won an award.

(B) She directed a play.

3 What will listeners most likely hear next?

(A) An interview

(B) An advertisement

정답 및 해설 p. 247

기출로 익히는 패러프레이징

기출 문제에 등장했던 상황과 문장을 보고 정답이 어떤 식으로 패러프레이즈 되는지 확인해보세요.

담화 내 단서 포착	패러프레이징 된 정답 찾기
Even though Newport already has two bridges crossing the river, traffic often backs up during rush hour. 뉴포트에는 강을 건너는 다리가 이미 두 개 있음에도 불구하고, 출퇴근 시간에 종종 교통이 정체됩니다.	**Q. 문제점?** **A.** Traffic congestion 교통 체증
Tune in tomorrow for an interview with Arthur Chen, one of the youngest company presidents in the world. 내일 세계에서 가장 젊은 기업 대표인 아서 챈과의 인터뷰를 놓치지 마세요.	**Q. 아서 챈은 누구?** **A.** A business executive 회사 간부
The greatest advantage of this location is that it's directly adjacent to the main train station in town. 이 장소의 최대 장점은 시내의 가장 큰 기차역에 바로 인접해 있다는 것입니다.	**Q. 장소의 장점?** **A.** Public transportation is close by. 대중교통이 인근에 있다.
Unlike other similar programs, it's very user-friendly. 유사한 다른 프로그램들과 달리, 매우 사용자 친화적입니다.	**Q. 웹사이트를 권하는 이유?** **A.** It is easy to use. 사용하기 쉽다.

주제별 기출 어휘

P4_24

제품/서비스 광고

feature 특징, 특색
state-of-the-art 최신식의, 최첨단의
durable 내구성이 좋은
warranty 품질 보증서
affordable (가격이) 적당한
exclusive 독점적인
price reduction 가격 인하
promotional event 홍보 행사, 판촉 행사
annual sale 연례 할인 행사
special offer 특별 할인가
save 절약하다, 아끼다
complimentary 무료의
easy to carry 휴대가 쉬운
For further[more] information 정보가 더 필요하면
on sale 할인 중인
discount on ~에 대한 할인
regular price 정가
Don't miss (out) ~ ~을 놓치지 마세요

채용 광고

opportunity 기회
professional 직업적인, 전문적인; 전문가
talented 재능이 있는
full-time worker 정규직 사원
previous work experience 이전 근무 경력
contact information 연락처
submit 제출하다
on-the-job training 직장 내 훈련, 현장 연수
be offered positions for the company 회사에서 직책을 제안 받다

일기예보/교통 방송

low[high] pressure 저[고]기압
humidity 습도
temperature 온도, 기온
clear out 날씨가 개다[맑아지다]
tune in (라디오 주파수·TV 채널을) 맞추다, 청취하다
stay tuned 주파수[채널]를 고정하다
public transportation 대중교통
detour 우회 도로
traffic congestion 교통 체증(= traffic jam)
heavy traffic 교통 혼잡
backup 막힘, 정체
be stuck in traffic 교통 체증에 걸리다
take the highway 고속도로를 이용하다
take an alternate route 대체 도로를 이용하다

뉴스/토크쇼

radio broadcast 라디오 방송
business news 경제 뉴스
commercial break 광고 방송
merge 합병하다
acquire (회사를) 인수하다, 얻다
expand 확장하다
official 공무원, (회사의) 임원, 직원
release (제품을) 출시하다(= launch)
based on ~에 근거하여, ~을 기초로 하여
update on ~에 대한 최신 소식
프로그램명+coming up after~ ~다음 프로그램
I'm your host, ~ ~저는 진행자인 ~입니다

ETS 문제로 훈련하기

P4_25

문장 핵심 파악하기

먼저 질문의 키워드에 동그라미로 표시하며 질문 내용을 파악하세요. 담화를 듣고 주어진 질문에 답한 후 빈칸을 채워 보세요.

1 What will the business do this week?

(A) Extend its hours of operation (B) Offer free delivery

Summertime is outdoor time! And this week Zee's Sporting Goods is holding its ________ Summer Festival of ________. Come in for huge savings on all of your outdoor gear. You'll find all the ________ you need for camping, fishing, hiking, and more. And to ________ ________ ________ for you to take advantage of these savings, Zee's will ________ ________ ________ every evening this week.

2 What will take place for the first time at the event?

(A) Live music (B) Celebrity interviews

Thanks for listening to *The Morning Show* on 105.6. In local entertainment, the annual ________ ________ starts today at the Convention Center, with over one hundred exhibitors offering ________ ________ for your next vacation. And ________ ________ ________ ________ this year, the expo will ________ several ________ performances by ________ from around the world. For more information, visit the Convention Center Web site.

실전에 가깝게 훈련하기

질문의 키워드에 동그라미로 표시한 후, 담화를 듣고 주어진 질문에 답하세요.

3 According to the speaker, what is new this year?

(A) Longer operating hours
(B) Additional exercise facilities
(C) Reduced waiting times
(D) Special family rates

4 What does the speaker say about the parking area?

(A) It fills up quickly.
(B) It is near the entrance.
(C) It is free for customers.
(D) It is open 24 hours a day.

정답 및 해설 p. 247

ETS 실전 테스트

1. What kind of business is being advertised?
   (A) A conference center
   (B) A catering service
   (C) A travel agency
   (D) A real estate firm

2. What added benefit does the speaker mention?
   (A) Lower prices
   (B) Faster service
   (C) Internet booking
   (D) Free gift with purchase

3. What are listeners invited to do on Tuesday?
   (A) Enter a contest
   (B) Submit an application
   (C) Tour a home
   (D) Attend a presentation

---

4. What project will start tomorrow?
   (A) Roadwork on a highway
   (B) Construction of an airport
   (C) A bridge repair
   (D) A subway line extension

5. What are listeners advised to do?
   (A) Avoid rush hour
   (B) Take another road
   (C) Use public transportation
   (D) Call a hotline

6. How long is the traffic situation expected to last?
   (A) Two weeks
   (B) Three weeks
   (C) One month
   (D) Two months

7. What event is being advertised?
   (A) A nutrition conference
   (B) A book signing
   (C) A cooking class
   (D) A restaurant opening

8. According to the advertisement, who is Lori Webster?
   (A) An actress
   (B) A chef
   (C) A doctor
   (D) A store owner

9. What can listeners win?
   (A) A meal at a restaurant
   (B) A private consultation
   (C) A gift certificate
   (D) Tickets to a show

---

10. What is Gretchen Richter's area of expertise?
    (A) Online marketing
    (B) Customer service
    (C) Business accounting
    (D) Corporate law

11. What is Ever Flash?
    (A) A camera brand
    (B) A software program
    (C) An electronic reading device
    (D) An automatic payment method

12. Why does the speaker say, "Only her employees were allowed to try out the product before its release"?
    (A) To explain why some experts are doubtful about a product
    (B) To find out if some product testing had to be canceled
    (C) To ask how many people work for a company
    (D) To invite the audience to test some merchandise

13. According to the speaker, why is a festival being held?

(A) To collect monetary donations
(B) To recruit local volunteers
(C) To promote a music competition
(D) To introduce city politicians

14. What special event will happen at this year's festival?

(A) Restaurants will serve free samples.
(B) A contest winner will be announced.
(C) A celebrity will give a speech.
(D) Musicians will perform.

15. What does the speaker advise the listeners to do?

(A) Tell their friends
(B) Bring a résumé
(C) Sign up online
(D) Take public transportation

---

16. What topic does the radio show focus on?

(A) Finance
(B) Travel
(C) Cooking
(D) Health

17. What is the speaker mainly talking about?

(A) Feedback from some radio listeners
(B) Requirements to participate in a race
(C) Information about an invited guest
(D) Details of a new sales strategy

18. What does the speaker imply when he says, "Most authors don't do that"?

(A) He does not like a suggestion.
(B) He would like an explanation.
(C) The listeners have a special opportunity.
(D) The listeners should use a different writing style.

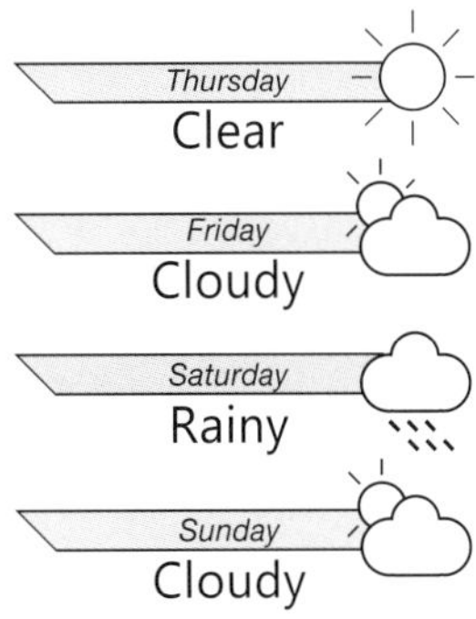

19. What does the speaker say about the recent weather?

(A) It was good during an event.
(B) It caused traffic delays.
(C) It was unusually cool.
(D) It set a record.

20. Look at the graphic. What day is a parade scheduled for?

(A) Thursday
(B) Friday
(C) Saturday
(D) Sunday

21. What will listeners hear about next?

(A) A summer festival
(B) Driving conditions
(C) A local business
(D) Health news

정답 및 해설 p. 249

UNIT 04 회의 발췌

다양한 직장 내의 회의에서 업무 관련 논의를 하거나 공지 사항을 전달하는 등의 내용이 출제됩니다.

기출 문제풀이 전략

P4_27

STEP 01 질문 파악 질문을 먼저 읽으면서 키워드를 파악하세요.

1 In what department does the speaker most likely work?
(A) Technology
(B) Advertising
(C) Customer service
(D) Training

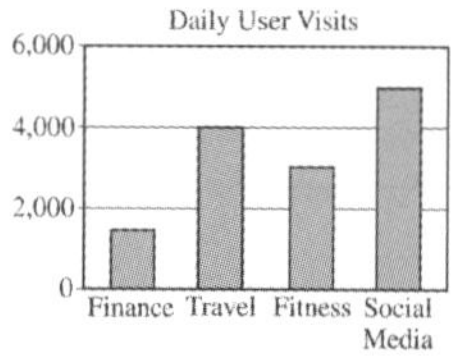

Daily User Visits

	Finance	Travel	Fitness	Social Media
Daily User Visits	(chart: approx. 1,500)	(approx. 4,000)	(approx. 3,000)	(approx. 5,000)

2 Look at the graphic. Which type of Web site does the speaker recommend?
(A) Finance (B) Travel
(C) Fitness (D) Social Media

3 What will the listeners most likely do next?
(A) Review a policy
(B) Research competitors
(C) Visit a Web site
(D) Discuss some designs

STEP 02 정답 고르기 담화를 들으며 키워드의 단서를 찾아 정답을 고르세요.

회의 주제 1 I'd like to start our meeting by discussing our advertising efforts for our new running shoes.
세부 사항 Take a look at the chart I passed out. It shows popular types of Web sites with advertising space for sale. Although social media sites get the most visits, I think we should go with the type that attracts our target audience. 2 Although these sites only have about 3,000 users per day, the people who visit those sites will likely be interested in our product.
주의/요청 사항 So 3 our next step is to plan the designs for those advertisements. Let's break into groups to discuss that.

1. 키워드: 화자의 부서
광고 활동에 대한 논의를 한다는 말에 유의 → 정답은 (B)

2. 키워드: 추천 웹사이트
하루 3천 명 정도가 방문하는 사이트라고 한 말에 유의 → 정답은 (C)

3. 키워드: 청자가 다음에 할 일
광고 디자인 기획을 위해 그룹으로 논의하자는 말에 유의 → 정답은 (D)

—
새 운동화 광고 활동에 대한 논의로 회의를 시작하겠습니다. 제가 나눠 드린 도표를 봐 주세요. 이 도표는 판매 광고 공간이 있는 인기 웹사이트 유형을 보여줍니다. 소셜 미디어 사이트가 가장 많은 방문객들이 찾는 곳이긴 하지만, 목표 대상을 끌어들이는 유형을 선택해야 한다고 생각합니다. 비록 이러한 사이트에는 일일 3천 명 정도의 사용자만 방문하지만, 해당 사이트 방문자들은 우리 제품에 관심을 가질 것입니다. 따라서 다음 단계는 그런 광고를 위한 디자인을 기획하는 것입니다. 그룹으로 나눠서 이 점에 대해 논의해 봅시다.

정답 및 해설 p. 257

CHECK UP

Step 1 다음 3개의 질문을 읽으며 키워드에 표시하세요.

Step 2 담화를 들으며 정답의 단서를 찾아 정답을 고르세요

P4_28

1 What was the company's goal?

(A) To lower production costs

(B) To create a more efficient product

2 Look at the graphic. Which phase of development is the company in?

(A) Financial planning

(B) Consumer testing

Project Timeline

	Jan	Feb	Mar	Apr
Financial planning	■			
Design		■		
Prototyping			■	
Consumer testing			■	■

3 What does the speaker ask the listeners to do?

(A) Attend a meeting

(B) Complete a survey

정답 및 해설 p. 257

기출로 익히는 패러프레이징

기출 문제에 등장했던 상황과 문장을 보고 정답이 어떤 식으로 패러프레이즈 되는지 확인해보세요.

담화 내 단서 포착	패러프레이징 된 정답 찾기
I'd like to take some time during this staff meeting to talk about the valuable information we received from the questionnaire. 이 직원회의에서 우리가 설문지에서 받은 귀중한 정보에 대해 이야기하는 시간을 갖고 싶습니다.	**Q. 담화의 주제?** **A.** Responses to a questionnaire 설문지에 대한 응답
You'll be required to use double-sided printing whenever you make copies. 복사할 때마다 양면 인쇄를 사용해야 합니다.	**Q. 청자들이 해야 할 일?** **A.** Change how they print documents 서류 인쇄 방식 변경
We'd like you to hand out fliers to all customers when they come into the store. 우리는 모든 고객들이 가게에 들어올 때 당신이 전단을 나눠주었으면 합니다.	**Q. 청자들이 요청 받는 일?** **A.** Pass out advertisements 광고지 배부
I'd like each of you to come up with a list that you can share with me when we meet individually next month to go over your job performance. 여러분 각자 다음 달 업무 평가를 위해 저와 개별적으로 만날 때 공유할 수 있는 목록을 제시하셨으면 합니다.	**Q. 청자들이 요청 받는 일?** **A.** Create a list 목록 작성

주제별 기출 어휘

영업 회의

upcoming launch 다가오는 출시
result in ~의 결과를 낳다
award-winning 상을 받은
satisfaction 만족
quality 품질
reduce 줄이다, 감소하다
fund 자금을 대다
client appreciation dinner 고객 감사 만찬
productivity 생산성
target customer group 목표 고객층
user-friendly 사용하기 쉬운
financial analyst 재무분석가
Studies have shown that ~ 연구 결과에 의하면
An analysis of the data shows that ~ 데이터 분석에 의하면
quarterly earnings 분기별 수익
conduct a market survey 시장조사를 하다
be aimed at ~을 목표로 하다
oversee a budget 예산을 감독하다
go over budget 예산을 초과하다
increase business 매출을 늘리다
customer records[information] 고객 정보
give[make] a presentation 발표하다
give a demonstration 시연하다

기타 회의

hand out 나눠주다(= pass out)
phase 단계
agenda 회의 의제
venue 장소
staff meeting 직원 회의
attendance 참석, 출석
performance 실적, 업적
go over ~을 검토하다(= review)
experienced employee 경력 있는 직원
take place 열리다, 개최되다
take part in ~에 참여하다
make it 참석하다
be responsible for ~에 대한 책임이 있다
on a daily basis 매일
presenter 발표자
work environment 작업 환경
performance review 인사고과
in preparation for ~에 대한 준비로
staffing 직원 채용
shareholder meeting 주주총회
new-employee information session 신입 직원 오리엔테이션
extended hours of operation 운영시간 연장
report an absence 결근계를 내다
relocate to ~로 이전하다
with that in mind 그것을 염두에 두고
give a heads-up 미리 알려주다
receive notification from ~로부터 통지를 받다
coordinator 조정자, 진행자
executive 중역(= director, officer, official)
the board of directors 이사회
following the lecture 강연 후에
keep up with ~에 뒤처지지 않게 따라가다
generate new ideas 새 아이디어를 내다
make improvements 개선하다
despite the short notice 갑작스런[촉박한] 통지에도 불구하고(= on such short notice)
adopt a new policy 새 정책을 채택하다

ETS 문제로 훈련하기

P4_30

문장 핵심 파악하기

먼저 질문의 키워드에 동그라미로 표시하며 질문 내용을 파악하세요. 담화를 듣고 주어진 질문에 답한 후 빈칸을 채워 보세요.

1 What problem does the speaker mention?

(A) A machine is not working. (B) A part was not delivered.

> Thanks for coming to this emergency ________ meeting, everyone. As you know, one of our labeling machines ________ ________ last night. We'll need to run the other labeling machine twenty-four hours a day to ________ ________ ________. So, I need some volunteers to work extra ________ for the rest of the week. Please let me know if you're interested in picking up another ________ as soon as possible.

2 What has changed about the Web site?

(A) A logo has been redesigned. (B) A new section has been added.

> If you've looked at the hospital Web site recently, you've probably noticed we've ________ ________ ________ about our medical staff. There's now a ________ ________ about your areas of specialization, and we want to upload ________ biographies and photos. So in the next few days, I'd like all of you to ________ a short paragraph about yourself. Once you've sent it to me, I'll put it online.

실전에 가깝게 훈련하기

질문의 키워드에 동그라미로 표시한 후, 담화를 듣고 주어진 질문에 답하세요.

3 What type of project is the speaker discussing?

(A) Remodeling a cafeteria
(B) Updating company policies
(C) Writing a new budget
(D) Developing nutrition guidelines

4 What does the speaker expect as a result of the project?

(A) More people will be hired.
(B) Employees will be promoted.
(C) Operating costs will decrease.
(D) Usage of a facility will increase.

ETS 실전 테스트

1. What is the speaker mainly talking about?
   (A) A new project
   (B) A company policy
   (C) Employee performance targets
   (D) Advantages of teamwork

2. According to the speaker, why do the listeners need to use an online application?
   (A) To view a list of clients
   (B) To manage group work
   (C) To report an absence
   (D) To upload an identification photo

3. What should the listeners do if an online application is not working?
   (A) Leave a message for a supervisor
   (B) Call technical support
   (C) Ask a colleague for assistance
   (D) Reboot a computer

---

4. What department does the speaker work in?
   (A) Accounting
   (B) Legal
   (C) Security
   (D) Human Resources

5. What does the speaker say the listeners need permission to do?
   (A) Meet in a designated area
   (B) Remove work documents
   (C) Bring guests into the building
   (D) Sign client contracts

6. What change does the speaker mention?
   (A) Doors will now be locked.
   (B) Management groups will be reorganized.
   (C) A cafeteria will offer breakfast.
   (D) A computer system will be upgraded.

7. What does Redwood Company produce?
   (A) Kitchen appliances
   (B) Furniture
   (C) Computers
   (D) Food products

8. What will listeners do today?
   (A) Set up their computers
   (B) Work with experienced staff members
   (C) Review company policies
   (D) Attend an industry conference

9. What are listeners encouraged to do during lunch?
   (A) Take a tour
   (B) Introduce themselves
   (C) Complete registration forms
   (D) Learn about job responsibilities

---

10. What event is the speaker discussing?
    (A) A conference
    (B) A merger
    (C) A client consultation
    (D) A department celebration

11. What does the speaker mean when he says, "This wasn't my idea"?
    (A) A coworker solved a problem.
    (B) A task should be reassigned.
    (C) Some results are surprising.
    (D) Some instructions were misunderstood.

12. According to the speaker, what will be completed by the end of the week?
    (A) A contract
    (B) A schedule
    (C) A research report
    (D) A budget forecast

13. Who most likely is the talk intended for?
(A) Sales representatives
(B) Recruitment agents
(C) Factory workers
(D) Department managers

14. What is the purpose of the talk?
(A) To present an award
(B) To announce a staff promotion
(C) To summarize some research
(D) To describe a policy

15. According to the speaker, what will Rob do?
(A) Review candidate résumés
(B) Record schedule information
(C) Provide copies of a budget report
(D) Prepare training materials

---

16. What is going to take place in June?
(A) A craft show
(B) A client dinner
(C) A company picnic
(D) A holiday party

17. Why does the speaker say, "we're not spending much on promotional items"?
(A) To complain about merchandise quality
(B) To thank some colleagues for their help
(C) To explain why a location is affordable
(D) To request budget revisions

18. What does the speaker ask Amal to do?
(A) Draft an activities schedule
(B) Hire some musical performers
(C) Post some flyers around a building
(D) Look up some catering options

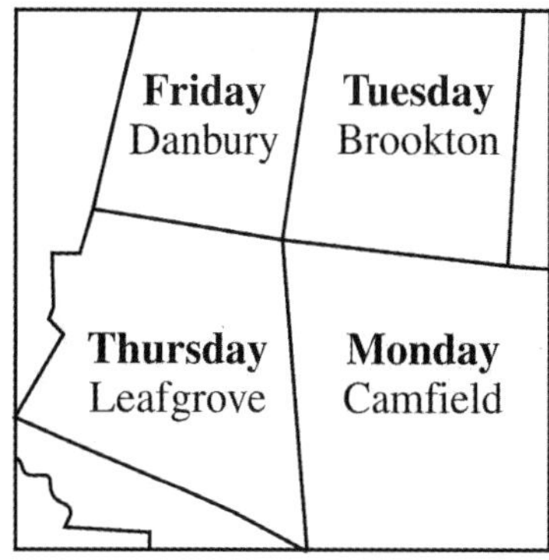

19. What industry does the speaker most likely work in?
(A) Recycling
(B) Education
(C) Agriculture
(D) Road maintenance

20. Look at the graphic. Which neighborhood will be affected by a schedule change?
(A) Danbury
(B) Brookton
(C) Camfield
(D) Leafgrove

21. What does the speaker hope to purchase?
(A) More comfortable uniforms
(B) Office furniture
(C) Better service vehicles
(D) Promotional materials

정답 및 해설 p. 260

UNIT 05 연설/강연/소개

연설이나 워크숍, 세미나 등에서의 강연, 그리고 행사나 방송 등에서 인물이나 제품을 소개하는 내용이 출제됩니다.

기출 문제풀이 전략

P4_32

질문 파악 질문을 먼저 읽으면서 키워드를 파악하세요.

1 Who is the speaker?	2 Why does the speaker say, "the old Wilson House will open as a museum"?	3 What can be found on a Web site?
(A) The owner of a travel agency (B) The mayor of the town (C) The organizer of a local festival (D) The host of a television program	(A) To recruit some volunteers (B) To correct a misunderstanding (C) To emphasize an accomplishment (D) To request that visitors follow some rules	(A) A donation form (B) A program schedule (C) Some photographs (D) The addresses of some properties

정답 고르기 담화를 들으며 키워드의 단서를 찾아 정답을 고르세요.

인물 소개 Good morning, 1 I'm Taro Harris, the host of *About Town* on Channel Six TV. Our special guest today is Simone Moreau.

세부 사항 She started a campaign to restore some of our city's historic landmarks. Last year, she met with the city council to request funding for repairs to several historic buildings. 2 One building that she's spent a lot of time and effort lobbying to restore is the Wilson House. And on Saturday, the old Wilson House will open as a museum! Let me tell you... the change to this property is remarkable.

추가 정보 3 You can see for yourself on our station's Web site—we've posted before and after photos of the house.

1. 키워드: 화자 신분

채널 6 TV의 진행자라는 말에 유의
→ 정답은 (D)

2. 키워드: 화자의 의도

복원을 위해 로비에 공을 들였다는 말에 유의 → 정답은 (C)

3. 키워드: 웹사이트에서 발견할 것

그 집의 전후 사진을 게시했다는 말에 유의 → 정답은 (C)

Paraphrasing before and after photos of the house → Some photographs

안녕하세요, 채널 6 TV의 〈어바웃 타운〉 진행자 타로 해리스입니다. 오늘 특별 손님은 시몬 모로입니다. 그녀는 우리 도시의 역사적인 명소들을 복원하기 위한 캠페인을 시작했는데요. 작년에 시의회를 만나 몇몇 역사적인 건물에 대한 수리 자금을 요청했습니다. 그녀가 복원하기 위해 로비에 많은 시간과 노력을 들인 건물은 바로 윌슨 하우스입니다. 그리고 토요일에, 유서 깊은 윌슨 하우스가 박물관으로 문을 열 것입니다!, 말씀드리자면, 이 건물의 변화는 놀랍습니다. 우리 방송국의 웹사이트에서 직접 보실 수 있습니다. 그 집의 전후 사진을 게시해두었습니다.

정답 및 해설 p. 267

CHECK UP

Step 1 다음 3개의 질문을 읽으며 키워드에 표시하세요.

Step 2 담화를 들으며 정답의 단서를 찾아 정답을 고르세요

P4_33

1 Who are the listeners?

(A) Business consultants

(B) Company managers

2 Why does the speaker say, "your colleagues are very capable"?

(A) To reassure the listeners

(B) To congratulate a team

3 What does the speaker remind the listeners to do?

(A) Stay within a budget

(B) Provide clear instructions

정답 및 해설 p. 268

기출로 익히는 패러프레이징

기출 문제에 등장했던 상황과 문장을 보고 정답이 어떤 식으로 패러프레이즈 되는지 확인해보세요.

담화 내 단서 포착	패러프레이징 된 정답 찾기
We're here tonight to celebrate the retirement of one of our most valued employees—Jessica Chavez. 우리는 오늘밤 우리의 가장 소중한 직원 중 한 명인 제시카 차베스의 은퇴를 축하하기 위해 여기 모였습니다.	**Q. 담화의 목적?** **A.** To say farewell to a colleague 동료에게 작별 인사하기
We'll be unveiling our newest compact car, the Spectrum S20, on October first. 10월 1일에 우리는 가장 최신 경차인 스펙트럼 S20을 선보입니다.	**Q. 10월 1일에 회사가 할 일?** **A.** Release a new product 신제품 출시
Finally, I need to thank the Bertram Association for their financial backing for my project. 마지막으로, 버트람 협회가 제 프로젝트에 재정 지원을 해 주신 데 대해 감사드려야겠습니다.	**Q. 버트람 협회를 언급한 이유?** **A.** They gave money to a project. 그들은 프로젝트에 자금을 댔다.
We'll hear from the mayor, Jim Sneed, about the thriving local business climate in our area. 짐 스니드 시장님으로부터 번성하는 우리 지역의 사업 환경에 대해 들어 보겠습니다.	**Q. 시장이 할 말?** **A.** The local economy 지역 경제

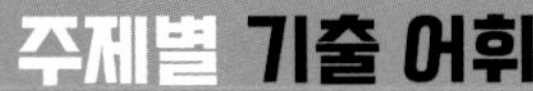

주제별 기출 어휘

연설/강연

subject 주제
give[make,deliver] a speech 연설하다
keep in mind 염두에 두다
business consultant 기업 컨설턴트
financial consultant 금융 컨설턴트
marketing analyst 마케팅 분석가
unveil 선보이다, 공개하다
financial backing 재정 지원
reputation 명성
preregister 사전 등록하다
turnout 참석자 수
in honor of ~을 기념하여
sign a document 서류에 서명하다
take action 조치를 취하다
paired with 짝을 지어
create a timeline 시간표를 만들다
consumer trends 소비자 경향
conference 컨퍼런스, 회의
convention 총회, 대회
reception (축하·환영) 연회
awards ceremony 시상식(= awards banquet)
retirement ceremony 퇴임식
anniversary 기념일
honor 명예, 영광; 경의를 표하다
thanks to ~ 덕분에
guest speaker 초대 연사
keynote speaker 기조 연설자
question and answer session 질의 응답 시간
donation 기부
recognize (공로를) 인정하다, 표창하다
devoted 헌신적인
charity 자선
welcome to+모임/장소 ~에 온 것을 환영하다
on behalf of ~을 대표해서
product demonstration 제품 시연
secure a budget 예산을 확보하다
in time for ~ 시간에 늦지 않게
give an update on ~에 대한 최신 정보를 제공하다
a few words of thanks 감사 인사 몇 마디
be pleased to ~하게 되어 기쁘다
be honored to ~하게 되어 영광이다
announce that ~이라는 것을 알리다
meet[achieve] a goal 목표를 달성하다
as a token of appreciation 감사의 표시로

인물 소개

special guest 특별 초대 손님(= featured guest)
expert 전문가(= specialist)
corporate 기업의
critic 비평가
stand out 두드러지다
come to the podium 연단으로 나오다
contribute 공헌하다, 기여하다
congratulate 축하하다
celebrate 축하하다, 기념하다
employee of the year 올해의 직원
give a round of applause 박수를 보내다
present A to B B에게 A를 주다[수여하다]
express thanks for ~에 대해 감사를 표하다
win an award 상을 받다
~ will be introduced ~이 소개될 예정이다
~ will be promoted ~이 승진될 예정이다
I'd like to introduce you to ~
여러분에게 ~을 소개하고 싶습니다

ETS 문제로 훈련하기

P4_35

STEP 01 문장 핵심 파악하기

먼저 질문의 키워드에 동그라미로 표시하며 질문 내용을 파악하세요. 담화를 듣고 주어진 질문에 답한 후 빈칸을 채워 보세요.

1 What is the purpose of the talk?

(A) To launch a new product (B) To honor an employee

Good evening, everyone, and thank you for coming to our annual ________ ________. As you know, I'm Sandra Dayton, president of Wonder Toys. I am very pleased to announce this year's ________ ________ ________ ________—Michael Tolliver. Mr. Tolliver ________ ________ ________ Wonder Toys for ten years, and in all of those ten years he has been one of our ________ ________. So, Mr. Tolliver, please come to the podium to ________ ________ ________.

2 What does the speaker say about his regional office?

(A) They increased sales. (B) They hired new employees.

Hello, everyone. ________ ________ ________ coming to the picnic on this beautiful Saturday afternoon. This is the company's way of saying thank you for all of your ________ ________. This quarter, our electronic equipment sales ________ ________ ________ among all the regional offices, which is up from fifth place ________ ________. We hope to continue ________ our sales of electronics. I hope you'll take the ________ to relax and enjoy the rest of the day.

STEP 02 실전에 가깝게 훈련하기

질문의 키워드에 동그라미로 표시한 후, 담화를 듣고 주어진 질문에 답하세요.

3 What does the speaker recommend?

(A) Creating a list
(B) Doing research
(C) Having alternate plans
(D) Learning from mentors

4 What are the listeners doing next week?

(A) Going on a trip
(B) Purchasing supplies
(C) Taking photographs
(D) Selecting a venue

정답 및 해설 p. 269

ETS 실전 테스트

1. Where is the speech most likely taking place?
(A) At an employee orientation
(B) At an awards ceremony
(C) At a job interview
(D) At a sales conference

2. In what field does the speaker work?
(A) Finance
(B) Medicine
(C) Engineering
(D) Computers

3. How long has the speaker worked in this field?
(A) Two years
(B) Three years
(C) Twelve years
(D) Twenty years

---

4. What topic does the television show usually discuss?
(A) Weekend entertainment
(B) The history of a city
(C) The opening of a local restaurant
(D) Political updates

5. Who is George Patel?
(A) A tour guide
(B) A city official
(C) An author
(D) A food critic

6. How can viewers win a prize?
(A) By registering on the station's Web site
(B) By becoming a sponsor
(C) By attending a special event
(D) By answering questions correctly

7. What is the topic of the talk?
(A) A construction project
(B) A community festival
(C) An upcoming election
(D) A sports competition

8. What does the speaker mean when he says, "our road and transit systems are overcrowded"?
(A) He is sorry for being late.
(B) He wants to move to another city.
(C) He disagrees with a proposal.
(D) He thinks a budget should be increased.

9. What does the speaker ask the listeners to do?
(A) Visit a Web site
(B) Sign a document
(C) Write a letter
(D) Reschedule an event

---

10. What type of work are the listeners being trained to do?
(A) Technology troubleshooting
(B) Literary translation
(C) Customer service
(D) Subscription sales

11. What are the listeners asked to do by February 12?
(A) Submit some receipts
(B) Read a handbook
(C) Register for a convention
(D) Prepare a timeline

12. According to the speaker, what will happen at the end of the program?
(A) Participants will give presentations.
(B) Winners will be announced.
(C) A hiring committee will meet.
(D) A party will be held.

13. What is the focus of the conference?
(A) Online advertising
(B) Medical technology
(C) Tourism
(D) Real estate

14. What does the speaker imply when he says, "I hope you brought the right shoes"?
(A) Participants will need to walk a lot.
(B) Formal wear is required.
(C) Rain is expected.
(D) There will not be time to change clothes.

15. What does the speaker say is difficult?
(A) Finding a venue
(B) Keeping a speech short
(C) Leaving a position
(D) Selling houses

---

16. What is the main purpose of this talk?
(A) To announce the opening of a store
(B) To introduce a new employee
(C) To describe some products
(D) To discuss the results of a research study

17. What type of goods does the speaker's company sell?
(A) Frozen foods
(B) Bathroom fixtures
(C) Women's clothing
(D) Kitchen appliances

18. What does the company want Ms. Villa to do?
(A) Design new kitchen appliances
(B) Open an overseas office
(C) Translate its company manuals
(D) Help it to understand customer Preferences

19. What does the speaker remind the listeners to do?
(A) Sign up for e-mail updates
(B) Pick up a handout
(C) Fill out a contact form
(D) Submit some feedback

20. Look at the graphic. Which tool will the listeners learn to use first?
(A) Tool 1
(B) Tool 2
(C) Tool 3
(D) Tool 4

21. What does the speaker say she is going to do next?
(A) Take some photographs
(B) Provide individual assistance
(C) Show an informational video
(D) Introduce a guest speaker

정답 및 해설 p. 270

UNIT 06 관광·견학/설명

관광지나 역사적 장소 등에서의 관광 안내나 공장, 농장 등의 특정 시설 견학 관련 담화, 그리고 사내 특정 행사에 대한 설명이나 시설, 기기 등의 사용법 및 절차 등을 설명하는 담화가 출제됩니다.

기출 문제풀이 전략

P4_37

STEP 01 **질문 파악** 질문을 먼저 읽으면서 키워드를 파악하세요.

1 Where is the talk taking place?	2 What are listeners given?	3 What does the speaker remind listeners to do?
(A) In a laboratory (B) In a coffee shop (C) In a factory (D) In a grocery store	(A) Product samples (B) Some photographs (C) An ingredient list (D) A site map	(A) Retrieve their belongings (B) Return their visitor passes (C) Sign a security form (D) Wear safety gear

STEP 02 **정답 고르기** 담화를 들으며 키워드의 단서를 찾아 정답을 고르세요.

행사/주제 소개 1 Our tour ends here, in the packaging area—the final step for our gourmet chocolates.

세부 사항 After all of the ingredients have been mixed, shaped, and cooled, the chocolates come here to be put in retail boxes and sent to stores. 2 I've got small boxes here for each of you—they contain some of our most popular chocolates, free of charge. Please spend some time here taking pictures and enjoying your gift.

주의/추가 정보 And before you exit the factory, 3 please remember to stop by the security desk and return your visitor's pass.

1. 키워드: 담화 장소

초콜릿의 마지막 단계, 포장 구역이라는 말에 유의 → 정답은 (C)

2. 키워드: 청자들이 받는 것

초콜릿을 무료로 준다는 말에 유의 → 정답은 (A)

Paraphrasing some of our most popular chocolates, free of charge → Product samples

3. 키워드: 청자들에게 상기한 일

방문자 출입증을 반납하라는 말에 유의 → 정답은 (B)

우리 투어는 여기 포장 구역에서 끝납니다. 우리의 맛있는 고급 초콜릿의 마지막 단계죠. 모든 재료를 섞고, 모양을 내고, 식힌 후에, 초콜릿은 여기로 와서 소매용 상자에 넣어 가게로 배송됩니다. 여기 여러분 한 분 한 분께 드릴 작은 상자들이 있습니다. 가장 인기 있는 초콜릿 몇 개가 무료로 들어 있어요. 여기서 사진도 찍고 선물도 즐기면서 시간을 보내세요. 그리고 공장을 떠나기 전에 보안 데스크에 들러 방문자 출입증을 꼭 반납해주세요.

정답 및 해설 p. 278

CHECK UP

Step 1 다음 3개의 질문을 읽으며 키워드에 표시하세요.

Step 2 담화를 들으며 정답의 단서를 찾아 정답을 고르세요

P4_38

1 Where is the talk most likely taking place?

(A) At a factory

(B) At a culinary school

2 What does the speaker describe?

(A) A product history

(B) A manufacturing process

3 What does the speaker ask some of the listeners to do?

(A) Turn off their phones

(B) Wear special clothing

정답 및 해설 p. 278

기출로 익히는 패러프레이징

기출 문제에 등장했던 상황과 문장을 보고 정답이 어떤 식으로 패러프레이즈 되는지 확인해보세요.

담화 내 단서 포착	패러프레이징 된 정답 찾기
We need a few volunteers to give other hikers a ride from the main parking area. 우리는 메인 주차장에서 다른 등산객들을 태워줄 자원 봉사자들이 몇 명 필요합니다.	**Q. 자원봉사자가 필요한 이유?** **A.** To provide transportation 교통편 제공
We do have a very good restaurant on the second floor of the museum. 박물관 2층에 아주 훌륭한 식당이 있습니다.	**Q. 청자들에게 추천하는 것?** **A.** A place to eat 먹을 곳
The rock floor is wet and slippery, so please watch your step. 바위 바닥이 젖어서 미끄러우니 조심해서 걸으시기 바랍니다.	**Q. 화자가 권하는 것?** **A.** Walking carefully 조심해서 걷기
Let's look first at the large piece of pottery that stands in the center of the room. 방 중앙에 놓여 있는 큰 도자기를 먼저 봅시다.	**Q. 견학자들이 다음에 할 일?** **A.** Look at art work 미술품 보기

주제별 기출 어휘

설명

instruction 지시, 설명
new hires 신입 직원들
focus group 포커스 그룹, 표적 집단
innovation 혁신
summarize 요약하다
specialize in ~을 전문으로 하다
strategy 전략
quality control 품질 관리
provide transportation 교통편을 제공하다
complete a survey 설문조사를 완료하다
valued customers 소중한 고객들
preference 선호(도)
attend an exposition 전시회에 참석하다
refrain from ~을 삼가다
sales strategy 영업 전략
concentrate on ~에 집중하다
attract buyers 구매자들의 마음을 끌다
questionnaire 설문지
be assigned to + 명사 ~에 지정되다, 배정 받다
assemble products 제품을 조립하다
conduct research 연구하다
make a final decision 최종 결정을 내리다
hiring process 채용 과정
give details 상세히 설명하다
give directions 지시 사항을 알려주다
promotional video 홍보 영상
point out an error 오류를 지적하다
mandatory training session 의무 교육 과정

관광/견학

go sightseeing 관광을 가다
tourist attraction 관광 명소
lead a tour 관광[견학]을 인솔하다
be famous for ~으로 유명하다
be crowded with ~으로 붐비다
destination 목적지
explore 둘러보다
distinctive 독특한, 특유의
spectacular 장관을 이루는, 볼 만한
laboratory 연구실, 실험실
free of charge 무료로
move on to ~로 이동하다
a tour of a factory 공장 견학
exit a factory 공장에서 나가다
visitor's pass 방문자 출입증
safety procedures 안전 규정[절차]
safety gear 안전 장치
manufacturing process 제조 과정
protective 보호하는, 보호용의
found 설립하다(= establish)
stay with the group 무리와 함께 있다
feel free to 편하게 ~하다, 주저 없이 ~하다
Watch your step. 조심하세요.(= Walk carefully.)
audio recording 음성 녹음
adjust the volume 볼륨을 조절하다
open to the public 대중에게 개방하다
preserve 보존하다
direct one's attention to the right 오른쪽으로 주의를 돌리다
Renovations are underway. 수리가 진행 중이다.
head towards ~로 향하다
special exhibit 특별 전시회
souvenir shop 기념품 가게
be not permitted[allowed] 허용되지 않다
be welcome to 기꺼이 ~해도 좋다
The tour will last + 시간. 관광은 (시간이) ~ 걸립니다.

ETS 문제로 훈련하기

P4_40

STEP 01

문장 핵심 파악하기

먼저 질문의 키워드에 동그라미로 표시하며 질문 내용을 파악하세요. 담화를 듣고 주어진 질문에 답한 후 빈칸을 채워 보세요.

1 What does the speaker remind the listeners to do?

(A) Pick up a map (B) Stay with the group

Good afternoon and welcome to this ________ ________ of Brownsville. As you may know, Brownsville is significant for the many buildings ________ from the time when it was ________. I'll be telling you a little about these ________ ________ as we tour the downtown area. This is a ________ ________, so please be sure to ________ ________ so you can hear me clearly.

2 What is the program intended to do?

(A) Improve safety (B) Involve more people

Good morning, and thanks for ________ ________ for our new, three-day adventure program here at Greentop Park. I'm Ken Sato, the head ranger. The ________ of our program is to get more people ________ in various ________ ________ available in the park, so it's great to see so many of you here for the first activity. Today we'll be ________ ________ Greentop Mountain, and rangers will be coming along to ________ the group up the trail.

STEP 02

실전에 가깝게 훈련하기

질문의 키워드에 동그라미로 표시한 후, 담화를 듣고 주어진 질문에 답하세요.

3 Why does the speaker say, "most people spend less than a minute on each question"?

(A) To express concern
(B) To explain why a survey was changed
(C) To congratulate the listeners
(D) To reassure the listeners

4 What does the speaker say will be provided later?

(A) A payment
(B) A meal
(C) A certificate
(D) A report

정답 및 해설 p. 279

ETS 실전 테스트

1. Where does the talk probably take place?
   (A) At a photography studio
   (B) At a restaurant
   (C) At a train station
   (D) At a clothing store

2. What does the speaker say employees will do first?
   (A) Go to lunch
   (B) Complete some forms
   (C) Put items on shelves
   (D) Try on a uniform

3. When does the speaker say employees can leave today?
   (A) At 2 P.M.
   (B) At 3 P.M.
   (C) At 5:30 P.M.
   (D) At 8:30 P.M.

---

4. Where does the talk take place?
   (A) At a farm
   (B) At a factory
   (C) At a cooking school
   (D) At a food market

5. What does the speaker encourage the listeners to do?
   (A) Take photographs
   (B) Ask questions
   (C) Select some fruit
   (D) Sign up for a newsletter

6. According to the speaker, what will happen at the end of the tour?
   (A) A shuttle bus will arrive.
   (B) A survey will be distributed.
   (C) A meal will be served.
   (D) A special guest will speak.

7. What does the speaker's company manufacture?
   (A) Furniture
   (B) Clothing
   (C) Cosmetics
   (D) Bags

8. What is the company planning to do?
   (A) Change a logo
   (B) Attend an exposition
   (C) Open a branch store
   (D) Offer new merchandise

9. What will the listeners most likely do next?
   (A) Participate in a discussion
   (B) Take notes
   (C) Complete an online survey
   (D) Sign up for an interview

---

10. Where does the speaker most likely work?
    (A) At a photography studio
    (B) At a bookstore
    (C) At a gardening center
    (D) At an art museum

11. What does the speaker imply when she says, "I get asked this question a lot"?
    (A) She doesn't know the answer.
    (B) She wants people to refrain from asking this question.
    (C) She knows people are curious.
    (D) She is the only person who can provide an answer.

12. What is *Blanchard's Gaze*?
    (A) A song
    (B) A book
    (C) A painting
    (D) A poem

13. What is the main purpose of the talk?
(A) To give directions to a visitors' center
(B) To describe a nature tour
(C) To introduce a guest speaker
(D) To explain the history of a national park

14. What are listeners invited to do?
(A) Ask questions
(B) Bring along food
(C) Take photographs
(D) Swim in some areas

15. What does the speaker recommend?
(A) Walking carefully
(B) Taking notes
(C) Drinking a lot of water
(D) Wearing comfortable shoes

---

16. Who most likely are the listeners?
(A) Retail salespeople
(B) Fitness coaches
(C) Factory workers
(D) Software engineers

17. According to the speaker, what will the listeners do on Friday?
(A) They will be meeting a new executive.
(B) They will attend a training session.
(C) They will go to a staff appreciation event.
(D) They will be filmed for a promotional video.

18. Why does the speaker say, "some tables and chairs have been set up on the patio"?
(A) To express surprise
(B) To correct a misunderstanding
(C) To point out an error
(D) To make a suggestion

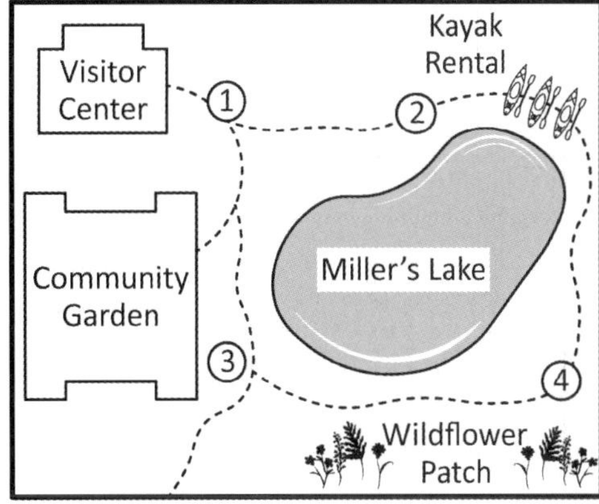

19. Why does the speaker thank the listeners?
(A) For volunteering to do some work
(B) For donating some money
(C) For bringing some refreshments
(D) For leading a tour

20. What happened recently?
(A) Some trees were planted.
(B) A visitor center was built.
(C) A storm caused some damage.
(D) There was a safety inspection.

21. Look at the graphic. Where will the listeners go next?
(A) To area 1
(B) To area 2
(C) To area 3
(D) To area 4

정답 및 해설 p. 281

PART 4

Directions: You will hear some talks given by a single speaker. You will be asked to answer three questions about what the speaker says in each talk. Select the best response to each question and mark the letter (A), (B), (C), or (D) on your answer sheet. The talks will not be printed in your test book and will be spoken only one time.

71. What kind of business is being advertised?
(A) A bank
(B) A law office
(C) An accounting firm
(D) An insurance agency

72. What has the business recently received?
(A) A grant
(B) An award
(C) A government contract
(D) A construction permit

73. According to the speaker, what can new customers receive in September?
(A) A complimentary tote bag
(B) Access to informational videos
(C) A free consultation
(D) An extended service agreement

74. What is the purpose of the announcement?
(A) To provide information about train service
(B) To suggest alternate travel arrangements
(C) To tell passengers to check a departure board
(D) To request that a passenger come to the service desk

75. What does the speaker remind the listeners to do?
(A) Remain in their seats
(B) Show their tickets
(C) Store their luggage
(D) Listen for station alerts

76. Why does the speaker apologize?
(A) A dining car is closed.
(B) Downstairs seating is full.
(C) Refunds will not be issued.
(D) Wi-Fi service is not working.

77. What is the main purpose of the message?
(A) To announce an art contest
(B) To confirm that the museum is open
(C) To advertise discounted tickets
(D) To explain why an exhibit has been canceled

78. What can the listeners find by following some signs?
(A) Extra seating
(B) A parking area
(C) An information booth
(D) A temporary entrance

79. How can the listeners help?
(A) By signing a petition
(B) By writing a letter
(C) By making a donation
(D) By placing an order

---

80. Who was a clothing item designed for?
(A) Gardeners
(B) Actors
(C) Athletes
(D) Doctors

81. What does the speaker imply when she says, "I haven't seen anything like this before"?
(A) She may be interested in a business deal.
(B) She thinks an employee deserves an award.
(C) She will need to consult a manual.
(D) She is happy with the success of a product.

82. Why is the speaker traveling to Chicago?
(A) To speak at a conference
(B) To take a city tour
(C) To attend a wedding
(D) To meet with some clients

---

83. What does Howell produce?
(A) Backpacks
(B) Health food
(C) Exercise machines
(D) Athletic clothing

84. What incentive is provided to encourage participation?
(A) Participants will be allowed to keep a product sample.
(B) Participants will be entered into a raffle for a prize.
(C) Participants will receive a gift certificate.
(D) Participants will be featured in a documentary film.

85. According to the speaker, who cannot participate?
(A) Howell employees
(B) Previous product testers
(C) People living abroad
(D) Professional athletes

---

86. What does the speaker say happened last year?
(A) A budget was exceeded.
(B) An award was received.
(C) Employees earned certifications.
(D) Profits increased.

87. What does the speaker imply when he says, "there aren't any other restaurants nearby"?
(A) A restaurant address is incorrect.
(B) A meeting should be canceled.
(C) A new restaurant will be successful.
(D) A menu should not be changed.

88. What will the listeners do next?
(A) Watch a commercial
(B) Write some reports
(C) Try some food samples
(D) Book a flight

GO ON TO THE NEXT PAGE

89. What are the listeners participating in?

(A) An audition
(B) A job fair
(C) A focus group
(D) A trade show

90. What does the speaker tell the listeners to do at the end of the session?

(A) Fill out a questionnaire
(B) Refer a friend
(C) Submit a résumé
(D) Pick up a newsletter

91. What will the listeners receive?

(A) A free membership
(B) Refreshments
(C) Newspaper subscriptions
(D) Gift cards

92. What does the business sell?

(A) Vehicle accessories
(B) Custom-made furniture
(C) Office supplies
(D) Fitness equipment

93. What does the speaker say about the clear floor mats?

(A) They are a top-selling item.
(B) They have gone up in price.
(C) They are no longer being made.
(D) They are available in several sizes.

94. What does the speaker imply when he says, "Omar, aren't you working every day next week"?

(A) Omar should correct a work schedule.
(B) Omar should request a promotion.
(C) Omar should consider taking a vacation.
(D) Omar should volunteer for a special task.

Sherbrooke	20 miles
Springfield	35 miles
Woodbridge	40 miles
Kanata	55 miles

95. Why does the speaker say he is calling?
(A) To request information about a client
(B) To explain a late arrival
(C) To reschedule an event
(D) To discuss transportation options

96. Look at the graphic. Which city is the speaker going to?
(A) Sherbrooke
(B) Springfield
(C) Woodbridge
(D) Kanata

97. What will the speaker most likely do next?
(A) Call technical support
(B) Purchase a ticket
(C) Ask for directions
(D) Send some slides

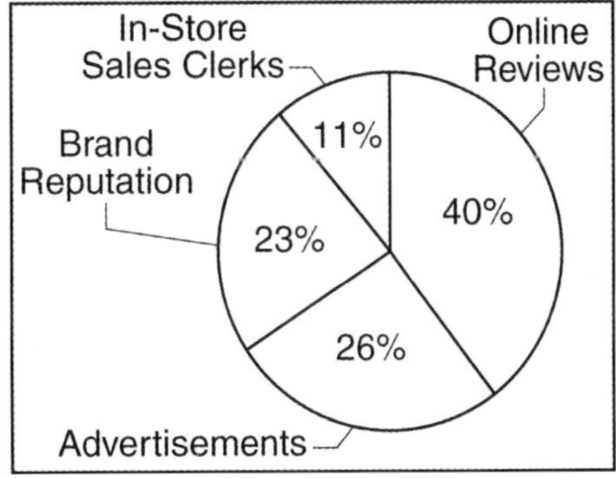

98. What product is the speaker discussing?
(A) A vacuum cleaner
(B) A washing machine
(C) A water heater
(D) A refrigerator

99. According to the speaker, how is their product better than their competitors' products?
(A) It is less expensive.
(B) It lasts longer.
(C) It is less noisy.
(D) It works faster.

100. Look at the graphic. Which factor does the speaker say the company should focus on?
(A) Online Reviews
(B) Advertisements
(C) Brand Reputation
(D) In-Store Sales Clerks

ETS FINAL TEST

ETS 실전 모의고사

LISTENING TEST

In the Listening test, you will be asked to demonstrate how well you understand spoken English. The entire Listening test will last approximately 45 minutes. There are four parts, and directions are given for each part. You must mark your answers on the separate answer sheet. Do not write your answers in your test book.

PART 1

Directions: For each question in this part, you will hear four statements about a picture in your test book. When you hear the statements, you must select the one statement that best describes what you see in the picture. Then find the number of the question on your answer sheet and mark your answer. The statements will not be printed in your test book and will be spoken only one time.

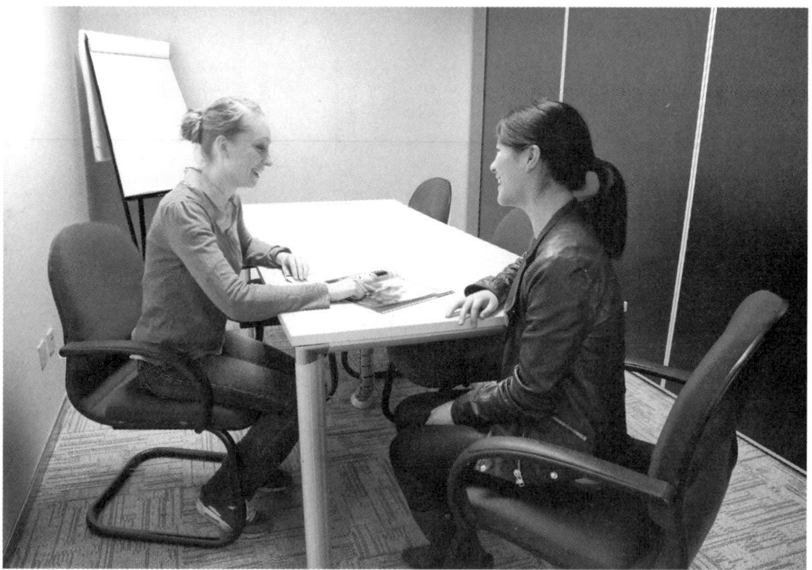

Statement (C), "They're sitting at a table," is the best description of the picture, so you should select answer (C) and mark it on your answer sheet.

1.

2.

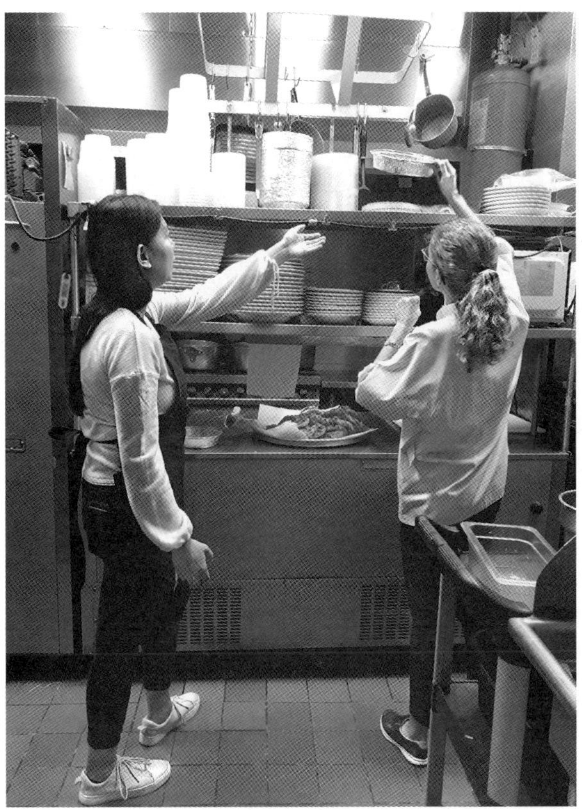

GO ON TO THE NEXT PAGE

3.

4.

5.

6.

ETS 실전 모의고사

GO ON TO THE NEXT PAGE

PART 2

Directions: You will hear a question or statement and three responses spoken in English. They will not be printed in your test book and will be spoken only one time. Select the best response to the question or statement and mark the letter (A), (B), or (C) on your answer sheet.

7. Mark your answer on your answer sheet.

8. Mark your answer on your answer sheet.

9. Mark your answer on your answer sheet.

10. Mark your answer on your answer sheet.

11. Mark your answer on your answer sheet.

12. Mark your answer on your answer sheet.

13. Mark your answer on your answer sheet.

14. Mark your answer on your answer sheet.

15. Mark your answer on your answer sheet.

16. Mark your answer on your answer sheet.

17. Mark your answer on your answer sheet.

18. Mark your answer on your answer sheet.

19. Mark your answer on your answer sheet.

20. Mark your answer on your answer sheet.

21. Mark your answer on your answer sheet.

22. Mark your answer on your answer sheet.

23. Mark your answer on your answer sheet.

24. Mark your answer on your answer sheet.

25. Mark your answer on your answer sheet.

26. Mark your answer on your answer sheet.

27. Mark your answer on your answer sheet.

28. Mark your answer on your answer sheet.

29. Mark your answer on your answer sheet.

30. Mark your answer on your answer sheet.

31. Mark your answer on your answer sheet.

PART 3

Directions: You will hear some conversations between two or more people. You will be asked to answer three questions about what the speakers say in each conversation. Select the best response to each question and mark the letter (A), (B), (C), or (D) on your answer sheet. The conversations will not be printed in your test book and will be spoken only one time.

32. Who most likely are the speakers?
(A) Sales associates
(B) IT technicians
(C) Company executives
(D) Accounting staff

33. Why is a director unavailable?
(A) She is at a conference.
(B) She is out for lunch.
(C) She is in a board meeting.
(D) She is on vacation.

34. What does the man say he will do next?
(A) Call a staff member
(B) Submit a work request
(C) Cancel a reservation
(D) Consult a manual

---

35. What kind of project is the woman's team working on?
(A) Creating a new product
(B) Forming a hiring committee
(C) Improving a manufacturing process
(D) Providing technical support

36. What does the woman say about a keyboard?
(A) It should be delivered soon.
(B) It can be washed.
(C) It is being discontinued.
(D) It needs to be repaired.

37. What does the woman show the man?
(A) Some sales figures
(B) Some research results
(C) A product sketch
(D) An instruction manual

---

38. Who most likely is the woman?
(A) A landscaper
(B) An architect
(C) An apartment manager
(D) An appliance salesperson

39. Why does the man say, "I'm expecting guests tomorrow"?
(A) To explain a change to his work schedule
(B) To emphasize the urgency of a request
(C) To apologize for an inconvenience
(D) To share some good news

40. What does the man ask about?
(A) A service fee
(B) A confirmation code
(C) Business hours
(D) Parking regulations

---

41. What type of job is the woman interviewing for?
(A) Digital film editor
(B) Graphic designer
(C) Repair technician
(D) Software developer

42. What does the woman say she enjoys about her current job?
(A) Conducting trainings
(B) Traveling frequently
(C) Meeting with clients
(D) Attending conferences

43. Where will the speakers go next?
(A) To a warehouse
(B) To a computer lab
(C) To a security office
(D) To a maintenance department

GO ON TO THE NEXT PAGE →

44. Who most likely is the woman?

(A) An event organizer
(B) A photographer
(C) A job recruiter
(D) A journalist

45. What problem does the man mention?

(A) He does not have much experience.
(B) He is busy with a special project.
(C) Some travel expenses are too high.
(D) A topic has not been chosen yet.

46. What does the woman say some information will be used for?

(A) Completing a résumé
(B) Updating a Web site
(C) Reserving some accommodations
(D) Preparing for an interview

---

47. Which industry do the speakers most likely work in?

(A) Health care
(B) Publishing
(C) Technology
(D) Accounting

48. Why is the woman unsure about the man's idea?

(A) Special skills are required.
(B) Other tasks should be a priority.
(C) A facility's machinery is too old.
(D) A manager's permission is needed.

49. What does the man offer to do?

(A) Schedule a meeting
(B) Collect some feedback
(C) Draft some articles
(D) Work an extra shift

---

50. What is the man shopping for?

(A) A mobile phone
(B) A business suit
(C) A suitcase
(D) A desk

51. What does the man say he is doing next month?

(A) Attending a conference
(B) Starting a new job
(C) Going on vacation
(D) Moving to a new apartment

52. What product feature does Chiharu mention?

(A) The material
(B) The size
(C) A battery
(D) A lock

---

53. Where do the speakers work?

(A) At a car dealership
(B) At a trucking company
(C) At an airline
(D) At a taxi service

54. What is the woman's opinion about upgrading some equipment?

(A) It will be difficult to find replacement parts.
(B) It will cost too much money.
(C) It will take too long to do.
(D) It will require too much training.

55. What does the man say he will do?

(A) Research competitors' strategies
(B) Plan a social gathering
(C) Contact some suppliers
(D) Review a budget report

---

56. Who is George Silva?
(A) A travel agent
(B) A store owner
(C) A news reporter
(D) A shop assistant

57. What did the speakers do last week?
(A) They started making candles in a workshop.
(B) They visited friends in New York.
(C) They sold their products at an outdoor market.
(D) They designed a Web site for their business.

58. What does the woman mean when she says, "I've already started making phone calls"?
(A) She does not want her calls to be interrupted.
(B) She has decided to hire another worker.
(C) She might change some travel plans.
(D) She is determined to find a solution.

---

59. What does the man say the farm stand customers like?
(A) Personal interaction
(B) Vegetarian recipes
(C) Seasonal discounts
(D) Unusual merchandise

60. How will the speakers prepare for next year?
(A) By renovating the farm stand
(B) By planting cover crops
(C) By purchasing additional farmland
(D) By improving an irrigation system

61. What will the woman do in the afternoon?
(A) Look at a catalog
(B) Check a storage area
(C) Compare prices
(D) Create a checklist

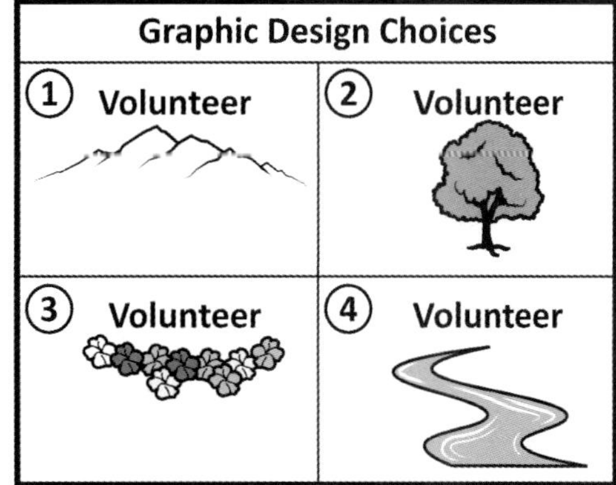

62. Where do the speakers most likely work?
(A) At an employment agency
(B) At a theater company
(C) At a parks department
(D) At a public library

63. Look at the graphic. Which design will the speakers use?
(A) Choice 1
(B) Choice 2
(C) Choice 3
(D) Choice 4

64. What does the woman say she will do next?
(A) Take some photographs
(B) Visit a park
(C) Contact some volunteers
(D) Place an order

GO ON TO THE NEXT PAGE

Best-Selling Fiction	
Xia Chen	*The Traitor's Granddaughter*
Nadia Aziz	*Life in Outer Space*
Alicia Garcia	*Exploring Australian Forests*
Susan Rosetti	*Amused and Confused*

65. Look at the graphic. Which book did the woman write?

(A) *The Traitor's Granddaughter*
(B) *Life in Outer Space*
(C) *Exploring Australian Forests*
(D) *Amused and Confused*

66. Who is the man?

(A) A book reviewer
(B) A literary agent
(C) A bookstore owner
(D) A publishing house executive

67. What does the woman agree to do?

(A) Sign copies of her book
(B) Modify a contract
(C) Give a speech
(D) Participate in an interview

Options
1. Volume
2. Share Screen
3. Settings
4. Chat

68. What will the woman do tomorrow?

(A) Attend a convention
(B) Conduct a webinar
(C) Download some software
(D) Lead a virtual tour

69. Look at the graphic. Which option does the man point out?

(A) Option 1
(B) Option 2
(C) Option 3
(D) Option 4

70. How can the woman receive additional support?

(A) By reading a user manual
(B) By paying for a premium package
(C) By sending the man a text message
(D) By calling customer support

PART 4

Directions: You will hear some talks given by a single speaker. You will be asked to answer three questions about what the speaker says in each talk. Select the best response to each question and mark the letter (A), (B), (C), or (D) on your answer sheet. The talks will not be printed in your test book and will be spoken only one time.

71. What does the speaker's company sell?
(A) Kitchen appliances
(B) Exercise apparel
(C) Beauty products
(D) Bedding items

72. What can the listeners do online?
(A) Enter a contest
(B) Look up product information
(C) Submit a photo
(D) Find a promotional code

73. What can the listeners receive with a purchase?
(A) A gift
(B) Free delivery
(C) Admission to an event
(D) An extended warranty

---

74. What type of business is the speaker calling?
(A) A hair salon
(B) A hotel
(C) A restaurant
(D) A computer store

75. What was the speaker unable to do on a Web site?
(A) Enter his phone number
(B) Select a staff member
(C) Find an address
(D) Change an appointment time

76. How can customers obtain a discount?
(A) By presenting a coupon
(B) By registering for a rewards program
(C) By receiving a service from a trainee
(D) By referring a new customer

---

77. Where do the listeners work?
(A) At a jewelry store
(B) At a fitness center
(C) At an electronics store
(D) At a photography studio

78. What does the speaker say is special about some new products?
(A) They will be made of recycled materials.
(B) They will have a lifetime warranty.
(C) They can be customized.
(D) They can be easily cleaned.

79. What will the listeners do next week?
(A) Attend a trade show
(B) Organize an auction
(C) Receive replacement member cards
(D) Learn to use some equipment

---

80. Where is the announcement being made?
(A) At a movie theater
(B) At a train station
(C) At a sports complex
(D) At a shopping center

81. What can plastic bottles be exchanged for?
(A) Gift cards
(B) Food
(C) Clothing
(D) Tickets

82. What will the auction proceeds be used for?
(A) Facility renovations
(B) New inventory
(C) Student scholarships
(D) Festival attractions

GO ON TO THE NEXT PAGE →

83. What will the listeners most likely do after the session?
(A) Pose for a photograph
(B) Go to lunch
(C) Look at a display
(D) Pick up a free poster

84. What type of work does Yuri Baxter do?
(A) He finds filming locations.
(B) He creates promotional items.
(C) He designs costumes for actors.
(D) He writes movie and television scripts.

85. Why does the speaker say, "this session is only 40 minutes long"?
(A) To ask the listeners to be patient
(B) To ask the listeners to find their seats
(C) To explain why a schedule was changed
(D) To explain why a topic was chosen

86. What department do the listeners most likely work in?
(A) Security
(B) Maintenance
(C) Manufacturing
(D) Sales

87. What does the speaker imply when she says, "heavy snow is expected in the region in the coming weeks"?
(A) Delivery delays should be expected.
(B) Some locations will be closed.
(C) The listeners will work fewer shifts.
(D) A product will be in high demand.

88. What does the speaker offer to the listeners?
(A) A mobile phone
(B) A bus pass
(C) Some vacation days
(D) A gym membership

89. What is the theme of the weekly radio show?
(A) Technology trends
(B) Retirement planning
(C) Business finance
(D) Real estate

90. What did the speaker do before the commercial break?
(A) He talked to some listeners on the air.
(B) He told a personal story.
(C) He gave advice on choosing a bank.
(D) He described a property for sale.

91. What will happen next?
(A) A contest winner will be announced.
(B) An expert will be interviewed.
(C) A traffic report will be given.
(D) A cohost will explain a process.

92. What is the city planning to do?
(A) Open a new power plant
(B) Install solar panels on government buildings
(C) Encourage the use of public transportation
(D) Upgrade the street lighting system

93. What does the speaker imply when she says, "our community's top priority is promoting energy efficiency"?
(A) A project requires additional staff.
(B) Work on another project has been suspended.
(C) The cost of a project is justified.
(D) A news report on a project is accurate.

94. What does the speaker ask the listeners to do?
(A) Arrange an interview
(B) Look at a chart
(C) Take some pictures
(D) Visit a construction site

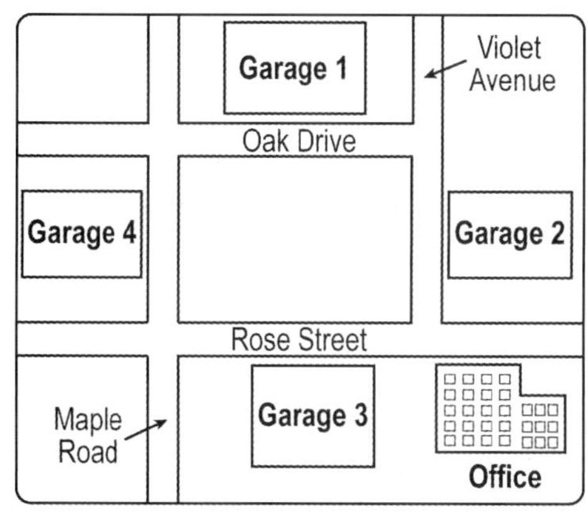

95. What industry does the speaker most likely work in?

(A) Banking
(B) Publishing
(C) Marketing
(D) Manufacturing

96. What does the speaker ask the listener to do?

(A) Make a reservation
(B) Give a presentation
(C) Provide some references
(D) Bring photo identification

97. Look at the graphic. Where does the speaker suggest parking?

(A) Garage 1
(B) Garage 2
(C) Garage 3
(D) Garage 4

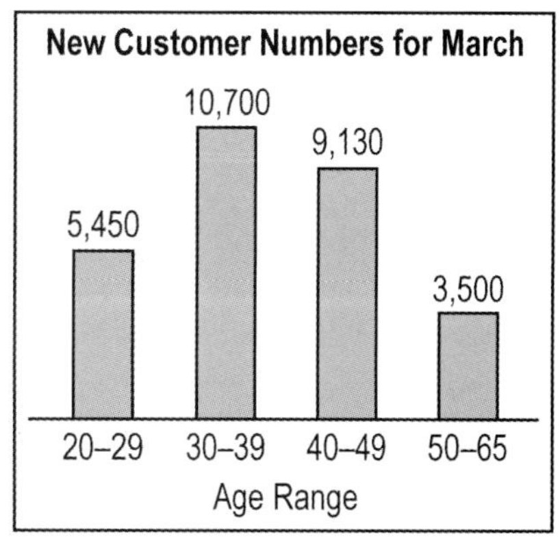

98. What kind of business does the speaker work for?

(A) A clothing retailer
(B) A storage company
(C) A software maker
(D) A publishing company

99. Look at the graphic. Which number does the speaker focus on?

(A) 5,450
(B) 10,700
(C) 9,130
(D) 3,500

100. What change does the speaker want to introduce?

(A) A redesigned company logo
(B) A greater product range
(C) A shorter delivery time
(D) A more diverse staff

ANSWER SHEET

Final Test

수험번호						

응시일자 : 20 년 월 일

성명	한 글	
	한 자	
	영 자	

Test 01 (Part 1~4)

1	ⓐ ⓑ ⓒ ⓓ	21	ⓐ ⓑ ⓒ	41	ⓐ ⓑ ⓒ ⓓ	61	ⓐ ⓑ ⓒ ⓓ	81	ⓐ ⓑ ⓒ ⓓ
2	ⓐ ⓑ ⓒ ⓓ	22	ⓐ ⓑ ⓒ	42	ⓐ ⓑ ⓒ ⓓ	62	ⓐ ⓑ ⓒ ⓓ	82	ⓐ ⓑ ⓒ ⓓ
3	ⓐ ⓑ ⓒ ⓓ	23	ⓐ ⓑ ⓒ	43	ⓐ ⓑ ⓒ ⓓ	63	ⓐ ⓑ ⓒ ⓓ	83	ⓐ ⓑ ⓒ ⓓ
4	ⓐ ⓑ ⓒ ⓓ	24	ⓐ ⓑ ⓒ	44	ⓐ ⓑ ⓒ ⓓ	64	ⓐ ⓑ ⓒ ⓓ	84	ⓐ ⓑ ⓒ ⓓ
5	ⓐ ⓑ ⓒ ⓓ	25	ⓐ ⓑ ⓒ	45	ⓐ ⓑ ⓒ ⓓ	65	ⓐ ⓑ ⓒ ⓓ	85	ⓐ ⓑ ⓒ ⓓ
6	ⓐ ⓑ ⓒ ⓓ	26	ⓐ ⓑ ⓒ	46	ⓐ ⓑ ⓒ ⓓ	66	ⓐ ⓑ ⓒ ⓓ	86	ⓐ ⓑ ⓒ ⓓ
7	ⓐ ⓑ ⓒ	27	ⓐ ⓑ ⓒ	47	ⓐ ⓑ ⓒ ⓓ	67	ⓐ ⓑ ⓒ ⓓ	87	ⓐ ⓑ ⓒ ⓓ
8	ⓐ ⓑ ⓒ	28	ⓐ ⓑ ⓒ	48	ⓐ ⓑ ⓒ ⓓ	68	ⓐ ⓑ ⓒ ⓓ	88	ⓐ ⓑ ⓒ ⓓ
9	ⓐ ⓑ ⓒ	29	ⓐ ⓑ ⓒ	49	ⓐ ⓑ ⓒ ⓓ	69	ⓐ ⓑ ⓒ ⓓ	89	ⓐ ⓑ ⓒ ⓓ
10	ⓐ ⓑ ⓒ	30	ⓐ ⓑ ⓒ	50	ⓐ ⓑ ⓒ ⓓ	70	ⓐ ⓑ ⓒ ⓓ	90	ⓐ ⓑ ⓒ ⓓ
11	ⓐ ⓑ ⓒ	31	ⓐ ⓑ ⓒ	51	ⓐ ⓑ ⓒ ⓓ	71	ⓐ ⓑ ⓒ ⓓ	91	ⓐ ⓑ ⓒ ⓓ
12	ⓐ ⓑ ⓒ	32	ⓐ ⓑ ⓒ ⓓ	52	ⓐ ⓑ ⓒ ⓓ	72	ⓐ ⓑ ⓒ ⓓ	92	ⓐ ⓑ ⓒ ⓓ
13	ⓐ ⓑ ⓒ	33	ⓐ ⓑ ⓒ ⓓ	53	ⓐ ⓑ ⓒ ⓓ	73	ⓐ ⓑ ⓒ ⓓ	93	ⓐ ⓑ ⓒ ⓓ
14	ⓐ ⓑ ⓒ	34	ⓐ ⓑ ⓒ ⓓ	54	ⓐ ⓑ ⓒ ⓓ	74	ⓐ ⓑ ⓒ ⓓ	94	ⓐ ⓑ ⓒ ⓓ
15	ⓐ ⓑ ⓒ	35	ⓐ ⓑ ⓒ ⓓ	55	ⓐ ⓑ ⓒ ⓓ	75	ⓐ ⓑ ⓒ ⓓ	95	ⓐ ⓑ ⓒ ⓓ
16	ⓐ ⓑ ⓒ	36	ⓐ ⓑ ⓒ ⓓ	56	ⓐ ⓑ ⓒ ⓓ	76	ⓐ ⓑ ⓒ ⓓ	96	ⓐ ⓑ ⓒ ⓓ
17	ⓐ ⓑ ⓒ	37	ⓐ ⓑ ⓒ ⓓ	57	ⓐ ⓑ ⓒ ⓓ	77	ⓐ ⓑ ⓒ ⓓ	97	ⓐ ⓑ ⓒ ⓓ
18	ⓐ ⓑ ⓒ	38	ⓐ ⓑ ⓒ ⓓ	58	ⓐ ⓑ ⓒ ⓓ	78	ⓐ ⓑ ⓒ ⓓ	98	ⓐ ⓑ ⓒ ⓓ
19	ⓐ ⓑ ⓒ	39	ⓐ ⓑ ⓒ ⓓ	59	ⓐ ⓑ ⓒ ⓓ	79	ⓐ ⓑ ⓒ ⓓ	99	ⓐ ⓑ ⓒ ⓓ
20	ⓐ ⓑ ⓒ	40	ⓐ ⓑ ⓒ ⓓ	60	ⓐ ⓑ ⓒ ⓓ	80	ⓐ ⓑ ⓒ ⓓ	100	ⓐ ⓑ ⓒ ⓓ

Test 02 (Part 1~4)

1	ⓐ ⓑ ⓒ ⓓ	21	ⓐ ⓑ ⓒ	41	ⓐ ⓑ ⓒ ⓓ	61	ⓐ ⓑ ⓒ ⓓ	81	ⓐ ⓑ ⓒ ⓓ
2	ⓐ ⓑ ⓒ ⓓ	22	ⓐ ⓑ ⓒ	42	ⓐ ⓑ ⓒ ⓓ	62	ⓐ ⓑ ⓒ ⓓ	82	ⓐ ⓑ ⓒ ⓓ
3	ⓐ ⓑ ⓒ ⓓ	23	ⓐ ⓑ ⓒ	43	ⓐ ⓑ ⓒ ⓓ	63	ⓐ ⓑ ⓒ ⓓ	83	ⓐ ⓑ ⓒ ⓓ
4	ⓐ ⓑ ⓒ ⓓ	24	ⓐ ⓑ ⓒ	44	ⓐ ⓑ ⓒ ⓓ	64	ⓐ ⓑ ⓒ ⓓ	84	ⓐ ⓑ ⓒ ⓓ
5	ⓐ ⓑ ⓒ ⓓ	25	ⓐ ⓑ ⓒ	45	ⓐ ⓑ ⓒ ⓓ	65	ⓐ ⓑ ⓒ ⓓ	85	ⓐ ⓑ ⓒ ⓓ
6	ⓐ ⓑ ⓒ ⓓ	26	ⓐ ⓑ ⓒ	46	ⓐ ⓑ ⓒ ⓓ	66	ⓐ ⓑ ⓒ ⓓ	86	ⓐ ⓑ ⓒ ⓓ
7	ⓐ ⓑ ⓒ	27	ⓐ ⓑ ⓒ	47	ⓐ ⓑ ⓒ ⓓ	67	ⓐ ⓑ ⓒ ⓓ	87	ⓐ ⓑ ⓒ ⓓ
8	ⓐ ⓑ ⓒ	28	ⓐ ⓑ ⓒ	48	ⓐ ⓑ ⓒ ⓓ	68	ⓐ ⓑ ⓒ ⓓ	88	ⓐ ⓑ ⓒ ⓓ
9	ⓐ ⓑ ⓒ	29	ⓐ ⓑ ⓒ	49	ⓐ ⓑ ⓒ ⓓ	69	ⓐ ⓑ ⓒ ⓓ	89	ⓐ ⓑ ⓒ ⓓ
10	ⓐ ⓑ ⓒ	30	ⓐ ⓑ ⓒ	50	ⓐ ⓑ ⓒ ⓓ	70	ⓐ ⓑ ⓒ ⓓ	90	ⓐ ⓑ ⓒ ⓓ
11	ⓐ ⓑ ⓒ	31	ⓐ ⓑ ⓒ	51	ⓐ ⓑ ⓒ ⓓ	71	ⓐ ⓑ ⓒ ⓓ	91	ⓐ ⓑ ⓒ ⓓ
12	ⓐ ⓑ ⓒ	32	ⓐ ⓑ ⓒ ⓓ	52	ⓐ ⓑ ⓒ ⓓ	72	ⓐ ⓑ ⓒ ⓓ	92	ⓐ ⓑ ⓒ ⓓ
13	ⓐ ⓑ ⓒ	33	ⓐ ⓑ ⓒ ⓓ	53	ⓐ ⓑ ⓒ ⓓ	73	ⓐ ⓑ ⓒ ⓓ	93	ⓐ ⓑ ⓒ ⓓ
14	ⓐ ⓑ ⓒ	34	ⓐ ⓑ ⓒ ⓓ	54	ⓐ ⓑ ⓒ ⓓ	74	ⓐ ⓑ ⓒ ⓓ	94	ⓐ ⓑ ⓒ ⓓ
15	ⓐ ⓑ ⓒ	35	ⓐ ⓑ ⓒ ⓓ	55	ⓐ ⓑ ⓒ ⓓ	75	ⓐ ⓑ ⓒ ⓓ	95	ⓐ ⓑ ⓒ ⓓ
16	ⓐ ⓑ ⓒ	36	ⓐ ⓑ ⓒ ⓓ	56	ⓐ ⓑ ⓒ ⓓ	76	ⓐ ⓑ ⓒ ⓓ	96	ⓐ ⓑ ⓒ ⓓ
17	ⓐ ⓑ ⓒ	37	ⓐ ⓑ ⓒ ⓓ	57	ⓐ ⓑ ⓒ ⓓ	77	ⓐ ⓑ ⓒ ⓓ	97	ⓐ ⓑ ⓒ ⓓ
18	ⓐ ⓑ ⓒ	38	ⓐ ⓑ ⓒ ⓓ	58	ⓐ ⓑ ⓒ ⓓ	78	ⓐ ⓑ ⓒ ⓓ	98	ⓐ ⓑ ⓒ ⓓ
19	ⓐ ⓑ ⓒ	39	ⓐ ⓑ ⓒ ⓓ	59	ⓐ ⓑ ⓒ ⓓ	79	ⓐ ⓑ ⓒ ⓓ	99	ⓐ ⓑ ⓒ ⓓ
20	ⓐ ⓑ ⓒ	40	ⓐ ⓑ ⓒ ⓓ	60	ⓐ ⓑ ⓒ ⓓ	80	ⓐ ⓑ ⓒ ⓓ	100	ⓐ ⓑ ⓒ ⓓ

ANSWER SHEET

파트별 모의고사

수험번호						

응시일자 : 20 년 월 일

성명	한 글	
	한 자	
	영 자	

Test 01 (Part 1~4)

No.		No.		No.		No.		No.	
1	ⓐ ⓑ ⓒ ⓓ	21	ⓐ ⓑ ⓒ	41	ⓐ ⓑ ⓒ ⓓ	61	ⓐ ⓑ ⓒ ⓓ	81	ⓐ ⓑ ⓒ ⓓ
2	ⓐ ⓑ ⓒ ⓓ	22	ⓐ ⓑ ⓒ	42	ⓐ ⓑ ⓒ ⓓ	62	ⓐ ⓑ ⓒ ⓓ	82	ⓐ ⓑ ⓒ ⓓ
3	ⓐ ⓑ ⓒ ⓓ	23	ⓐ ⓑ ⓒ	43	ⓐ ⓑ ⓒ ⓓ	63	ⓐ ⓑ ⓒ ⓓ	83	ⓐ ⓑ ⓒ ⓓ
4	ⓐ ⓑ ⓒ ⓓ	24	ⓐ ⓑ ⓒ	44	ⓐ ⓑ ⓒ ⓓ	64	ⓐ ⓑ ⓒ ⓓ	84	ⓐ ⓑ ⓒ ⓓ
5	ⓐ ⓑ ⓒ ⓓ	25	ⓐ ⓑ ⓒ	45	ⓐ ⓑ ⓒ ⓓ	65	ⓐ ⓑ ⓒ ⓓ	85	ⓐ ⓑ ⓒ ⓓ
6	ⓐ ⓑ ⓒ ⓓ	26	ⓐ ⓑ ⓒ	46	ⓐ ⓑ ⓒ ⓓ	66	ⓐ ⓑ ⓒ ⓓ	86	ⓐ ⓑ ⓒ ⓓ
7	ⓐ ⓑ ⓒ	27	ⓐ ⓑ ⓒ	47	ⓐ ⓑ ⓒ ⓓ	67	ⓐ ⓑ ⓒ ⓓ	87	ⓐ ⓑ ⓒ ⓓ
8	ⓐ ⓑ ⓒ	28	ⓐ ⓑ ⓒ	48	ⓐ ⓑ ⓒ ⓓ	68	ⓐ ⓑ ⓒ ⓓ	88	ⓐ ⓑ ⓒ ⓓ
9	ⓐ ⓑ ⓒ	29	ⓐ ⓑ ⓒ	49	ⓐ ⓑ ⓒ ⓓ	69	ⓐ ⓑ ⓒ ⓓ	89	ⓐ ⓑ ⓒ ⓓ
10	ⓐ ⓑ ⓒ	30	ⓐ ⓑ ⓒ	50	ⓐ ⓑ ⓒ ⓓ	70	ⓐ ⓑ ⓒ ⓓ	90	ⓐ ⓑ ⓒ ⓓ
11	ⓐ ⓑ ⓒ	31	ⓐ ⓑ ⓒ	51	ⓐ ⓑ ⓒ ⓓ	71	ⓐ ⓑ ⓒ ⓓ	91	ⓐ ⓑ ⓒ ⓓ
12	ⓐ ⓑ ⓒ	32	ⓐ ⓑ ⓒ ⓓ	52	ⓐ ⓑ ⓒ ⓓ	72	ⓐ ⓑ ⓒ ⓓ	92	ⓐ ⓑ ⓒ ⓓ
13	ⓐ ⓑ ⓒ	33	ⓐ ⓑ ⓒ ⓓ	53	ⓐ ⓑ ⓒ ⓓ	73	ⓐ ⓑ ⓒ ⓓ	93	ⓐ ⓑ ⓒ ⓓ
14	ⓐ ⓑ ⓒ	34	ⓐ ⓑ ⓒ ⓓ	54	ⓐ ⓑ ⓒ ⓓ	74	ⓐ ⓑ ⓒ ⓓ	94	ⓐ ⓑ ⓒ ⓓ
15	ⓐ ⓑ ⓒ	35	ⓐ ⓑ ⓒ ⓓ	55	ⓐ ⓑ ⓒ ⓓ	75	ⓐ ⓑ ⓒ ⓓ	95	ⓐ ⓑ ⓒ ⓓ
16	ⓐ ⓑ ⓒ	36	ⓐ ⓑ ⓒ ⓓ	56	ⓐ ⓑ ⓒ ⓓ	76	ⓐ ⓑ ⓒ ⓓ	96	ⓐ ⓑ ⓒ ⓓ
17	ⓐ ⓑ ⓒ	37	ⓐ ⓑ ⓒ ⓓ	57	ⓐ ⓑ ⓒ ⓓ	77	ⓐ ⓑ ⓒ ⓓ	97	ⓐ ⓑ ⓒ ⓓ
18	ⓐ ⓑ ⓒ	38	ⓐ ⓑ ⓒ ⓓ	58	ⓐ ⓑ ⓒ ⓓ	78	ⓐ ⓑ ⓒ ⓓ	98	ⓐ ⓑ ⓒ ⓓ
19	ⓐ ⓑ ⓒ	39	ⓐ ⓑ ⓒ ⓓ	59	ⓐ ⓑ ⓒ ⓓ	79	ⓐ ⓑ ⓒ ⓓ	99	ⓐ ⓑ ⓒ ⓓ
20	ⓐ ⓑ ⓒ	40	ⓐ ⓑ ⓒ ⓓ	60	ⓐ ⓑ ⓒ ⓓ	80	ⓐ ⓑ ⓒ ⓓ	100	ⓐ ⓑ ⓒ ⓓ

Test 02 (Part 1~4)

No.		No.		No.		No.		No.	
1	ⓐ ⓑ ⓒ ⓓ	21	ⓐ ⓑ ⓒ	41	ⓐ ⓑ ⓒ ⓓ	61	ⓐ ⓑ ⓒ ⓓ	81	ⓐ ⓑ ⓒ ⓓ
2	ⓐ ⓑ ⓒ ⓓ	22	ⓐ ⓑ ⓒ	42	ⓐ ⓑ ⓒ ⓓ	62	ⓐ ⓑ ⓒ ⓓ	82	ⓐ ⓑ ⓒ ⓓ
3	ⓐ ⓑ ⓒ ⓓ	23	ⓐ ⓑ ⓒ	43	ⓐ ⓑ ⓒ ⓓ	63	ⓐ ⓑ ⓒ ⓓ	83	ⓐ ⓑ ⓒ ⓓ
4	ⓐ ⓑ ⓒ ⓓ	24	ⓐ ⓑ ⓒ	44	ⓐ ⓑ ⓒ ⓓ	64	ⓐ ⓑ ⓒ ⓓ	84	ⓐ ⓑ ⓒ ⓓ
5	ⓐ ⓑ ⓒ ⓓ	25	ⓐ ⓑ ⓒ	45	ⓐ ⓑ ⓒ ⓓ	65	ⓐ ⓑ ⓒ ⓓ	85	ⓐ ⓑ ⓒ ⓓ
6	ⓐ ⓑ ⓒ ⓓ	26	ⓐ ⓑ ⓒ	46	ⓐ ⓑ ⓒ ⓓ	66	ⓐ ⓑ ⓒ ⓓ	86	ⓐ ⓑ ⓒ ⓓ
7	ⓐ ⓑ ⓒ	27	ⓐ ⓑ ⓒ	47	ⓐ ⓑ ⓒ ⓓ	67	ⓐ ⓑ ⓒ ⓓ	87	ⓐ ⓑ ⓒ ⓓ
8	ⓐ ⓑ ⓒ	28	ⓐ ⓑ ⓒ	48	ⓐ ⓑ ⓒ ⓓ	68	ⓐ ⓑ ⓒ ⓓ	88	ⓐ ⓑ ⓒ ⓓ
9	ⓐ ⓑ ⓒ	29	ⓐ ⓑ ⓒ	49	ⓐ ⓑ ⓒ ⓓ	69	ⓐ ⓑ ⓒ ⓓ	89	ⓐ ⓑ ⓒ ⓓ
10	ⓐ ⓑ ⓒ	30	ⓐ ⓑ ⓒ	50	ⓐ ⓑ ⓒ ⓓ	70	ⓐ ⓑ ⓒ ⓓ	90	ⓐ ⓑ ⓒ ⓓ
11	ⓐ ⓑ ⓒ	31	ⓐ ⓑ ⓒ	51	ⓐ ⓑ ⓒ ⓓ	71	ⓐ ⓑ ⓒ ⓓ	91	ⓐ ⓑ ⓒ ⓓ
12	ⓐ ⓑ ⓒ	32	ⓐ ⓑ ⓒ ⓓ	52	ⓐ ⓑ ⓒ ⓓ	72	ⓐ ⓑ ⓒ ⓓ	92	ⓐ ⓑ ⓒ ⓓ
13	ⓐ ⓑ ⓒ	33	ⓐ ⓑ ⓒ ⓓ	53	ⓐ ⓑ ⓒ ⓓ	73	ⓐ ⓑ ⓒ ⓓ	93	ⓐ ⓑ ⓒ ⓓ
14	ⓐ ⓑ ⓒ	34	ⓐ ⓑ ⓒ ⓓ	54	ⓐ ⓑ ⓒ ⓓ	74	ⓐ ⓑ ⓒ ⓓ	94	ⓐ ⓑ ⓒ ⓓ
15	ⓐ ⓑ ⓒ	35	ⓐ ⓑ ⓒ ⓓ	55	ⓐ ⓑ ⓒ ⓓ	75	ⓐ ⓑ ⓒ ⓓ	95	ⓐ ⓑ ⓒ ⓓ
16	ⓐ ⓑ ⓒ	36	ⓐ ⓑ ⓒ ⓓ	56	ⓐ ⓑ ⓒ ⓓ	76	ⓐ ⓑ ⓒ ⓓ	96	ⓐ ⓑ ⓒ ⓓ
17	ⓐ ⓑ ⓒ	37	ⓐ ⓑ ⓒ ⓓ	57	ⓐ ⓑ ⓒ ⓓ	77	ⓐ ⓑ ⓒ ⓓ	97	ⓐ ⓑ ⓒ ⓓ
18	ⓐ ⓑ ⓒ	38	ⓐ ⓑ ⓒ ⓓ	58	ⓐ ⓑ ⓒ ⓓ	78	ⓐ ⓑ ⓒ ⓓ	98	ⓐ ⓑ ⓒ ⓓ
19	ⓐ ⓑ ⓒ	39	ⓐ ⓑ ⓒ ⓓ	59	ⓐ ⓑ ⓒ ⓓ	79	ⓐ ⓑ ⓒ ⓓ	99	ⓐ ⓑ ⓒ ⓓ
20	ⓐ ⓑ ⓒ	40	ⓐ ⓑ ⓒ ⓓ	60	ⓐ ⓑ ⓒ ⓓ	80	ⓐ ⓑ ⓒ ⓓ	100	ⓐ ⓑ ⓒ ⓓ